# R/C SPORTS AIRCRAFT

## from Scratch

# R/C SPORTS AIRCRAFT

## AIRCRAFT
### *from Scratch*

## Alex Weiss

## Cartoons by Bob Graham

Nexus Special Interests

This book is for Rupert, who has shared so many flying experiences with me.

Nexus Special Interests Ltd.
Nexus House
Boundary Way
Hemel Hempstead
Hertfordshire HP2 7ST
England

First published by Nexus Special Interests Ltd. 1996

ISBN 1-85486-140-9

Printed and bound in Great Britain by Bookcraft (Bath) Ltd.

# Contents

## INTRODUCTION
**The aim of the book** xi
**Avoiding maths** xii
**Acknowledgements** xiii

## CHAPTER 1  GETTING GOING
**Why build from scratch?** 1
**Deciding what you want** 1
  How difficult is it? - The aesthetics - What is a 'sports' model? - Knowing your
  limitations - Flying field considerations - Number of channels
**Modifying existing designs** 3
  Sketching on plans
**Using components from current/crashed models** 4
**Changing the size of proven designs** 6
**What to build** 6
  Low wing layouts - High wing configurations - Other wing positions - A three
  view sketch - Propeller ground clearance and aircraft rotation
**Sports scale** 10
  Sources of scale information - Compromises and simplification

## CHAPTER 2  CHOOSING A CONFIGURATION
**Conventional layouts** 13
  Monoplanes - Biplanes
**Offbeat aircraft** 14
  Flying wings - Deltas - Canards
**Engine location** 16
  Multi engines
**Undercarriages** 18
  Noselegs versus tail draggers

## CHAPTER 3  A SUITABLE SIZE
**Transportability** 21
  Choosing the dimensions - Wingspan and aspect ratio - Fuselage length
  and cross section - Tail size and position - All moving tails - Fin size -
  V or butterfly tails
**Balancing the model** 28
  Centre of gravity location - The aerodynamic mean chord (AMC) -
  Biplane and canard centres of gravity
**Effect of size on flight performance** 32

# Contents

## CHAPTER 4  PROVIDING POWER

**Possible sources of power**                                              33
  Two stroke glow engines – Four stroke glow engines – Diesels – Petrol engines –
  Silencers
**Installing I/C engines**                                                 36
  Upright, inverted or sidewinder – 45° mounting – Pushers – Pylon mounting –
  Slot propellers – Engine bearers and plates – Plastic and metal engine mounts –
  Fuel systems – Propellers
**Electric power**                                                         40
  Motors – Batteries – Folding propellers
**Installing electric motors**                                             43

## CHAPTER 5  DEFEATING DRAG

**The basic facts**                                                        45
**Drag**                                                                   45
  Parasite drag – Form drag – Interference drag – Skin friction – The boundary
  layer – Laminar boundary layer – Turbulent boundary layer – Transition point –
  Factors affecting parasite drag – Air speed – Shape – Interference drag –
  Surface area and smoothness – Induced drag – Factors affecting induced drag –
  Total drag – Variation of drag with speed – Speed for minimum total drag
**Speed and speed range**                                                  48
  Thrust – Speed range

## CHAPTER 6  LOTS OF LOVELY LIFT

**Generating lift**                                                        51
**Types of aerofoil**                                                      51
  High-lift aerofoils – General purpose aerofoils – High-speed aerofoils –
  Centre of pressure – Movement of the centre of pressure – Amounts of lift –
  Variation of lift with angle of attack – Stalling angle of attack – Variation
  of drag with angle of attack – Variation of lift/drag ratio with angle of attack
**Aerofoil sections**                                                      54
  Aerofoils – Symmetrical aerofoils – Flat plate – NACA 0009 – NACA 0018 –
  Semi-symmetrical aerofoils – NACA 2412 and 2415 – Eppler 374 – Other
  cambered aerofoils – Curved plate – Clark Y – Göttingen 797 –
  NACA 6412 – NACA 2R212 Reflex – Your own special aerofoil
**Wing planform**                                                          60
  Wing vortices – Aspect ratio – Aspect ratio and induced drag – Aspect ratio, lift
  and stalling – Use of high aspect ratio – Sweep-back – Effect of sweep-back on
  lift and drag – Tip-stalling, aileron response and pitch up – Alleviating tip-stalling –
  Pros and cons of various planforms
**Wing position**                                                          67
  Dihedral and anhedral
**Wing loading**                                                           68
**High-lift devices**                                                      68
  Flaps – Types of flaps – Simple flaps – Split flaps – Fowler flaps – Slats and slots

## CHAPTER 7  CONTROL CHARACTERISTICS

**Manoeuvrability**                                                        73

Aerobatic capability - Speed - Payload - Take-off and landing characteristics -
Flight duration

**Stability**                                                                                           75
The three axes – Longitudinal axis – Directional axis – Lateral axis – Static
and dynamic stability – Static stability – Dynamic stability – Subsidence and
divergence – Longitudinal stability – Position of the centre of pressure –
Angle of attack – Wing loading – Looping accelerations – Turbulence –
Transient disturbances – Degrees of longitudinal stability – Too stable –
Not stable enough – Unstable – Design of the tailplane – Lateral and directional
stability – Lateral stability – Positive lateral stability – Negative lateral stability –
Neutral lateral stability – Dihedral angle – Sweep-back – High keel surface –
High wing and low centre of gravity – Directional stability – Directional
stability and the spin – Interaction between lateral and directional stability –
Spiral instability – Oscillatory instability – Roll with yaw – Degrees of stability –
Automatic stability

**Trim**                                                                                                83
Wing and tail incidences – Wing incidence – Tailplane aerofoils – Downwash –
Longitudinal dihedral – Engine thrust lines – Up/down thrust – Side thrust

**Control surfaces**                                                                                    86
Effectiveness – Elevators – Ailerons – Inset ailerons – Adverse yaw and aileron
drag – Strip ailerons – Spoilers as ailerons – Aileron reversal – Rudders –
Options for avoiding elevator/rudder contact – Coupled aileron and rudder –
Elevons – Ruddevators and flaperons – Airbrakes – Balancing – Mass balancing –
Aerodynamic balancing – Overbalance – All moving tails – Moving control
surfaces

**Flutter**                                                                                             94
Torsional flexural flutter - Torsional aileron flutter - Flexural aileron flutter -
Elevator and rudder flutter

## CHAPTER 8  MAKING THE MOST OF MATERIALS

**The basic materials**                                                                                 99
Choosing the size of material – Balsa – Obechi – Liteply – Ply – Spruce – Beech –
Cardboard

**The plastics**                                                                                        102
Foam – Foam board – Plastics and vacuum forming – ABS – Acetate – Acrylic –
Polycarbonate – PVC – Styrene – Other plastics – Expanded polystyrene –
Polyester – Polycarbonate – Glass reinforced plastic – Designing in strength –
Estimating moulding thickness – Estimating weight – Strength –  Exotic
materials

**Metals**                                                                                              107
Aluminium alloy – Piano wire – Brass

**The choice of adhesives**                                                                             108
**Building in lightness**                                                                               110
The stress points

## CHAPTER 9  AIRFRAME ALTERNATIVES

**The fuselage**                                                                                        111
**Formers**                                                                                             111

# Contents

**Simple boxes**      **111**
All sheet – Open frame

**Oval and circular shapes**      **113**
Horizontal and vertical crutches – Stringers – Sheeted – Planked – Rolled tubes

**Advanced shapes and materials**      **114**
Metal – GRP and wooden cowls

**Wings**      **115**
Parallel chord – Tapered – Elliptical – Wing tips – Biplanes and triplanes –
Multi engined aircraft

**Aerofoils**      **117**
Flat plates – Curved plates – Flat bottomed aerofoils – Symmetrical
and semi-symmetrical aerofoils – Under cambered aerofoils – Washout

**Wing construction**      **119**
Leading and trailing edges – Spars – Ribs – Rib thickness and spacing –
Capping strips – Sheeting – Foam wings – Cut-outs in foam wings –
Joining wing panels – Sweep-back

**Attachment of wings to the fuselage**      **124**
Cabane struts – Wing struts and rigging

**Tailplanes and fins**      **126**
All sheet – Built up – Sheet cored – Foam – V or butterfly tails –
Attachment to the fuselage

**Types of undercarriage**      **128**
Fixed – Sprung

**Retracts**      **130**
Retraction mechanism – Mounting – Wheel wells – Undercarriage doors

**Tricycle or tail dragger**      **130**
Noselegs – Tail draggers

**Wheels**      **131**
Wheel spats

**Installation**      **132**

**Operating off water**      **133**
Floats – Seaplanes – Wing tip floats

**Operating off snow**      **135**

## CHAPTER 10  CONTROL CONFIGURATIONS

**Primary controls**      **137**
Elevators – Ailerons – Aileron hinges – Differential and Frise ailerons –
Spoilers as ailerons – Elevons – Rudders – All moving tails – Airbrakes –
Simple and split flaps

**Hinging**      **142**

**The radio equipment**      **142**
Planning the installation – Number and positioning of servos

**Control runs**      **143**
Push rods – Bell cranks – Snakes – Closed loop controls – Horns – Clevises –
All moving tails

## CHAPTER 11  FINAL FINISHING OFF

**Cockpits**      **147**

Canopies – Open cockpits – Pilots

**Hatches**     148

**Stores**     148

**Types of covering**     149
Tissue – Nylon – Heat shrink fabric and film – Glass skinning

**Painting**     150
Decoration – Fuel-proofing

## CHAPTER 12   DRAWING THE DESIGN

**Manual methods**     153
Making copies – Drawing instruments – Drawing boards

**Computer Aided Drawing (CAD)**     154

**Detailed design**     154
Indicating different materials – Drawing aerofoils – Transferring the information

**Getting it published**     157

## CHAPTER 13   THE FIRST FLIGHT

**Before the first flight**     159
Balance – Rigging – Checking the weight – Control throws – The use of rates –
Choosing the propeller – Taxying trials – The video – A first hop

**The first flight**     162
Flaps on take-off and landing – Raising flaps in flight – Controllability –
Stall characteristics – Spinning and spin recovery – The first landing

**Assessing flight performance**     164
What changes to make – Side and down thrust – Stability characteristics

## GLOSSARY     167

## BIBLIOGRAPHY     171

## INDEX     173

# Introduction

## The aim of the book

Much has been written over the years about the glorious hobby of building and flying radio controlled model aircraft, so why yet another book? A lifetime's experience has shown that there is very little available about the design and construction of powered sports models, whether utilising internal combustion engines or electric motors.

This book has been written particularly for those who have already built and flown two or three radio controlled models, either from commercially available kits or from published plans, and are looking for a way of extending the knowledge and pleasure they obtain from the hobby. The choices available to the builder of any new aircraft are considered and a brief look taken at the various aerodynamic considerations.

The text also examines the numerous possible aircraft configurations and provides guidance on how to produce the right model with the desired flight performance. It reviews the many different construction techniques which may be selected when building the airframe. Each of the major sub-systems is considered in turn, reviewing the various options. The book shows how to draw up a plan and submit details of your model for publication. It concludes with a chapter on test flying a brand new design.

Excluded from consideration are helicopters, gliders, very large models which require some care in stress analysis, and the specialised field of ducted fan and turbojet powered models. Nevertheless, much of the information contained in these pages is also applicable to all of these classes of models, except for helicopters.

The text explores three possible categories of scratch building. The first category includes making minor improvements and modifications

**Figure 1** *Perhaps the ultimate in sports scale modelling, this Tornado GR1, in Royal Aircraft Establishment colours, features wings which can be swung in flight and retractable undercarriage.*

to an existing kit or plan and many modellers will have already dabbled in this area. The second involves building a new aircraft from parts of crashed models, such as a wing from one and a tail from another, combined with a replacement fuselage. Finally, there is the creation of an original and unique model, involving a range of design, construction and aerodynamic considerations.

This book is not just for those modellers who tinker with modifications or wish to design from scratch. Most people have their own preferred construction method and views on what is an attractive model. Anyone involved in our hobby can benefit from a greater understanding of design and construction principles. Such people may only ever consider building a proven design from a plan or kit, but should get a better grasp of why the designer arrived at the particular compromises found in the model.

Much of the contents of the book has been simplified to make it more readable and easy to use. Aerodynamicists will have to accept that much has been left unsaid and many difficulties glossed over. Mention will be made in passing of Mr Reynolds, famed for his number. Beyond

# Introduction

**Figure 2** *A classical high wing trainer is a good place to start a first scratch design.*

this mention, Reynolds' number is avoided like the plague. Suffice it to say, that he was able to show that, all other things being equal, bigger aeroplanes fly better from an aerodynamic point of view than smaller ones, particularly when they fly faster as well. There can be few radio modellers who do not recognise the truth of these facts from their own practical experience.

## Avoiding maths

Aeromodelling is supposed to be a pleasurable hobby, although some would consider it masochistic when returning home with their latest pride and joy in a black bin liner. Mathematics is considered by the majority of modellers to be

even worse than a crash. As far as is humanly possible, it has been avoided throughout this book. The use of nomographs avoids the need to make tedious calculations and for those who enjoy it, any maths is reduced to simple four function calculations (addition, subtraction, multiplication and division) on a pocket calculator.

As an example of how simple it is to use a nomograph, take a look at Figure 3. Having estimated the maximum speed of a new model and knowing the engine rpm for maximum power, what propeller pitch should be used? A ruler is laid on an engine rpm of 15,000 and a speed of 120 kph (75 mph), giving a propeller pitch of 22 mm (8½"). Easy, isn't it? The nomograph is particularly well suited to providing the answer to the "what if?" question. For example, just by angling the ruler to a different speed a different propeller pitch will be recommended.

Born before the Second World War, I have still managed to embrace the metric system and abandon the imperial one. However, recognising that some people still cling to the older system, all units are either given in both metric and imperial. The key units used are shown in Table 1.

AT LEAST THERE ISN'T ANY MATHS TO CONTEND WITH !!

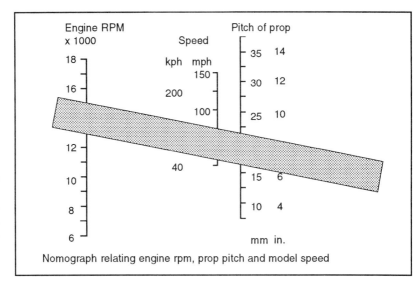

**Figure 3**
*Nomographs are easy to use and they avoid the need for tedious calculations. Simply slide the ruler until it intersects the two known figures and read off the third.*

Nomograph relating engine rpm, prop pitch and model speed

A glossary at the end of this book describes the technical terms used, the vast majority of which will be familiar to the average R/C modeller, together with a list of abbreviations found in the text. A detailed index will help the reader to access a particular piece of information.

## Acknowledgements

The writing of this book has taken inspiration, help and a fair amount of time. The inspiration came from several people. First are Gordon Whitehead, whose book *Scale Aircraft* I still consider to be a 'bible', and Chris Bashford, whose articles on aerodynamics in the 1960s and 1970s fostered my interest in the subject. This interest was furthered by Martin Simons' glider oriented treatise *Model Aircraft Aerodynamics*. Inevitably David Boddington has also affected my approach to R/C flying. His writings as 'Button Man' inspired me to get involved in radio control, albeit single channel, quickly followed by 'Galloping Ghost'. Mention must also be made of Peter Russell's *Straight & Level* column in *RCM&E*. It has been filled with interesting facts and figures, some of which have been invaluable in the compilation of this book.

A name rarely mentioned in the aeromodelling field, but well known in full size aviation is that of A.C. Kermode. Among his numerous books, *Flight without Formulae* was first published in 1940 by Pitmans and has been continuously in print ever since. A fifth edition, updated by Bill Gunston, was produced in 1989 and again reprinted as recently as 1995. Completely devoid of any maths, *Flight without Formulae* has provided much of the motivation for this book.

Many books and articles were consulted in the preparation of this text, and special mention needs

| Parameter | Metric Unit | Imperial unit |
|---|---|---|
| Length | Metres, centimetres and millimetres | Feet and inches |
| Weight | Kilograms and grams | Pounds and ounces |
| Wing area | Square decimetres | Square feet |
| Wing loading | Grams per square decimetre | Ounces per square foot |
| Speed | Kilometres per hour | Miles per hour |
| Engine capacity | Cubic centimetres | Cubic inches |
| Material weight | Grams per square metre<br>Grams per cubic centimetre | Ounces per square foot<br>Ounces per cubic inch |

**Table 1**
*The metric units used in this book and their imperial equivalents.*

# Introduction

**Figure 4** *Peter Russell's 362 delta was my first foray into the world of flying unconventional aircraft.*

to be made of Ron Warring's excellent *Glassfibre Handbook*, David Thomas' *Radio Control Foam Modelling* and Tubal Cain's *Model Engineer's Handbook*. Information from these books, which are all available from *Nexus Special Interests*, has formed the basis of the specialist sections in this volume.

John Hearne, John Lynham, and Kevin Walton have all generously given time to have their models photographed for inclusion in this book. Rupert Weiss, Bill-Kits, Handy Systems and Derek Hardman of Solarfilm also provided valuable information and photographs. I should add that I have no connection, commercial or otherwise, with any of the products or companies mentioned in this book. Finally, my wife has stoically put up with my obsession with completing this text, keeping me well supplied with sustenance during my long hours of work. She also heroically proof read the text, making many useful suggestions for improvement.

# 1  Getting going

## Why build from scratch?

As if flying radio controlled aircraft isn't a demanding enough hobby, why on earth should anyone wish to launch a completely unproved aircraft into the air? Fundamentally, there are three main answers to the question. First there is great satisfaction to be had from bringing a unique model to the flying field, and this feeling can increase if other people build from your plan. Secondly, modifying proven designs or even designing R/C models from scratch is a very pleasurable aspect of the hobby in its own right, bringing about mental gymnastics to arrive at a satisfactory result. Thirdly, the pleasure resulting from the successful first flight of an own design is hard to beat – a close second to sex! It is also worth noting that you can make money by getting a design published. Although you will never get rich, you may well be able to subsidise your hobby and pacify either your conscience or your partner when making your next expensive purchase of a new engine, radio or kit.

To modify an existing design or build an entirely new model from scratch, all you need is a little courage, some imagination and a pencil and paper. A collection of catalogues from the modelling trade is helpful when you are searching for details of a particular part, although a number of the tables in this book are devoted to providing baseline information on materials. The extra time devoted to the modification or original design stage of the hobby brings its rewards when your first own creation successfully takes to the air.

For the more advanced designer, a personal computer with a computer aided drawing program can save a lot of time. An associated word processor and a SLR camera can put you well on the path to getting one of your designs published in a hobby magazine.

**Figure 5** *Bo Garstad's Draken, Nexus Plan RM1355 provided the basis for this fun scale model of the Columbia Space Shuttle, built by my middle son and described in RCM&E in March 1982. Little has changed from the original design except the fin outline and the colour scheme.*

## Deciding what you want

So you've made the decision that you're going to have a go at creating something unique. The question is ... where to start? Think about what you want. Anything can be made to fly: well, almost anything. Many of the modelling shows around the country include flights by such weird objects as flying wheelbarrows and even airborne pigs. Perhaps for the more experienced! The simplest place to start is by modifying someone else's design.

Figure 5 shows the Columbia Space Shuttle based on Bo Garstad's all sheet three channel Draken. While the shape of the fin is drastically different, its area has not been altered. As a result, the flying characteristics remained unchanged. However, with a black and white paint scheme, the resulting model was a unique and satisfying first attempt at something different for the builder. Moving on to a complete design from scratch, we will look at most of the popular aircraft configurations for powered sports and sports scale models later in this chapter.

# Chapter 1

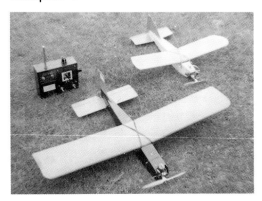

**Figure 6** *My first design was O-Ranger, dating back to the early 1970s, which had Galloping Ghost proportional control. It used proportional rudder and elevator with progressive throttle.*

## How difficult is it?

It's much easier than you might think to design your own model, assuming you have some experience of building and flying other people's designs. Some modellers are perfectly happy to build directly from a sketch on the back of the proverbial cigarette packet. Others will draw something out on a roll of lining paper and build on top of their drawing. A number will sit down at a drawing board, or PC with the latest computer aided drawing (CAD) package, and produce plans to professional standards. There is no right way. You can choose whatever suits you. Chapter 12 does, however, give advice on how to end up with a practical plan from which to build a model.

**Figure 7** *CAD, although not essential, is becoming increasingly popular for those with access to a PC. A computer is also useful for typing manuscripts if you want to get your plan published.*

**Figure 8** *The Flair Magnatilla is a classic vintage looking sports model, complete with circular aluminium cowl.*

## The aesthetics

How important is the look of the finished model? It is said that beauty is in the eye of the beholder and this is also true in aircraft design. Initially, you may find it difficult to imagine what a two dimensional drawing will look like when built up as a three dimensional aeroplane. Experience is the best aid here, matched to the degree of inquisitiveness which makes people study aircraft plans and compare them with photographs of the resulting product. The sheer joy of putting your own hallmark on your model, as Geoffrey de Havilland did with his fin/rudder shapes, can be a reward in itself.

## What is a 'sports' model?

This book is designed as a handbook for the vast majority of modellers who wish to build powered sports or sports scale models. Defining what a sports model is can be quite difficult. It is not a contest model such as an out and out competitive aerobatic machine or a winning pylon racer. It is not a faithful scale model, though it may be a simple representation of a scale model. It is not a ducted fan or turbojet powered model.

A reasonable interpretation is that it is a practical model which may not accurately represent any particular full sized aircraft and which is relatively simple to fly. Its primary purpose is to be flown, rather than admired on the ground. It may be designed for aerobatics, training, carrying a payload, such as a parachutist or load of toffees, trying twin engines or just looking like an old timer and flying gently around the sky. It

**Figure 9** *Smarty Pants, a Howard Metcalfe design is a typical small high wing sports model. Its configuration provides forgiving flight characteristics and makes it a good trainer.*

may be a biplane or a monoplane. It is a model which can be built and flown successfully for fun by you, the average modeller. It may be powered by a petrol, glow, diesel or electric motor. It includes training aircraft and does cover what Peter Russell has defined as OBA or offbeat aircraft such as canards and deltas, even though they may be rather harder to fly.

## Knowing your limitations

Most experienced fliers will have come across the beginner who is building a scale Spitfire or Lancaster as a first model. Similar dangers face the budding scratch builder. As this book will emphasise later, the best place to begin is with some simple modifications to someone else's design. It may not exactly be total scratch building, but it does result in a unique model. Many readers of this book will, no doubt, have already tried this initial stage. It can quickly be followed

**Figure 10** *Experienced modellers recognise that the Spitfire is not a good model to start with if you are a beginner.*

by an original design based on a well proven configuration. Remember, however, if you fly biplanes, it's hardly sensible to try to design a delta as your first model, and vice-versa.

## Flying field considerations

The length and surface finish of your flying field, not to mention the proximity of obstacles, such as trees, should have a serious impact on your choice of models. Noise limitations are another major factor, which may lead to the selection of an electric motor, or a well silenced four stroke engine, as the power plant. A rough field may mean the elimination of any undercarriage, while a field of restricted size is better suited to a small, manoeuvrable model. Only you can evaluate these considerations and then decide the sort of aircraft you want to build.

## Number of channels

Consideration of the radio control system for any model can have quite an impact on the choice of design parameters. A two channel radio can be used to control either rudder and elevator or aileron and elevator, although in a slow flying, old timer type of design, throttle could be used instead of elevator. Moving on to three channels allows throttle, motor and either rudder or aileron to be incorporated, while four channels give a full house set of controls. However, things do not end there. A mixer allows elevons or a butterfly tail to become a part of the design, while five or more channels enable flaps, retracts, air brakes, bomb dropping or whatever takes your fancy to be designed into the model.

# Modifying existing designs

When having a go at designing your own model, taking the first step is usually the hardest. Certainly few people are likely to sit down at a drawing board with a blank sheet of paper and produce their first design from scratch. The recommended approach, whether working from a kit or an existing plan, is to make some small changes. Then you will have the pleasure of a unique model, albeit based on someone else's design.

**Figure 11** *The Flair Magnatilla in the foreground is built to plan, the other modified by Kevin Walton to look like a Fokker EIII.*

Figure 11 shows the tail end of a Magnatilla, built from the Flair kit, in the foreground. In the background is the same model with changes to the tail surfaces to make it look like a Fokker E3. The areas of the fin/rudder and tailplane/ elevator were not altered, and thus the flying characteristics remained unchanged. However, the modified model, which also featured a curved upper fuselage, became a fun scale Fokker and provided a lot of enjoyment for the builder of this unique model.

### Sketching on plans

Looking at the existing plan is a good place to start making alterations to a model. Basically, at this stage, we are talking about minor structural changes, alterations to the outline of the design to give it a new and individual look. As long as their areas are not significantly changed, the outline and the look of the fin and tailplane can be changed extensively. Figure 12 shows how the modifications were done.

The grey area is the fin and rudder of the existing Magnatilla design with the dotted outline showing their proposed replacements. A similar approach was taken with the tailplane and elevator. A quick look shows that the areas and positions have changed little. Thus the 'new' design should perform roughly as the original.

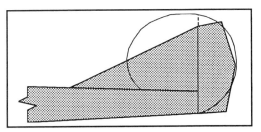

**Figure 12** *The fin and rudder outlines can easily be altered without affecting their areas or the performance of the aircraft.*

Assuming the tail surfaces on the original model were all sheet, there are no structural changes to think about either. This technique can be applied to most existing designs.

There is, in fact, lots of scope for different changes. As well as new fin/rudder and tailplane/ elevator shapes, different wing tips, the use of a foam wing instead of a built up one, or vice versa, and some alterations to the internal fuselage structure can all continue the confidence building process.

## Using components from current/ crashed models

Many of us have a workshop or loft full of models awaiting repair. It is not uncommon to find an undamaged wing or tail surface and occasionally a fuselage, each belonging to a different aircraft. Unfortunately there are no complete aircraft. This is the time to introduce the idea of designing a 'Bitsa', a new model created from the remaining bits of old crashed aircraft.

**Figure 13** *My Bullpup has rather more extensive changes. Developed from J. Bowmer's Wifurskin, Nexus Plan RC914X, it has different fin, tailplane and wing tip shapes as well as internal constructional changes.*

BuT You SAID " USE COMPONENTS FROM CRASHED MODELS " !

An undamaged wing can be a favourite starting point, not only because this component is often the most long lived, but also because it is less likely to be oil/fuel soaked on an internal combustion engined model. This time we will consider the plan view of the model. Assume you have a wing from an old model (let's call it model A), and a tailplane from another (model B), albeit somewhat larger than the tail

that was originally fitted to model A. You can use both these old parts and the plan shows a new fuselage that is somewhat thinner than the original.

The result, shown in Figure 15, is a Bitsa that uses bits of model A and bits of model B, together

**Figure 14** *My first Bitsa. Eric Clutton's famous Sharkface, seen in original form in the background of Figure 6, with a one third bigger wing and proportional control on rudder and elevator.*

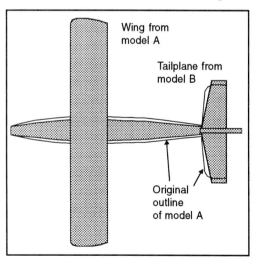

**Figure 15** *A new fuselage for an existing wing from one model and the tailplane from another is a useful step forward for the budding designer.*

## Chapter 1

with your own design of fuselage to hold the bits together. Again, the budding designer gets some experience of designing, without having to go the whole hog.

## Changing the size of proven designs

Sometimes, an existing design catches the eye, but is either too large or too small to become the next model on the building list. Changing the size will not change the aerodynamics of the model significantly, except that wings become more efficient the bigger they are and vice versa. The construction, however, is a different matter. Scale up a design to give double the wingspan and the wing area will increase four times. Scale up the building materials proportionately and the weight will go up eight times. With four times the wing area and eight times the weight, we would double the wing loading: not a happy state of affairs.

In Figure 16, the left-hand graph shows how much we should increase the linear dimensions of the materials used to maintain strength. Our model with double the wingspan will end up at just under three times the weight and four times the wing area. This is a good situation likely to result in an improved flight performance due to

the reduced wing loading. The right-hand graph is a similar one for use when scaling down. A sensible selection of materials to the nearest standard size is all that is required.

## What to build

Perhaps the first questions to ask when deciding on a new model are what motor is to be used and how many radio functions? Next, is the model to be designed as a conventional model or some unusual configuration such as a delta, canard, twin-boom or flying wing? Should it fly fast or slowly and how manoeuvrable should it be? Finally, does it have to look pretty or can the design be strictly functional?

Having considered each of these questions, what is the new model going to look like? This is where you should commence sketching on some scrap paper until you find the sort of layout you want. How will you know when you've got the right answer? Well, when you've built a few models, you get a feeling about it and if it looks right, it usually is.

### Low wing layouts

If you look at Figure 18, you will see side views of two different low wing models, both with the same wing and tailplane and both featuring a

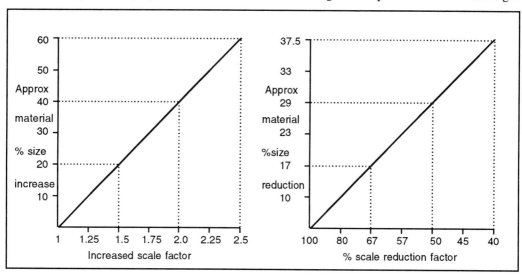

**Figure 16** *When the size of a model is increased, the dimensions of the materials should not be increased in the same proportion to maintain the strength of the structure. The same holds true when the size of a model is reduced.*

**Figure 17** *The Mongrel, designed by Brian Peckham, looks just like a full sized, modern, low wing, light aircraft, yet it is not a scale model. It is available from* Nexus Plans Service *as Plan RM 168.*

tricycle undercarriage. The first has its engine mounted between the side cheeks of the fuselage, a commercial teardrop canopy and a short strake leading to a pleasantly curved fin and rudder. Suppose this was your first sketch but was not quite what you wanted. You try again with an engine and spinner blending into the fuselage, an integral cockpit rising out of the fuselage and an angular fin and rudder.

Now consider tailwheel aircraft. Again there are two side view sketches in Figure 19. The top one shows a model with engine and spinner faired into the nose, a large integral cabin and the rear fuselage sloping down to a curved fin and rudder with a small tailwheel. Perhaps you prefer to use a teardrop canopy with a swept back fin/rudder and tail skid. You now have four alternative side layout sketches for your low wing model. Perhaps with some minor changes you will finally feel happy to select one of them.

## High wing configurations

The same process can be applied to a design for a high wing model, still using the same wing and tailplane as previously. Figure 20 overleaf shows two high wing models with tricycle undercarriages. The first is a cabin layout with its engine located between the front fuselage cheeks. The upper rear of the fuselage is straight and horizontal, with the underside of the fuselage sloping up markedly. The fin and rudder are both nicely rounded. Maybe you feel it looks a

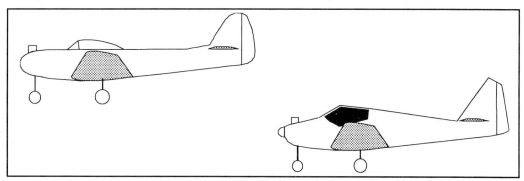

**Figure 18** *Two typical low wing designs, both different but each using the same wing and tailplane.*

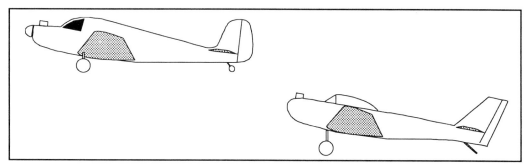

**Figure 19** *Changing the configuration to a tail dragger can have a remarkable impact on the look of the model despite again using the same wing and tailplane.*

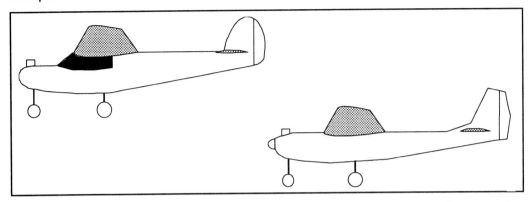

**Figure 20** *A change to a high wing configuration, but utilising the same wing/tail configuration, gives further variations.*

bit old fashioned and try another sketch. This has a shallower fuselage altogether with a spinner blending into the front of the fuselage. There is also a small strake in front of the angular fin and rudder.

The last pair of sketches, in Figure 21, are high wing models but this time tail draggers. The first has a pronounced chin under the engine, which could be installed inverted. The cabin is in front of and above the wing while the rear fuselage slopes down sharply to a large swept back fin with a tail skid beneath it. The other model has no cockpit and a much slimmer fuselage which blends into the spinner. Fitted with a tailwheel, the shape of the fin and rudder assembly is noticeably triangular.

Having examined eight possibilities based on only two variations: high wing or low wing and nosewheel or tailwheel, it is clear that sketching

small side views can quickly result in a layout that you personally find pleasing.

**Other wing positions**

Now, consider a parasol wing layout, a mid wing design and a biplane, shown in Figure 22. All three use similar fuselages, except that the parasol and biplane have open cockpits, while the mid wing design has a teardrop canopy. In the case of the biplane, the wings have been reduced proportionately in size since there are two of them, but the tailplane position still remains unchanged.

**A three view sketch**

So, you've finally made your choice of side view for your new model. Apply the same idea to the plan view and then sketch a small three-view, preferably on squared paper. Amend the lines until

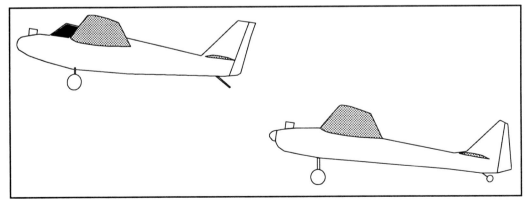

**Figure 21** *Retaining the high wing configuration but changing to a tail dragger undercarriage configuration gives yet another set of options.*

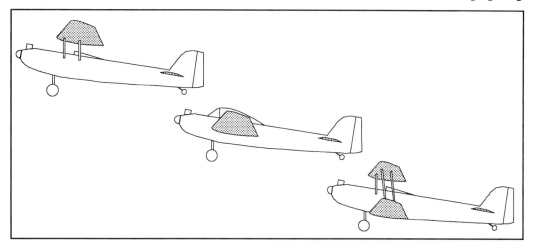

**Figure 22** *Possible parasol, mid wing and biplane configurations provide further interesting possibilities.*

they seem clean and satisfying, and then think about sizes and areas for the wing, tail and fin. Chapter 3 contains a number of graphs and nomographs which enable these to be selected. Figure 23 shows what might be your first attempt. The model is a high wing trainer fitted with aileron, elevator, rudder and throttle. A side view, plan and front elevation have all been sketched in. It has a tricycle undercarriage fixed to the fuselage. A small amount of dihedral should provide some lateral stability. Don't forget to put in a scale as this will help when converting the sketch to full size. From this 3-view, a full-size outline drawing can be prepared. Just scale it all up, having first marked out the principal dimensions on a datum line. Chapter 12 shows how to prepare working drawings.

## Propeller ground clearance and aircraft rotation

To avoid the engine stopping on take-off because the propeller has fouled the ground, it is important to think about the undercarriage geometry at the design stage. The impact on the design of nosewheels and tail draggers has already been shown. Looking at the top left model in Figure 24, it is clear that provided the propeller centre line is set sufficiently high above the ground, no fouling of the propeller on the take-off run is likely. Bearing in mind noseleg flexing, a clearance of 5 cm (2") is satisfactory unless trying to take-off from long grass or a very rough strip, when a 50% increase is beneficial.

With the tail dragger it is important that there is good propeller clearance when the fuselage

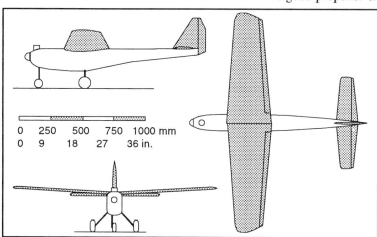

0   250   500   750   1000 mm
0    9     18    27    36 in.

**Figure 23** *A sketch for a first model design for a high wing, four function trainer.*

9

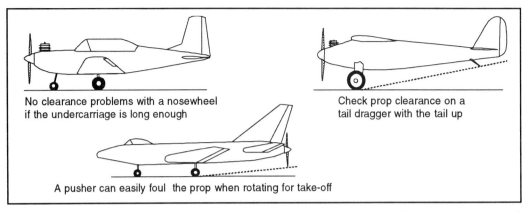

No clearance problems with a nosewheel if the undercarriage is long enough

Check prop clearance on a tail dragger with the tail up

A pusher can easily foul the prop when rotating for take-off

**Figure 24** *A propeller hitting the ground can stop the engine and abort a take-off at best. At worst, it will result in a broken prop. It is essential that the prop clears the ground under all circumstances.*

and wings are in the take-off attitude. Again the clearance of the tip of the propeller in this attitude should be the same as for a nosewheel model. The most difficult situation occurs with the pusher layout. As the aircraft rotates, it is common to see the propeller foul the ground. This is particularly so with deltas and swept wing aircraft, where the angle of rotation is often large. In all cases, a check on the plan at the design stage can save a lot of heartache later.

## Sports scale

Many people are put off the thought of producing a scale model by the amount of research and detail required, the building time and fear of an overweight model. Yet those very same people like the idea of a model which looks like a real aeroplane. Thus, a sports scale design needs only to capture the flavour of the full sized prototype to give much satisfaction. A fun scale Spitfire can have enlarged tail surfaces, a wing with most of the leading edges straight rather than curved, but still retaining the elliptical tips, near full span ailerons and an engine cylinder and silencer which hang out in the airstream. A fixed under-carriage, or no undercarriage at all also simplifies the construction. Yet, on the ground or in the air, a well painted model will immediately be recognisable as a Spitfire. Building time will be a fraction of that for a full scale model and once airborne, the flight characteristics should be much more docile, not least because the wing will almost certainly be more lightly loaded.

Now consider a modern jet fighter like the Tornado. Powered by a ducted fan, with retracts and swing wings, the model is destined for the fanatical flier who has access to a tarmac strip. Yet a good Tornado look alike can be designed and built, with the engine driving a conventional propeller in the nose or at the rear of the fuselage and the wings fixed in sweep-back terms. Once airborne with the propeller invisible, the model will be instantly recognisable as a Tornado.

### Sources of scale information

There are plenty of sources of information about full-size aircraft which provide sufficient information to produce a realistic sports scale model. An 'Airfix' or other 1/72nd scale plastic kit is an excellent starting point, giving a three dimensional impression as well as a small three-view. *The Observer's Book of Aircraft* is another excellent source of three-view plans. Books about aircraft can be purchased from book shops

**Figure 25** *Rupert Weiss designed this fun scale North American B70 with a pusher propeller at the rear. The excessively long undercarriage is necessary to give clearance on take-off and landing.*

Figure 27 *This RPV exhibited at an airshow looks just like a model and could be the stimulus for a new design.*

Figure 26 *Immediately identifiable as an F14 Tomcat, this design makes no pretence at scale. The wings (in the swept back position) are combined with the tailplane to form a pure delta.*

or borrowed from a library. The Military and Aviation Book Club's range of books includes a number of suitable titles. Magazines such as *Aeroplane Monthly* and Nexus Special Interests' *R/C Scale Aircraft* also provide a good source.

The RAF museum at Hendon and the Old Warden collection of aircraft provide excellent opportunities to see and photograph aircraft at full size. There are many other museums and airshows around the country which provide similar opportunities.

## Compromises and simplification.

Compromises will always have to be made when designing any flying model. There is no such thing as a perfect design, just a set of choices that result in a better model than others in its class. For example, looks often get sacrificed in the search for out-and-out performance. Similarly, plenty of stability and lots of manoeuvrability cannot be built into the same model.

Simplification can save weight and construction time as well as producing a more reliable performance. A typical example is the use of strip ailerons instead of inset ones. How far simplification is taken will depend on you, but if the first rule of aviation is to build in lightness, the second is to simplify everything.

# 2. Choosing a configuration

## Conventional layouts

### Monoplanes

What could be more natural than to want to start a first completely new design by choosing the well proven monoplane layout, with the engine at the front, and fin and tailplane at the back? It is the low risk route which most full size and model designers have preferred since the 1930s. It is the easiest to design and the most likely to lead to success. It is also the layout that the majority R/C modellers prefer. A conventional monoplane design is unlikely to lead to any undesirable characteristics either from a building or a flying point of view.

Fun-fly models are a specialist form of monoplane. They can be considered as low aspect ratio, low wing loading models with a moderately to low powered engine up front. They usually also have short fuselages. Their key features

**Figure 28**  *A pair of Fun-Fly 15s with their large, low aspect ratio wings. (Photo courtesy Bill-Kits)*

are high manoeuvrability, excellent aerobatic capability and a small turning circle. Their maximum speed is usually limited either by

IT'S MY LATEST DESIGN ... I THOUGHT I'D PLAY SAFE SO IT'S GOT FIVE WHEELS, FOUR WINGS, THREE ENGINES AND TWO FINS !!!

**Figure 29** *My JH2 Stringbox with its triple fins and twin tail showing clearly. It is a slow and graceful flier in the air. The plan, No RM 259, is available from* Nexus Plans Service.

engine capacity or control flutter; usually by a combination of both.

The advantages of conventional monoplanes include:

- Familiarity with construction techniques
- Weight of tail surfaces balanced by engine
- Radio equipment near centre of gravity allows easy access by removing wing
- Only one wing to build
- Easy orientation in the air

### Biplanes

There is something about a biplane which is magical in its appeal. Maybe it's the association with the dawn and golden ages of aviation. Maybe it's the lazy way they appear to float around the sky. Maybe it's their manoeuvrability and small turning circle. They also have the benefit of a smaller wingspan for a given wing area and loading, despite the fact that the biplane configuration is less efficient than a monoplane, due to interference between the two wings. Biplanes also produce more drag, particularly from their struts and bracing wires.

For some modellers, the thought of building two wings, or even three in the case of a triplane, is enough to put them off the thought of ever building a multi-wing model. On the other hand, there are many advantages to this configuration. Biplanes are generally slow flying models without a large speed range. They are manoeuvrable and easily aerobatic. The down side is that when the engine stops they may have less than perfect gliding characteristics.

**Figure 30** *For a really offbeat aircraft, what could be better than an autogyro? This is my Al's Autogyro ready to start engines. It can be built from Nexus Plan RC1695.*

## Offbeat aircraft

### Flying wings

Flying wings have much to recommend themselves in terms of ease of construction. There are no tail surfaces to construct and often not even a fuselage. They are exciting and unusual models which perform well and always cause comment when seen on the flying field. The lack of tail minimises both weight and drag which both help to offset the inherent loss of lift caused by the need for a reflex aerofoil section.

Many people are put off by potential problems of tailless models. In particular they are concerned about the control and centre of gravity areas, not to mention orientation difficulties when flying them. Neither problem is insuperable. Special aerofoils have been developed over the years which are particularly well suited to the special needs of these aircraft and details are given in Chapter 6.

**Figure 31** *Pteradon is a three function 380 powered electric flying wing, one of a series of tailless models designed for a range of different power plants.*

**Figure 32** *The Dragon Delta has a spectacular rolling performance and a very wide speed range. It is available as Nexus Plan RM 373.*

**Figure 34** *The canard on this delta sits close to the front of the wing. It has been placed to try and generate some vortex lift.*

## Deltas

The delta is a particular form of flying wing, named because it looks like the Greek letter for 'D', which is 'Δ' or 'delta'. Its peculiarities include well swept wings and a low aspect ratio. The former can lead to Dutch roll problems if the fin size is inadequate. Both result in high drag at large angles of attack. This latter characteristic demands a powerful engine for the size of model so that speed can be maintained in tight turns and looping manoeuvres. It also allows control of high sink rates on finals by the application of plenty of power. On the positive side, the speed and roll rate of deltas are both exceptionally high and separate the men from the boys, the women from the girls.

The high speed achieved by deltas has resulted in them being banned from virtually every pylon racing class. They also have some unfamiliar characteristics. They have very high stalling angles of attack, which mean getting the nose well up on finals and giving careful thought to the undercarriage layout to allow the aircraft to rotate on take-off and avoid scraping its tail on touchdown.

## Canards

The word canard means 'duck' in French, though why this term has been applied to aircraft which fly tail first is unclear. The driving force that first led to canard layouts was the theory that the configuration is more efficient because both the wing and foreplane provide lift, and the wing becomes unstallable. Being ahead of the wing, the lifting foreplane is set to operate at a higher angle of incidence than the wing. Thus the foreplane stalls first and pitches the aircraft nose down, automatically unstalling the foreplane. The wing never reaches its stalling angle. In practice the wing is also never able to provide its maximum lift, because the foreplane stalls before it can do so.

Modern designs of full size aircraft are moving rapidly towards the canard configuration, matched to a delta wing. Examples include the Eurofighter 2000, Swedish Grippen, French Raphael and later marks of Mirage. The reasons for this are mainly concerned with the benefits to manoeuvre and the generation of vortex lift. In addition the structural strength and space within the wing are both an advantage.

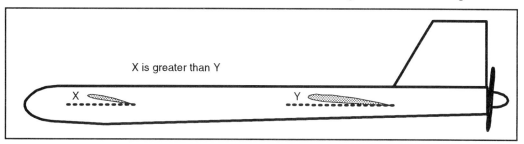

X is greater than Y

X

Y

**Figure 33** *A canard can be tractor, or, as in this case, a pusher model. The foreplane is always set at a higher incidence than the main wing.*

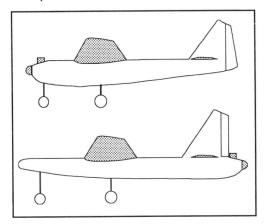

**Figure 35** *Typical tractor and pusher layouts show the impact of engine location on fuselage design.*

## Engine location

The primary position for an engine is in the nose or in the tail of the aircraft, although location on a pylon above the wing has some benefits. Looking first at the tractor configuration at the top of Figure 35, this is the most commonly found layout and the reasons are not hard to understand.

The location allows the weight of the engine to balance that of the tail surfaces. It provides slipstream over the elevator and rudder increasing their effectiveness at low airspeeds; particularly useful during take-off and landing. Slipstream over the centre section of the wing also increases the lift it generates. With a conventional monoplane or biplane, the fuel tank is positioned behind the engine and reasonably close to the aircraft's centre of gravity, thus minimising trim changes as fuel is consumed.

The pusher layout avoids oil from the exhaust spreading over the model if mounted in the tail, but requires the radio to be installed right at the front of the model to try to balance the engine's weight. There is no slipstream over any of the control surfaces and on the take-off run the propeller ground clearance is reduced as the aircraft rotates, often necessitating an extra long undercarriage to avoid the engine stopping. The engine will tend to run rich when the nose is raised and the tank will be well aft of the centre of gravity unless a pumping arrangement is employed.

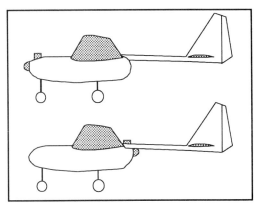

**Figure 36** *A pair of twin boom models showing that whether they use a tractor or pusher layout there is little difference in the fuselage shape.*

In a twin boom layout, however, these snags disappear. Twin booms can be used for pusher or tractor layouts as shown in Figure 36 top and bottom. However, servo runs to the elevator and rudders may be more complex and adequate stiffness must be built into the booms.

### Multi engines

The use of more than one engine adds expense and complexity to any model, but the sound of two or more internal combustion engines running in near synchronisation is well worth the effort. Asymmetric problems in the case of engine failure mean that twin designs require a good degree of flying competency. There is also significantly more work in building a twin as

**Figure 37** *A twin boom layout can be used with either a tractor or a pusher engine. It usually means the use of twin rudders. This particular model was fitted with twin engines in tandem.*

**Figure 38** *John Hearne's fun scale Hercules features a stringered fuselage, foam nose and wing, balsa sheet tail surfaces and built-up nacelles.*

nacelles need to be designed and constructed, and fuel systems duplicated.

A key consideration is the requirement for a large rudder or rudders to ensure adequate directional control in single engine flight. This can be aided by canting the engines outwards by a small amount as shown in Figure 39.

The figure also shows a layout using twin fins, each angled slightly out and located in the slip-stream to help counteract asymmetric forces. When one engine stops, the fin in the slipstream of the remaining engine automatically tries to stop the yaw caused by the asymmetric thrust.

However, those who have tried a twin or even a three or four engined model say the thrill of success is difficult to better. For those still concerned about asymmetric problems, there are two alternatives. The first is to use electric power, when the chances of an engine failure are negligible. The alternative is a tandem

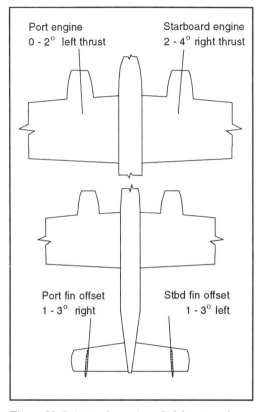

**Figure 39** *Pointing the engines slightly outwards can minimise the effects of asymmetric power on a twin. The figures given are for engines which turn anti-clockwise viewed from the front. Offset fins are another excellent way of reducing asymmetric difficulties.*

configuration in which one engine is mounted behind the other; both engines lying on the centre line of the aircraft. This does allow unmatched engines to be employed, conventional wisdom suggesting that the smaller engine should be the rear one. Figure 40 shows three possibilities:

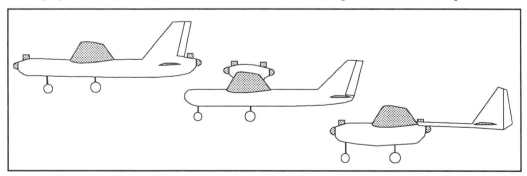

**Figure 40** *Three alternative twin engine push-pull configurations which allow engines of unequal size to be used.*

from left to right, the engines mounted in the nose and tail, a pair of engines installed in a push/pull configuration in a pylon above the wing and finally a twin boom layout.

## Undercarriages

The simplest landing gear solution from a builder's point of view is not to use any undercarriage at all. This involves a hand launch and landing on the belly of the fuselage or a skid. Next in complexity is the tail dragger, which may feature a fixed, castoring or steerable tailwheel or just a tail skid. Somewhat heavier than the tail dragger is the tricycle undercarriage with a fixed or steerable nosewheel. Thought may be given to the use of retracts, which require an additional channel to operate them, adding to the complexity of the aircraft. They also require a reasonably smooth landing strip and the skill to land on it and to touch down smoothly.

Finally, even heavier and producing more drag are floats and skis. These need to be accurately fixed in the pitching plane to ensure the aircraft is able to take-off and land safely from water or snow as appropriate. They provide a completely different approach to flying, though both can also be used to take-off and land on damp grass.

### Noselegs versus tail draggers

The noseleg configuration has a number of advantages and also a few snags when compared with a tail dragger. These will affect the choice of undercarriage layout. First, a nosewheel equipped model will try to track straight on take-off and landing; a most helpful characteristic. The configuration also minimises the possibility of bouncing back into the air after an excessively fast or heavy landing.

However, a nosewheel layout is generally heavier than a tail dragger configuration. It also imposes severe stress on the noseleg and its mounting when operating from less than ideally smooth runways, or during those misjudged arrivals which are supposed to be perfect landings. Furthermore, it is essential that the mainwheels are located only just behind the centre of gravity to allow the model to rotate on take-off, presenting the wing to the airflow at the optimum angle

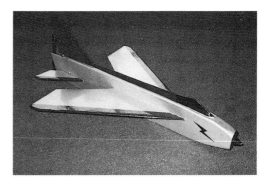

**Figure 41** *With only a small engine, this two channel fun scale Lightning is really too small for an undercarriage and anyway it wouldn't look right in the air.*

of attack. Do not forget that a three channel model with ailerons, elevator and throttle can have the ailerons connected to a steerable nosewheel to provide directional control on the ground.

Any tail dragger touching down at too high a speed can easily result in a bounce back into the air. This is because the centre of gravity lies behind the mainwheels and tries to push the tail down, increasing the wing's angle of attack and thus generating more lift. The cause of this phenomenon should be clear from Figure 42.

There are two further conflicting problems with tail draggers. The first is that if the wheels are too close to the centre of gravity, the model will have an uncontrollable tendency to nose

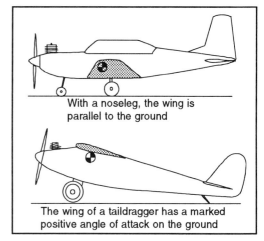

With a noseleg, the wing is parallel to the ground

The wing of a taildragger has a marked positive angle of attack on the ground

**Figure 42** *It is essential to understand the various advantages of nosewheel and tail dragger undercarriage configurations before deciding which to use.*

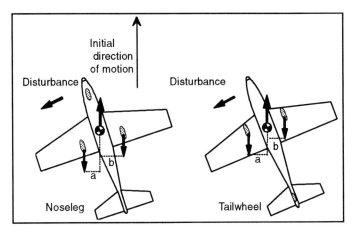

over on take-off and landing. Moving the mainwheels forward will increase the tendency to perform a ground loop; an uncontrollable swing. A sensible compromise position, good elevator authority and plenty of pilot experience are the key ways of avoiding these difficulties on take-off and landing.

Consider the pair of aircraft taking off in Figure 43. Both have hit a tussock of grass with their port mainwheel, which tries to swing the models to port (anti-clockwise). Initially, the inertia of the aircraft will try to keep them moving in the original direction. For a nosewheel configuration, the distance **b** is greater than **a**, and thus the drag from the starboard mainwheel tends to straighten the aircraft. With a tailwheel, **a** is greater than **b**, and the drag from the port wheel increases the swing.

# 3. A suitable size

## Transportability

Possibly the most important single factor in deciding the size of a new model is whether it will fit in your car, van or trailer for transportation to your flying site. This limitation is most apparent with large models; particularly single piece ones and, of course, is more of a problem for those owning small vehicles. Other important considerations are the size of your workshop, the type of engine to hand and the amount of cash available for the new model. Of course, it is always possible to buy a new engine for the latest design. Sports models will, by definition, need to weigh less than 7kg (15.4 lb.)

to avoid the legal requirement to obtain a CAA exemption and fit a fail-safe. At the other extreme, a wingspan of (600mm) 24" is likely to be a practical minimum although some even smaller micro R/C models have and will continue to be built.

### Choosing the dimensions

There are really two places to start when sizing a model. The first is a question of personal preference. Everyone has an idea of how large a model they want to build. The second is defined largely by engine size and performance. Obviously, engine size alone is not sufficient,

I DIDN'T THINK ABOUT FITTING IT IN THE CAR !

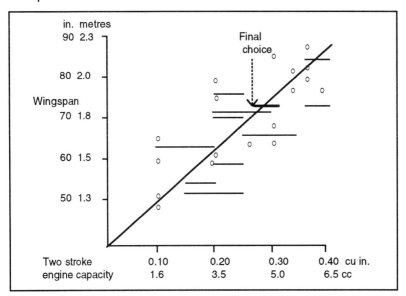

**Figure 44** *Sizing a model from the practical experience of other designers.*

as a small fast aeroplane will need the same size engine as a larger, slow flying aircraft.

As a practical example, during a design study for a twin engined model, a list was prepared of every plan for a twin available in the Nexus and some other ranges. The engine size and wingspan were noted and the results plotted on the graph shown in Figure 44. The circles represent models quoting a single size of engine; the straight lines those for a range of sizes. The diagonal line from the bottom left to the top right of the graph is the best fit line though all the plots. Having selected a size for the model, 1.88m (74") span, the graph suggested a range of suitable two stroke engines from 4 - 5cc (0.25 - 0.30 cu. in.).

Thinking about these two parameters, either select a given wingspan, or a particular engine size for a new model. We will now consider two possibilities; a 1.6m (63") span medium performance model, and then a model to be powered by an average 6.5cc (0.40 cu. in.) two stroke motor.

Starting with a 1.6m (63") span, a chord of around 25cm (10") looks right, giving a wing area of 40 sq. dm (4 square feet). For a reasonable wing loading of say 70 g per sq. dm (22½ oz per sq. ft), this means an all-up weight of 2.55 kg (90 ounces). Assuming average performance, a forty two stroke is about the right power level for such an aeroplane. However, looking at

Figure 45, the dotted line shows that a two stroke engine of 4cc (0.25 cu. in.) capacity would give a modest performance whilst one of 10cc (0.60 cu. in.) would suit a fully aerobatic model.

Now considering a model to be powered by that 6.5cc (0.40 cu. in.) engine, the dotted/dashed line on the figure suggests a model with a wing area between 30 and 55 sq. dm (3¼ and 5½ square feet); the former suitable for a fast aerobatic model and the latter for a slow flying relaxation or trainer model.

Figure 46 gives some baseline figures for a typical monoplane. With a wingspan of around six times the mean chord (C), the fuselage can be proportioned to about three quarters of this dimension. The tail and control surface areas are all related to the wing area. Later chapters discuss the sizing of these items in more detail and, of course, all that is being offered here are some initial guidelines. Dimension X must be sufficient to give adequate propeller clearance. This will depend on the surface of your flying field, but should be at least 50mm (2") plus half the length of the propeller if flying from grass strips. Dimension Y is important in ensuring that the model can rotate on take-off without scraping its tail.

For most people, calculation of the centre of gravity appears simple as it can be put between 25% and 33% of the mean wing chord without

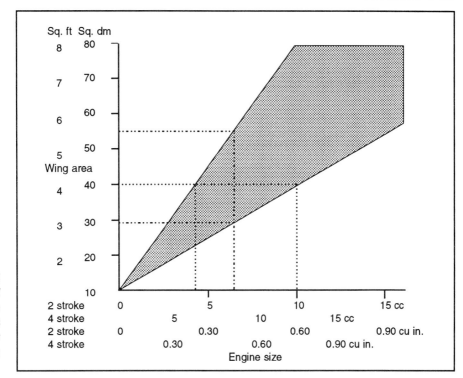

**Figure 45**
*The typical relationship between engine size and wing area.*

further calculation. The lower figure should be used when the fuselage is relatively short or the tailplane size is small in relation to the wing size. Later in this chapter we will look at a better way of finding a safe position for the centre of gravity on any model.

A key feature in providing ease of transportation is to design in the removal of selected parts of the model, rather than having a single piece airframe. The norm is to remove the wings and

in most models the wing will come off as a single item, giving access to the radio installation and thus reducing the need for a hatch. For the largest models, the ability to remove the tailplane is also a factor worth considering, although this is normally unnecessary.

Matched against the ease of transportation is the time taken to re-rig a model at the flying site. This is not usually a problem with monoplanes, but a biplane may have inter-plane struts to add

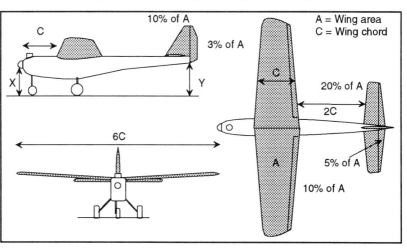

**Figure 46** *For that first design, the figures given are just a sensible starting point. X should give adequate propeller clearance and Y should ensure the tail clears the ground on rotation at take-off.*

Chapter 3

**Figure 47** *A triplane can often fit into a car fully assembled due to its short wingspan. This is the Flair Triplane, which looks realistic despite being a free-lance design.*

**Figure 49** *A Spitfire wing, designed to give the best possible manoeuvrability, compared to a typical glider wing shows the variation in aspect ratio for these two types of aircraft.*

to the complication of fitting two wings to the fuselage. A delta or flying wing, on the other hand may be quite satisfactory as a single piece model. Final decisions will be crucially affected by the size of vehicle available and the number of models/people to be carried in it. A little forethought may well avoid a disappointment when the model is finished, as may the construction of a box to carry the model on a roof rack. Some lucky people choose their car to fit their model!

**Wingspan and aspect ratio**

The wingspan of the proposed model will be dependent on two factors. The first is the designer's personal choice and the role of the new model. The other is the desired aspect ratio and wing area. In general, the higher the aspect ratio, the better the gliding performance and the worse the manoeuvrability. Having selected an engine and as a result decided on a desired wing area, the aspect ratio will determine the wingspan and average chord.

By simple multiplication using Figure 48, wingspan multiplied by chord equals wing area, and equally, wingspan divided by chord equals

aspect ratio. The importance of aspect ratio is that, all other things being equal, the higher the aspect ratio (the longer and thinner the wing) the lower the induced drag produced by the wing and the more difficult it is to build a strong wing structure. Thus, a delta may well have an aspect ratio of less than 2, a typical sports model one of around 6 and for a high performance glider a figure of 12 or more is common.

While it is straightforward to find the average chord with a wing featuring a straight leading and trailing edge, things do become slightly harder when this is not the situation. However, using the eye, it is not difficult to straighten the outline of the wing to give a reasonable approximation, which may then be used to find the mean chord which lies at the half span point.

**Fuselage length and cross section**

The importance of fuselage length is that it provides leverage for the tailplane and fin. For a typical monoplane the fuselage length will be around three-quarters of the wingspan. All other things being equal, the longer the fuselage, the more stable the resulting aircraft is likely to be in the pitching and yawing planes. The cross

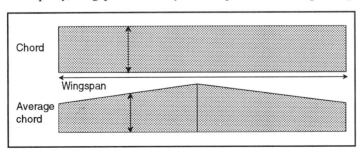

**Figure 48** *Aspect ratio compares the wingspan to the size of the chord or average chord.*

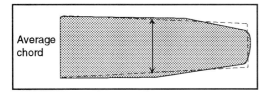

**Figure 50** *With an odd shaped wing, a new outline of the wing should be drawn approximating straight leading and trailing edges as well as the wing tip.*

section chosen is entirely up to the designer but must be large enough to house the radio and also give adequate strength.

A square or rectangular section is by far the easiest to design and build, but is less than aesthetically pleasing in many cases. Round or oval fuselages tend to be more attractive to the eye, but usually introduce two way curves into the structure which are not the easiest to build. More information on this subject is given in Chapter 9.

Consideration should also be given at this stage to the layout of the main items within the fuselage and a typical example is shown in Figure 52. These items comprise the engine and its associated fuel tank, the radio receiver, servos, battery and switch. Sufficient space is essential including padding for the fragile receiver. Of course, their location in terms of getting the centre of gravity in the right place without resorting to ballast is also important.

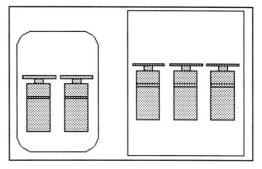

**Figure 51** *Will the required number of servos (usually two or three abreast) fit across the fuselage?*

## Tail size and position

The choice of tailplane size boils down fundamentally to a question of stability. Too small a tail and the resulting aircraft will be all but impossible to control. Too large will introduce a rear end weight penalty as well as an unnecessary increase in drag, neither of them attractive. The weight penalty can be difficult to balance, especially with a short nosed model.

The other crucial factor which affects the size necessary is the length of the rear fuselage between the wing and the tailplane itself. The size of the tailplane always includes the elevator as well. Starting with the fuselage length, Figure 53 suggests a size of tailplane as a percentage of wing size. Figure 54 enables an actual size of tailplane to be read, knowing the area of the wing.

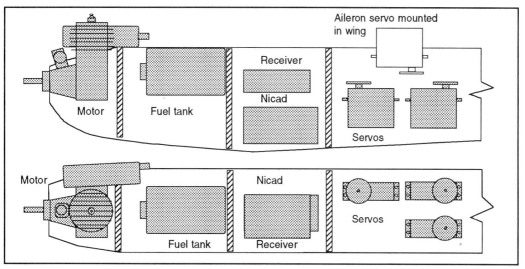

**Figure 52** *The positions of all the main items must be considered in plan view and elevation.*

# Chapter 3

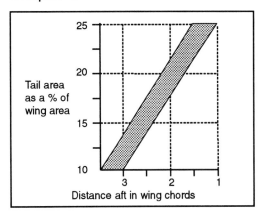

**Figure 53** *The size of the tailplane depends on its distance from the wing.*

A good starting figure seems to be around fifteen per cent of the wing area, possibly smaller if the distance between the tailplane and the wing is greater that two wing chords and, conversely larger if that distance is shorter. The tail area is calculated in a similar way to wing area, by multiplying the tail span by the average tail chord.

The key points to remember are that stability is increased by:

- Large tailplanes
- Long fuselages
- Forward centres of gravity

The vertical position of the tailplane also requires some serious consideration. Located, as it usually is, behind the wing, its performance can be adversely affected by downwash and turbulent flow from the wing. There are five basic vertical positions for a tailplane. These are shown in Figure 55. The higher ones avoid the downwash and turbulence, but may be blanked in a stall with a low aspect ratio or sharply swept

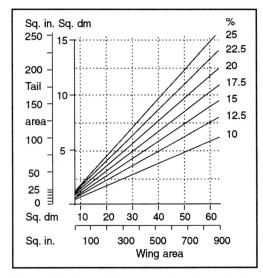

**Figure 54** *The tailplane area depends on the size of wing, length of fuselage and type of model.*

wing planform. For models without an undercarriage, a high position can also avoid potential damage if landing on rough ground. Clearly, the choice of position of the tailplane will also be affected by the vertical location of the wing.

### All moving tails

Historically, all moving tailplanes and fins have been most popular with gliders and ducted fan models, but they can be an interesting feature of many models providing lots of pleasure. However, there are dangers, of which flutter is potentially the most lethal. The axis of rotation of the surface and its centre of gravity must be positioned carefully, with a rigid slop-free linkage to the servo. The fuselage attachment must be strong and secure, yet allow easy movement.

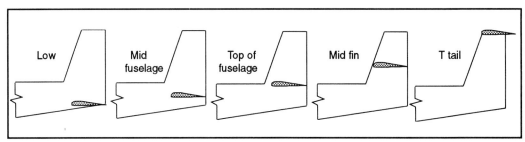

**Figure 55** *The five basic vertical positions for a tailplane starting left with a position below the fuselage and ending right with a T tail mounted on top of the fin.*

26

## Fin size

The size of the fin can be calculated in the same way as the size of the tailplane, and again is assumed to include the area of the rudder. Twin fins can be used and offer advantages for twin engined models, as they can be located in the prop wash of the engines. The construction and control runs will, however, be more complicated. Each fin should be half the size of a single one.

## V or butterfly tails

Finally a butterfly of V tail can be chosen, combining the functions of fin and tailplane. An area around 10% greater than a conventional tailplane, with each side angled up 30° is a good reference point. There are several attractions to butterfly tails. The two surfaces provide less drag (both parasitic and interference) than the two halves of a tailplane plus a fin. Second, they keep the tail well clear of the ground. This can be a great asset for models without an undercarriage, particularly when landing on rough ground. The

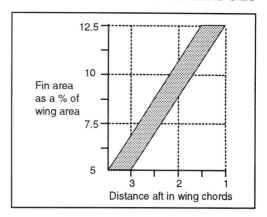

**Figure 56** *The size of the fin is dependent on its distance aft of the wing.*

linkage to them is unusual and an on-board rudder/elevator mixer is needed. Butterfly tails can be upright or inverted as shown in Figure 57 overleaf. When operating in rudder mode, they do have some of the undesirable characteristics associated with aileron adverse yaw. There is, therefore, some advantage to be gained from the use of differential rudder movement.

" I THOUGHT I'D TRY A BUTTERFLY TAIL !! "

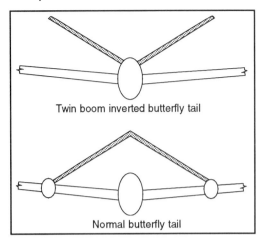

**Figure 57** *As well as an upright V, the tail can also be mounted inverted with a twin boom layout.*

## Balancing the model

Not surprisingly, many people find the final weight estimation of a paper design a difficult task, but a logical approach to the subject, a pair of scales

and experience all help. Consider first the major items and note their weights. The figures shown in Table 2 are for a four channel 4cc (0.25 cu. in.) two stroke powered model. All items can be weighed on kitchen scales and old fuselages, wings and tailplanes can be checked to get an idea of weight for a given size of item. Next draw a scale sketch of the side view of the fuselage and accurately mark the position of the major items. Alternatively, this information may be marked in on the plan. The weight of each item is then added to the sketch, allowing the balance of the outline design to be estimated. Figure 58 shows this stage.

### Centre of gravity location

As the aircraft designer, you can now put your own skills to the test, both in calculating where the centre of gravity should be located and also in getting it to that position without the use of lead ballast. In simple terms, it is useful to think of the fuselage as a seesaw which has to be balanced. Obviously, the engine and the

| Item | Wt g | Wt oz | Item | Wt g | Wt oz |
|------|------|-------|------|------|-------|
| Engine | 225 | 8 | 600 mAh battery | 110 | 4 |
| Propeller | 30 | 1 | *Fuselage* | 450 | 16 |
| Spinner | 25 | 1 | *Wing* | 175 | 6 |
| Fuel tank | 30 | 1 | *Undercarriage* | 340 | 12 |
| Receiver | 55 | 2 | *Tailplane* | 60 | 2 |
| 4 Servos | 170 | 6 | **Total** | **1660** | **59** |

**Table 2** *A typical weight budget for a new design. Items in italics are only estimates at this stage.*

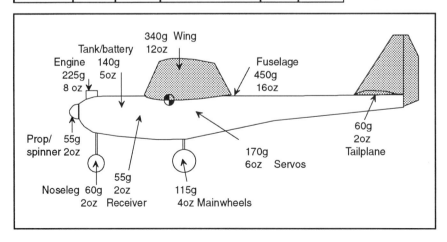

**Figure 58** *The location and weights of the various components marked in on the side view of the aircraft.*

tailplane are usually at the extremes of the fuselage and Figure 59 shows this straight-forward view.

In fact, every single item in the aircraft contributes to the balance and should be located so that the centre of gravity of the completed model is in the right place. Thus for the design shown above, the final balance figures are shown in Table 3, based on the distance of each item from the centre of gravity. It is useful to fill out a similar table for any new model.

Perhaps the more difficult question is exactly where to locate the centre of gravity. This critical factor will now be examined in detail.

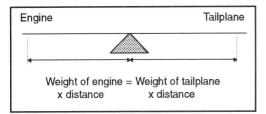

**Figure 59** *The location of the various major components must be chosen to balance the aircraft.*

### The aerodynamic mean chord (AMC)

The first thing is to establish where the aerodynamic mean chord lies. Remember it is not the same as the average wing chord, which lies at the half span for a straight-sided wing. This is fairly easily done by using the nomograph overleaf to locate the position of the mean aerodynamic wing chord. In this case, the single wing length and the ratio of the tip chord to the root chord of the wing must be measured.

An alternative is to use a graphical method (no maths, remember!). On a plan of the wing, extend the root chord forward and aft by an amount equal to the tip chord and vice versa. Then join the ends of the root and tip extended lines with diagonals and where they cross is the point where the aerodynamic mean chord lies. For wings which do not have straight line outlines, use the approximation technique shown in Figure 50. Both approaches give equally good answers.

Having established the position of the aerodynamic mean chord, we now need to find the ideal position of the centre of gravity along it.

| Item | Wt g | Dist mm | Dist x Wt | Wt Oz | Dist in. | Dist x Wt |
|---|---|---|---|---|---|---|
| Engine | 225 | 25 | 5625 | 8 | 1 | 8 |
| Propeller | 30 | 35 | 1050 | 1 | 1½ | 1½ |
| Spinner | 25 | 35 | 875 | 1 | 1½ | 1½ |
| Fuel tank | 30 | 25 | 750 | 1 | 1 | 1 |
| Noseleg | 60 | 25 | 1500 | 2 | 1 | 2 |
| 600 mAh battery | 110 | 25 | 2750 | 3¾ | 1 | 3¾ |
| Receiver | 55 | 15 | 825 | 2 | ½ | 1 |
| Wing | 340 | 0 | 0 | 12 | 0 | 0 |
| **Total forward** | | **g x mm** | **13375** | | **oz x in.** | **18¾** |
| 4 Servos | 170 | 10 | 1700 | 6 | ½ | 3 |
| Fuselage | 450 | 15 | 6750 | 16 | 3/5 | 9½ |
| Mainwheels | 115 | 10 | 1150 | 4 | ½ | 2 |
| Tailplane | 60 | 65 | 3900 | 2 | 2½ | 5 |
| **Total aft** | | **g x mm** | **13500** | | **oz x in.** | **18½** |

**Table 3** *It is useful to prepare a table showing how the model might balance. The answers are close enough for the design to continue. The discrepancy between the metric and imperial figures is due to rounding up and down.*

29

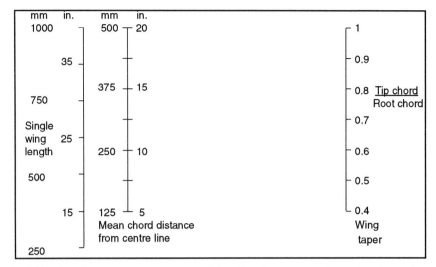

**Figure 60** *A nomograph for establishing the position of the aerodynamic mean chord.*

We must measure the following data:
- The length of the wing aerodynamic mean chord (AMC)
- The length of the tailplane aerodynamic mean chord
- Distance from 15% along the wing AMC to 15% along the tailplane AMC
- Wing area
- Tailplane area

We must then
- Divide the tail area by the wing area
- Divide the distance from 15% along the wing AMC to 15% along the tail AMC by wing AMC

Armed with these results, we can then lay a ruler on the nomograph in Figure 63 to arrive at a position for the centre of gravity along the aerodynamic mean chord. Complicated yes, but not requiring much maths. Re-read this paragraph before putting it into practice.

In the example shown, the dotted line connects a potential design with a 0.1 tail area and a distance of 2 average chords giving the location of the centre of gravity a distance along the aerodynamic mean chord of 24%. For a flying wing or a delta without a tailplane, the centre of gravity should be at the fifteen per cent point. Easy isn't it?

The nomograph works regardless of the units used; centimetres, millimetres or inches. Remember, however, that all the nomograph gives is a safe starting point and that flight

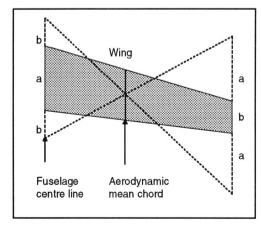

**Figure 61** *The location of the aerodynamic mean chord is readily established by graphical methods.*

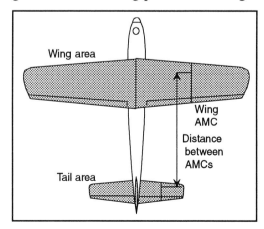

**Figure 62** *The key parameters to be established in order to locate the position of the centre of gravity.*

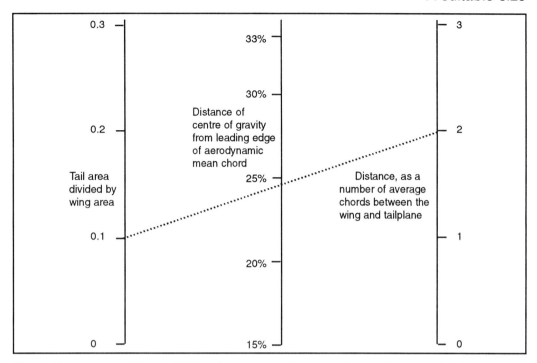

**Figure 63** *A nomograph for establishing the position of the centre of gravity for the maiden flight.*

experience may indicate a rearward movement of the centre of gravity, particularly for aerobatic models. It is also essential to ensure that the centre of gravity shift due to fuel usage is not too great, or to take this fact into account in deciding its final position.

If a model has a large forward fuselage, like the semi-scale jet layout shown in Figure 64, an allowance should be made for this additional forward lifting area. A 1% forward shift for each 10% of additional area (shown in grey on Figure 64) is a fair rule of thumb.

### Biplane and canard centres of gravity
In the case of a biplane (or triplane), if there is no stagger, the position of the centre of

gravity can be calculated as for a monoplane, but adding the areas of the two wings together. Where there is a stagger, the aerodynamic mean chord is simply drawn between the leading edge of the forward wing and the trailing edge of the rear one.

Slightly more awkward, but no more difficult to position, is the centre of gravity on a canard. In this case, the areas of the wing and foreplane must be calculated. The distance between the fifteen per cent points on the two aerodynamic mean chords must also be measured.

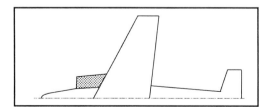

**Figure 64** *Some models need an allowance made for an excessive fuselage forward area.*

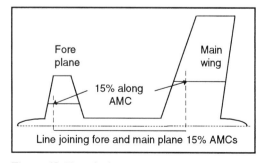

**Figure 65** *The calculations necessary to establish the centre of gravity position for a canard.*

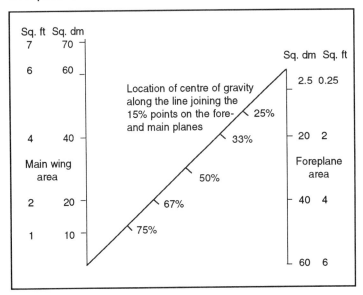

**Figure 66** *Nomograph for ascertaining the position of the centre of gravity for canards.*

The position of the centre of gravity along the line joining the foreplane and wing fifteen per cent points can be read off the nomograph in Figure 66, which has the areas of the wing and foreplane on the two vertical axes, and the location of the centre of gravity on the third.

## Effect of size on performance

The size of a model has quite an impact on its flight characteristics. For a start, the larger the aircraft the slower it appears to fly, as those watching jumbo jets in the air must have observed. This is because a large aircraft takes longer to travel its own length than a small one moving at the same speed. Also, a small model gets to the limit of observable flight faster, thus needing to be turned towards the pilot more often. On the other hand, small aircraft tend to be more manoeuvrable. For a given wing loading, a small aircraft has less inertia and thus can accelerate and turn more easily. It will also have a smaller radius of turn. For these reasons trainers should be reasonably large as small aircraft demand speedy reflexes. It should be self apparent that the larger the model, the stronger the various components must be and vice versa. Thus the materials used will have to be increased or decreased in size appropriately. As mentioned in Chapter 1 Figure 16, the increase or reduction in the dimensions of materials used is not pro rata to the size of the model.

# 4.  Providing power

## Possible sources of power

There are many means of powering an R/C model. Excluded from this book are gravity and thermals, used by our glider brethren, and orographic uplift, the source employed by slope soarers. Also excluded as not being a part of the sports scene are multi cylinder piston engines, turbojets and ducted fans. These are usually fitted into complex scale models.

The choice of power source is likely to have a major impact on the design and construction of any model, so a summary of the basic features of the various choices is a good place to start. Table 4 shows some of the key factors to be considered for your new pride and joy.

For internal combustion engines, it is becoming increasingly clear that noise is an issue that must be faced up to by all. As effective silencers tend to be bulky and run hot, it is important to consider their location and installation. Noise has also been one of the drivers which has caused an upsurge in the popularity of electric flight. There is now a wide selection of electric power systems available which enable an excellent flight performance to be achieved.

### Two stroke glow engines

For a powered model, there is little doubt that two stroke motors are the most widespread. Of simple and lightweight construction, they are

**Figure 67** *Top left are a pair of small diesels, both without throttles. Top right is a sports two stroke glow motor. Bottom left is a racing two stroke and right a typical four stroke.*

| | Engine weight | Fuel weight | Vibration level | Power to weight | Ability to swing large propeller | Noise level |
|---|---|---|---|---|---|---|
| **Glow 2 stroke** | Low | Modest | Medium | Very high | Poor | V. high |
| **Glow 4 stroke** | Medium | Low | High | High | Average | High |
| **Diesel** | Medium | Low | High | High | Good | High |
| **Petrol 2 stroke** | High | V. low | Medium | High | Average | V. high |
| **Petrol 4 stroke** | High | V. low | High | Medium | Good | High |
| **Electric** | V. Low | V. high | Trivial | Low | Poor | V. low |
| **Geared electric** | Low | V. high | Trivial | Low | Excellent | V. low |

**Table 4** *The main characteristics of the various types of power plant for R/C sports aircraft.*

straightforward to operate and provide an excellent power-to-weight ratio. Mention must be made of the Wankel engine, of which the OS version of 5cc (0.30 cu. in.) is the only one in production in 1996. Wankels are compact cylindrical shaped motors which turn small propellers at high rpm, even compared to conventional two strokes. That apart there are few practical differences.

There have, in the past, been occasional geared two stroke engines, which add to the weight of the motor, but do increase the ability to swing a large propeller. Their virtual demise has been brought about by the introduction of the practical four stroke engine.

Current motors provide a power output of between 75 watts (one tenth of a horsepower) per cubic centimetre (0.06 cu. in.) for sports motors and four times that amount for racing or ducted fan engines. Fuel consumption can vary by a factor of two to one between sports motors and high powered variants of the same capacity. All two strokes require a good silencer, and often a second one if they are to meet the BMFA noise limit of 82dB at seven metres. The disadvantage of all glow motors is the need to fuel-proof the complete airframe to protect its paint finish from attack by methanol and nitro methane.

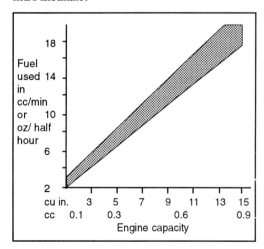

**Figure 68** *An examination of the fuel consumption of a typical sports two stroke glow motor allows selection of the correct size of fuel tank for the flight duration required.*

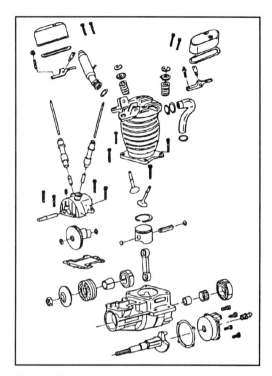

**Figure 69** *The four stroke engine has the added complexity of a pair of valves and springs, rocker arms and push rods, not to mention a cam shaft and reduction gearing to drive it.*

### Four stroke glow engines

Four stroke engines are more complex in their design and construction, and heavier for a given capacity than two strokes. They are also more expensive to purchase. On the other hand, they are much more economic in terms of fuel consumption, typically by a factor of two, and are inherently less noisy. These latter two factors can help to reduce the total installed weight to a similar figure to that of a two stroke engine, and the lower fuel consumption helps to offset the increased initial purchase price.

### Diesels

Diesel engines, or compression ignition engines as they are sometimes called, rely on the compression of the fuel/air mixture to cause ignition. They used to be very popular in the UK in the period after the Second World War, but their prevalence reduced with the introduction of the easy starting glow plug engine, first from the USA and later from Japan.

There are both pros and cons with diesels. First, they do not require any battery to power a glow plug for starting, reducing the amount of equipment to be carried in the flight box. Secondly, they are able to swing larger propellers than an equivalent capacity glow motor, a great plus for models with large radial cowls. Their fuel consumption is around half that of a glow two stroke and the fuel is less likely to attack the finish of the airframe.

On the down side, these engines do tend to be slightly heavier and produce more vibration than their glow equivalents. There is an additional compression control to set and they do produce a black oily goo from their exhausts. They can be harder to start and operate as there are two controls, mixture and compression, both of which need to be set correctly. These skills are not difficult to learn. Diesels have historically been harder to throttle reliably and have been manufactured only in smaller sizes, up to 5cc (0.30 cu. in.). However, recent developments have resulted in successful diesels up to at least 10cc (0.61 cu. in.) capacity.

## Petrol engines

Petrol engines are the most economic of all to operate, as petrol is cheap and consumption miserly. However, there is the added complication of a magneto or coil to produce the spark, the need to ensure that the spark does not interfere with the radio, and the requirement to avoid the use of silicon fuel tube, as it reacts negatively with petrol. The equipment to generate a spark adds both to the weight and expense of this form of power. Petrol engines are much more common in larger sizes of 15cc (0.90 cu. in.) upwards and are particularly prevalent in the form of converted chain saw motors. As with diesel engines, kits are available to convert glow motors to petrol usage.

## Silencers

There are three main types of commercially available silencer.

- Side mounted
- Dumpy/dustbin
- Tuned pipe

In addition, some people choose to fit home made silencers. Furthermore, second silencers are becoming increasingly popular. It is essential that the engine mounting allows convenient location of the silencer, and also that the weight of the silencer and its effect on the location of the centre of gravity are taken into account.

The title of this section might better be silence than silencers as the exhaust is not the only source of noise from a model I/C engine. Certainly, it is important to consider how the silencer will fit into the airframe; the more so if a second silencer is to be fitted. Will the silencer be mounted inside the model or externally? If the former, how will it be cooled? Modern silencers are bulky and get very hot. They must

**Figure 70** *A large Super Tigre engine, converted for petrol using ProSpark ignition, showing the coil and its battery pack. (Photo courtesy Handy Systems.)*

**Figure 71** *Top left anti-clockwise, a conventional silencer with an add-on unit, a helicopter type, a dumpy silencer, an add-on second silencer, a short tuned pipe, a home-made unit and a small conventional silencer.*

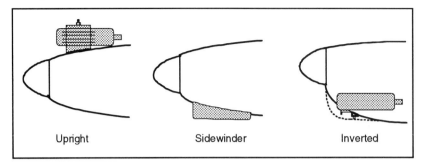

**Figure 72** *The three main positions for an engine viewed from the side. A forty-five degree position is also becoming increasingly popular.*

Upright          Sidewinder          Inverted

be securely installed, preferably so that any exhaust oil is thrown clear of the model.

The noise from propellers can be significant, so that the size and pitch of the propeller need consideration, particularly if the model has a large cross section fuselage. Generally, the larger the prop, both in diameter and pitch, the less noise the engine will emit. The next paragraph deals with engine mounts and it is worth remembering that anti-vibration mounts can also reduce noise. Finally, open structure airframes with taut covering can act as excellent loudspeakers amplifying any noise produced by the engine. This can be quite marked on a nylon covered, open structure wing and result in a noisier model than the same design with a foam wing.

## Installing I/C engines

Many of the considerations about how to install an engine will depend on the type of motor available or to be purchased for the model. The following is a list of the main factors.

- Engine size
- Glow, diesel or petrol
- Two stroke or four stroke
- Power output
- Location of engine
- Location of exhaust
- Mounting lugs
- Vibration level
- Fuel consumption

### Upright, inverted or sidewinder

Conventional wisdom says that an upright engine installation is the best for ease of starting and running. You may well ask why any other configuration should even be considered. Generally, the answer is that it's simply a question of aesthetics. Figure 72 shows that a typical two stroke sidewinder or inverted engine installation can provide a much more pleasing nose shape.

In the case of the sidewinder, when viewed from the favourable side, only a bit of the silencer shows hanging down beneath the fuselage. For the inverted installation, just the top of the cylinder head is visible, but the whole of a conventional two stroke silencer can now be seen from one side.

The cylinder head can, of course, be hidden completely, as shown by the dotted line. It is important to remember the increased length of a four stroke engine when compared with a two stroke one, the increase being caused by the space occupied by the valve gear.

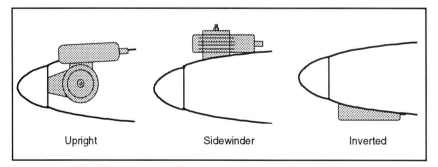

**Figure 73** *The three positions for an engine seen from above showing the difference in visibility of a typical two stroke engine/silencer combination.*

Upright          Sidewinder          Inverted

**Figure 74** *The use of a commercial engine mount to position the engine at 45° to the vertical. It enables the silencer of this two stroke engine to be kept comfortably clear of the fuselage.*

### 45° mounting

A compromise that has found favour is to angle the motor over at 45° to the vertical. This can result in a very neat installation, but does normally require the use of a commercial engine mount or some other form of bulkhead mounting.

### Pushers

From a constructional point of view, there is not a lot of difference between a tractor and a pusher installation. The two main factors are the silencer mounting and some thought about the fuel system in the case of a pusher. If a conventional two stroke silencer is mounted on a pusher, the exhaust exit faces into the air stream and will cause some back pressure. Turning the silencer through 180° will usually result in it fouling the propeller. A dumpy or dustbin silencer is often

**Figure 75** *This pusher engine and downward exhausting helicopter silencer is mounted on beech bearers.*

an ideal solution to this dilemma. On the fuel side, a nose-up attitude after take-off will result in the engine running richer, rather than the leaning out found on tractor layouts. Furthermore, the fuel tank is likely to be further from the centre of gravity resulting in a greater shift as fuel is consumed.

### Pylon mounting

For seaplanes and powered gliders in particular, it is not uncommon to find the engine, together with its fuel tank, mounted in a pylon above the wing. This layout has its advantages in these particular circumstances but does demand a stiff pylon, long enough to keep the propeller clear of the airframe. It also usually means a significant amount of up thrust (or down thrust if a pusher) is necessary to compensate for the high thrust line.

### Slot propellers

On deltas in particular, the slot propeller has found some favour. In this case, the engine is located half-way down the fuselage, with a slot cut for the propeller to rotate. Starting such an installation can provide some interesting problems and usually requires a starting belt and pulley. The big advantage lies in the solution to balancing the delta, which always seem to end up nose heavy if the engine is in the front. Pusher layouts cause problems of their own due to the large angles of attack used when deltas take-off and land, and the resulting requirement for an exceptionally long undercarriage.

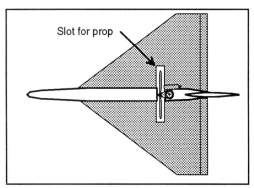

**Figure 76** *A delta with a slot propeller layout may use the engine in a tractor or pusher configuration.*

# Chapter 4

## Engine bearers and plates

The use of a pair of beech engine bearers is one of the oldest methods of attaching an internal combustion engine to a model. The main snag is the need for accurate cut-outs in the relevant formers, the need to adjust the spacing of the bearers to suit the chosen engine and the difficulty of making adjustments to the engine thrust line.

Bearers can still be used as mountings for an engine plate made from ply, paxolin or aluminium and this type of installation has much to recommend it for any new model. The plate can be replaced if the side thrust is incorrect or if a different, more or less powerful engine is needed. Finally, wedges can be fitted beneath the plate to adjust the up/down thrust.

## Plastic and metal engine mounts

Commercial engine mounts have most of the advantages of engine plates. They are supplied in a wide range of sizes to suit most engines and some are adjustable for spacing of the engine mounting lugs. Fairly recently, ones with absorbent mounting have been produced to help reduce engine vibration and noise. Side and up/down thrust can still be adjusted and many make provision for attaching a noseleg to the engine firewall. Because of their strength, the plastic ones are generally only suitable for smaller sized engines.

**Figure 77** *A four stroke engine mounted on a removable aluminium plate, which may be replaced if a change of side thrust is needed.*

**Figure 78** *Using a commercial plastic mount for this inverted 40 four stroke allows a neat installation which can be covered by a GRP cowl.*

## Fuel systems

It is essential, and should be self-evident, that the fuel supply must be located as close to the engine as possible, and at the correct vertical position in relation to the engine, unless a pumping system is used. While a pump gives freedom to position the fuel tank at the centre of gravity, it does tend to increase the weight, complexity and cost of the total fuel system. It is therefore not a particularly common solution.

The tank should be located so that the engine spray bar is level with the fuel when the tank is two-thirds full. It should be securely mounted, horizontally as close to the engine as possible. Particularly on two strokes, fuel tank pressurisation from the silencer is used to ensure positive fuel transfer and pipe routing needs to be planned.

**Figure 79** *Fuel tanks come in all shapes and sizes. The cross section may be round, rectangular, oval or square.*

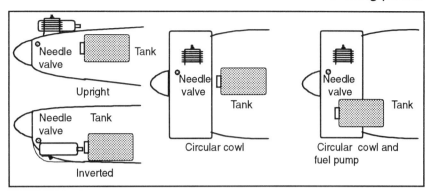

**Figure 80** *The location of the fuel tank is a critical factor if the engine is to perform satisfactorily. A fuel pump can give greater tank positional flexibility.*

Fuel tanks can be purchased in a variety of shapes and a range of sizes. They can also be hand-made from tinplate or brass sheet if an awkward space has to be filled. Chicken hopper tanks have their uses where it is difficult to obtain a constant head of fuel. The main tank may be pressurised, as normal, and the bottom tank should contain about 25% of the total fuel carried. While fuel will continue to feed during looping manoeuvres, prolonged inverted flight will result in an engine cut.

## Propellers

While manufacturers always recommend a range of propeller diameters and pitches to suit their engines, it is useful to be able to see at a glance the propeller sizes that should suit a new size of motor.

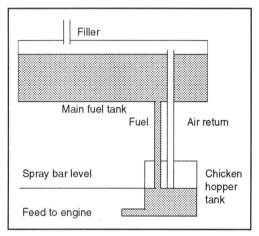

**Figure 81** *The operation of a chicken hopper system depends on an air lock preventing the lower tank flooding.*

| cc | cu in | 7×4 | 7×6 | 8×4 | 8×6 | 9×4 | 9×5 | 9×6 | 9×7 | 10×4 | 10×6 | 10×7 | 11×4 | 11×6 | 11×7 | 11×8 | 12×4 | 12×5 | 12×6 | 12×7 | 12×8 | 13×5 | 13×6 | 13×8 | 14×6 | 14×7 | 14×8 |
|---|---|---|---|---|---|---|---|---|---|---|---|---|---|---|---|---|---|---|---|---|---|---|---|---|---|---|---|
| 1.5 | 0.09 | ■ | ■ | ■ | | | | | | | | | | | | | | | | | | | | | | | |
| 2.5 | 0.15 | ■ | ■ | ■ | ■ | | | | | | | | | | | | | | | | | | | | | | |
| 3.5 | 0.19 | | | ■ | ■ | ■ | | | | | | | | | | | | | | | | | | | | | |
| 4.0 | 0.25 | | | | ■ | ■ | ■ | ■ | ■ | | | | | | | | | | | | | | | | | | |
| 5.0 | 0.30 | | | | | | ■ | ■ | | | ■ | ■ | | | | | | | | | | | | | | | |
| 5.7 | 0.35 | | | | | | | ■ | ■ | | ■ | ■ | | ■ | | | | | | | | | | | | | |
| 6.5 | 0.40 | | | | | | | ■ | | | ■ | ■ | ■ | ■ | ■ | ■ | | ■ | | | | | | | | | |
| 7.5 | 0.45 | | | | | | | | ■ | | | ■ | ■ | ■ | | ■ | ■ | | ■ | ■ | | | | | | | |
| 8.0 | 0.50 | | | | | | | | | | | ■ | | ■ | ■ | | ■ | ■ | ■ | | | | | | | | |
| 10 | 0.61 | | | | | | | | | | | | | ■ | ■ | ■ | ■ | ■ | ■ | ■ | ■ | ■ | | | | | |
| 15 | 0.90 | | | | | | | | | | | | | | | | | | | | | ■ | ■ | ■ | ■ | ■ | ■ |

**Table 5** *Suggested propeller sizes for a wide range of two stroke glow engines.*

| in | 4 | 5 | 6 | 7 | 8 | 9 | 10 | 11 | 12 | 13 | 14 | 15 | 16 |
|---|---|---|---|---|---|---|---|---|---|---|---|---|---|
| cm | 10 | 12 | 15 | 18 | 20 | 23 | 25 | 28 | 30 | 33 | 36 | 38 | 40 |

**Table 6** *Imperial to metric equivalent conversion for propeller diameter and pitch.*

The benefit to the designer comes when arranging undercarriage details to give the necessary ground clearance and also when considering a model with a large circular cowl. The lower diameter, higher pitch propellers for any engine size are better suited to fast models with high wing loadings. Chapter 13 explains how to make the right selection. Two stroke motors generally are capable of swinging the smallest propellers at the highest speeds.

Props come not only in a wide range of diameters and pitches, but also a number of shapes and materials, not to mention three bladed ones. Some of the choices are shown in Figure 82.

Four stroke engines have the ability to turn larger propellers than two strokes and also prefer weighty ones to give some flywheel effect during the non-firing stroke. Table 7 suggest some suitable sizes.

**Figure 82** *Wood and a variety of plastics are used in the manufacture of propellers.*

Diesels have the best low speed torque characteristics of all I/C engines and are able to provide a good performance on a really large propeller. This is particularly useful on models with large radial cowls.

When selecting a three bladed propeller, a reduction in diameter by a third might be expected, but due to a lower efficiency, a decrease of only 20 – 25% is recommended. The range of three blade propellers is much more limited than that of two blade ones. The choice of two blade pushers is also very limited.

| Three blade | | 2 blade pushers | |
|---|---|---|---|
| 8 x 6 | 12 x 6 | 7 x 4 | 10 x 8 |
| 9 x 7 | 12 x 8 | 8 x 6 | 11 x 6 |
| 10 x 7 | 14 x 7 | 9 x 6 | 11 x 7 |
| 10 x 8 | 15 x 8 | 10 x 6 | 11 x 8 |
| 11 x 7 | 16 x 8 | 10 x 7 | 14 x 6 |

**Table 9** *Only ten different sizes of three bladed propellers and a similar number of pusher two bladers were available in the UK at the time of publication.*

## Electric power

Last, but by no means least, is electric power. Rapidly growing in popularity, the advantages of this power source are noteworthy. It is virtually silent in operation: such a benefit in these noise conscious days. Furthermore, it is vibration free and obviates the need for fuel-proofing. While power-to-weight ratios cannot yet match those of internal combustion engines, progress has

| cc | cu in | 10 x4 | x6 | x7 | 11 x4 | x6 | x7 | x8 | 12 x4 | x5 | x6 | x7 | x8 | 13 x5 | x6 | x8 | 14 x6 | x7 | x8 | 15 x6 | x8 | 16 x6 | x8 |
|---|---|---|---|---|---|---|---|---|---|---|---|---|---|---|---|---|---|---|---|---|---|---|---|
| 6.5 | 0.40 | ■ | ■ | ■ | ■ | ■ | ■ | | ■ | ■ | | | | | | | | | | | | | |
| 7.5 | 0.45 | | | | ■ | ■ | ■ | ■ | ■ | ■ | ■ | | | | | | | | | | | | |
| 8.5 | 0.50 | | | | | ■ | ■ | ■ | ■ | ■ | ■ | ■ | | | | | | | | | | | |
| 10 | 0.60 | | | | | | | | | | ■ | ■ | | ■ | ■ | | ■ | ■ | ■ | ■ | ■ | | | |
| 15 | 0.90 | | | | | | | | | | | | | | | | ■ | ■ | ■ | ■ | ■ | | | |
| 20 | 1.20 | | | | | | | | | | | | | | | | | | ■ | ■ | ■ | ■ | ■ | ■ |

**Table 7** *Suitable propeller sizes for some of the more popular four stroke glow engines.*

| cc | cu in | 7 | 8 | | 9 | | | | 10 | | | | 11 | | | | 12 | | | | 13 | |
|---|---|---|---|---|---|---|---|---|---|---|---|---|---|---|---|---|---|---|---|---|---|---|
| | | x6 | x4 | x6 | x4 | x5 | x6 | x7 | x4 | x5 | x6 | x7 | x4 | x6 | x7 | x8 | x4 | x5 | x6 | x7 | x8 | x5 | x6 |
| 1.5 | 0.09 | ■ | ■ | ■ | ■ | | | | | | | | | | | | | | | | | | |
| 2.5 | 0.15 | | | | ■ | ■ | ■ | ■ | | ■ | | | | | | | | | | | | | |
| 3.5 | 0.20 | | | | ■ | ■ | ■ | ■ | ■ | ■ | ■ | ■ | | ■ | | | | | | | | | |
| 4 | 0.25 | | | | | ■ | ■ | ■ | ■ | ■ | ■ | ■ | ■ | ■ | ■ | ■ | | | | | | | |
| 5 | 0.30 | | | | | | | | | ■ | ■ | ■ | ■ | ■ | ■ | ■ | | ■ | ■ | | | | |
| 6 | 0.35 | | | | | | | | | | | | ■ | ■ | ■ | ■ | ■ | ■ | ■ | ■ | ■ | ■ | ■ |

**Table 8**  *A range of possible propeller sizes for diesel engines.*

been rapid in recent years. For those wishing to explore the subject in more detail, Nexus Special Interests' book *Fly Electric* by David Chinery provides excellent reading.

The ubiquitous rapid rechargeable nicad is used to store the electrical power. Its weight, and its restraint in the event of a heavy landing, are the two major challenges facing electric power. A final advantage is the ability to fly a twin engined model without fear of an engine cut and the trials and tribulations of an asymmetric landing.

While all the information given in this book is as applicable to electric models as it is to designs for internal combustion engines, the one area where electric flight lags well behind is in the power-to-weight ratio of the total system. For a given power output for a period, say, of five minutes, the weight of an I/C motor, fuel and tank is still dramatically less that for an electric motor and battery. Thus, in a design for electric flight, the weight of the airframe must be as low as it is humanly possible and the wing loading watched carefully.

**Figure 83** *From left to right, a 380 sized motor with gearbox, a 540 and a 540 with belt reduction drive.*

## Motors

As with internal combustion engines, electric motors come in a wide variety of sizes and shapes, with an equally wide range of power ratings. They can also be fitted with or without gearboxes. Unfortunately, unlike internal combustion engines, it is much harder to understand their sizes. Mabuchi use 280, 380, 540, 550 & 750 to define the sizes of their range of motors, while Astro use .035, .05, .15, .25, .40 & .90. Graupner use 400, 600 & 700. As with glow motors, there are hot motors and 'cooking' ones. From the design point of view, the following factors are important:

- Size
- Weight
- Power output
- Revs at maximum power
- Voltage
- Current consumption

The first two define the size of the engine mount, the third affects the size and weight of the model that can be flown, the fourth impacts on the choice of propeller size while the last two are major considerations in arriving at the size of battery.

The choice of whether to use a gearbox will depend primarily on the maximum speed of the model. Gearboxes give more thrust at slower speed, but are unsuitable for faster models. Geared systems are thus best suited to slower flying aircraft. They are also an advantage where the design features a large radial cowl. More information on the selection of propellers is contained in Chapter 13.

| Capacity mAh | Wt g | Wt oz | Size mm (Dia x ht) | Size in. |
|:---:|:---:|:---:|:---:|:---:|
| 500 | 19 | 0.7 | 14.6 x 50 | 0.6 x 2 |
| 700 | 22 | 0.8 | 14.6 x 50 | 0.6 x 2 |
| 850 | 25 | 0.9 | 14.6 x 50 | 0.6 x 2 |
| 1200 | 28 | 1 | 17 x 43 | 0.7 x 1.7 |
| 1400 | 52 | 1.8 | 23 x 42.2 | 0.9 x 1.7 |
| 1600 | 40 | 1.4 | 26.2 x 50 | 1 x 2 |
| 1700 | 54 | 2.3 | 25 x 45 | 1 x 1.8 |
| 2000 | 45 | 1.6 | 26.2 x 50 | 1 x 2 |
| 4000 | 55 | 1.9 | 33 x 61 | 1.3 x 2.4 |

**Table 10** *Typical sizes and weights of individual nicad cells for electric flight.*

## Batteries

At the time of writing, the nickel cadmium rechargeable battery rules supreme, both for electric flight and for powering airborne receivers and servos. This may change as battery technology continues to improve at a rapid rate, fuelled by the needs of portable power tools and telephones. In any case the weight and size of nicads is reducing year by year. Table 10 shows the state of the technology early in 1996. By way of comparison a nickel metal hydride cell will produce 1.2 volts, has a 30 − 50% performance advantage over the best nicads, no memory effects and is free from toxic or hazardous effects when the time comes for disposal.

The power available from a flight pack and how long it can provide power can be varied in two ways. Each nicad cell has a nominal voltage of 1.2 volts and a number of cells make up a battery or flight pack. The more cells used the greater the total voltage, though this must match the voltage rating of the selected motor. The larger each cell, the more current it can happily produce. It can also produce the same current as a smaller cell, but for a longer time.

The power passed to the motor in watts is a multiple of the voltage and the current. More of either will increase the power output. The duration of the powered part of the flight depends on the current drawn and the size of the cells in the battery. Remember that increasing the number of cells has two effects. For a given motor, it will increase the power output, but because more current flows, the duration will reduce. For most applications, a seven cell pack is normal, with six cells a good choice for lighter

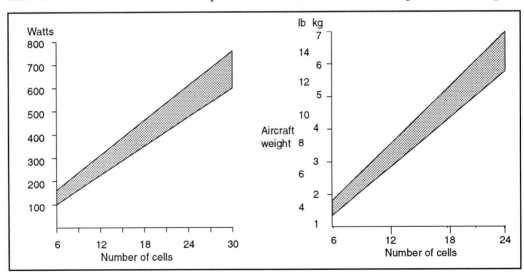

**Figure 84** *The amount of power available for electric flight can be increased by using more cells. Knowing the number of C sized cells, the total weight of the aircraft can be planned.*

weight and longer endurance, albeit with reduced power output. Larger numbers of cells are popular for high performance motors in larger models. Using popular C sized cells with capacities between 1000 to 1700 mAh, the number of cells can be related to the available power. Continuing to use the same size of cells, Figure 84 shows how the number of them can readily be related to the all-up weight of the model to ensure an adequate performance. Of course, less cells are needed in a slow flying old timer than a fast aerobatic model.

### Folding propellers

With so many electric powered models being flown without undercarriages to reduce weight to a minimum, folding propellers have become a popular choice. The current range available is shown in Table 11.

## Installing electric motors

Since electric motors produce virtually no vibration, installation is quite straightforward. A tube of card, balsa or thin ply, that fits around the motor may be used. Alternatively, a commercial electric mount or the fixing lugs

| 3.5mm shaft | 5mm shaft | |
|---|---|---|
| 6 x 3 | 6 x 6 | 11 x 7 |
| 6 x 6 | 8 x 4.5 | 11 x 7.5 |
| 7 x 3 | 8 x 6 | 12.5 x 6 |
| 8 x 4.5 | 9 x 5 | 12.5 x 6.5 |
| 8 x 6 | 9 x 7 | 13.5 x 7 |
| 9 x 5 | 10 x 6 | 14 x 8 |

**Table 11** *There are currently eighteen different sizes of folding propellers with two different shaft sizes designed specially for electric flight.*

found on many gearboxes can be attached to suitable hard points. Wiring to the battery needs planning as it must be thick enough to carry the high current, and will normally run via a switch and speed controller. It is best to mount the battery near the centre of gravity as it is by far the heaviest component. A further significant amount of weight can be saved by replacing the receiver battery with a battery elimination circuit (BEC). This unit powers the receiver and servos from the main motor battery, cutting off the motor before the battery voltage falls below the level needed to run the radio.

IT'S MY LATEST DIESEL ELECTRIC POWERED SEAPLANE ....
... THE BATTERIES ARE AUTOMATICALLY RECHARGED!

# 5. Defeating drag

## The basic facts

For normal powered straight and level flight, a model must generate sufficient lift to balance its weight and enough thrust to counteract the drag it produces. This is demonstrated in Figure 85.

## Drag

A model in steady level flight produces drag which must be balanced by the thrust from the propeller. For a given thrust, the amount of drag determines the speed of the aircraft. It is clearly important to minimise the amount of drag. To do this requires a basic understanding of what causes drag and why it varies. The total drag produced by a model in flight divides into two main forms, parasite drag and induced drag.

### Parasite drag

Parasite drag is a result of the airframe passing through the air. It has three different causes. These are form drag produced by the profile of the model, drag caused by interference at the joints of its main components and skin friction as the air rubs over the surface of the model.

### Form drag

The pressure of the airflow past a model causes drag. The amount depends on how much the smooth flow of the air is disrupted. An extreme occurs when a flat plate is placed at right angles to the airflow. Any object, no matter how well streamlined, is a source of form drag when it is moving.

### Interference drag

Drag is produced when several air streams meet at the point where one component of a model is attached to another, such as the wing/fuselage and the fin/tailplane joints.

### Skin friction

The resistance to the motion of air over the surface of a model causes drag. The amount of skin friction depends on the smoothness of the surface. The more polished and smooth the surface, the lower the friction.

## The boundary layer

Contact between the airflow and the skin of the model creates a thin layer of retarded air. This is called the boundary layer. The amount of drag

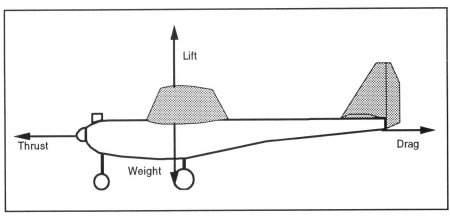

**Figure 85**
*Thrust equals drag and lift equals weight in straight and level flight.*

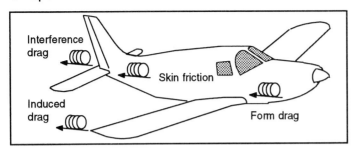

**Figure 86** *Any model in flight is affected by the three types of parasite drag as well as induced drag.*

it causes depends on the type and thickness of the flow in the layer. The thickness of an average boundary layer varies between about 1.5mm and 6mm ($^1/_{16}$" and ¼"). The amount of drag produced depends on whether the flow in the boundary layer is laminar or turbulent and where it transfers from one to the other.

### Laminar boundary layer

Laminar flow is an orderly motion in which successive layers of air slide past each other like a pack of cards thrown along a flat surface. The thinner the boundary layer, the easier it is to obtain laminar flow and consequently lower drag.

### Turbulent boundary layer

In a turbulent boundary layer the smooth laminar flow gives way to lots of tiny vortices and eddies. This increases the thickness of the boundary layer and causes more drag.

### Transition point

The point on a wing where the boundary layer changes from laminar to turbulent is called the transition point. Because of the large increase in drag with a turbulent boundary layer, some care is needed to preserve laminar flow over as much of a wing as possible. This depends on the choice of aerofoil, the accuracy of building and the smoothness of the surface finish.

## Factors affecting parasite drag

At model aircraft sizes and speeds, form drag is the dominant form of parasite drag and is affected by four main factors.

### Air speed

Parasite drag rises very rapidly as air speed increases. Each time the air speed doubles the parasite drag quadruples. Trebling it increases this drag nine times.

### Shape

The smoother the change of direction of the airflow around the object, the lower the drag. If the shape produces a turbulent airflow, the resulting drag is high. The effect of streamlining an object of given cross section is shown in Figure 88. A flat plate produces most drag, a cylinder about half this figure and a streamlined shape as little as 5%. The ratio of length to breadth of any streamlined body is called the fineness ratio. For typical model speeds a fineness ratio of about 4:1 is satisfactory. The ratio can clearly be increased either by decreasing cross section or increasing length.

### Interference drag

The effect of the interaction between conflicting airflows, at the point where one component of the model attaches to another, can be minimised

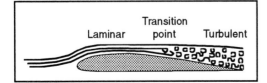

**Figure 87** *Laminar flow in the boundary layer changes to turbulent at the transition point.*

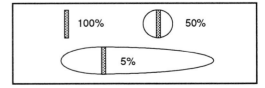

**Figure 88** *Streamlining can radically reduce drag and is fundamental to almost any model design.*

by fairing components into each other. Suitably shaped fillets should be fitted around the wing/fuselage, tailplane/fuselage and fin/fuselage joints.

### Surface area and smoothness

The amount of skin friction drag is determined mainly by a model's surface area and its surface smoothness. Skin friction is, however, very small in comparison with the form drag of model aircraft. It is likely to stay so unless maximum model speeds reach dramatically higher levels than the current 320 kph (200 mph).

## Induced drag

When any wing generates lift it also produces induced drag. When the air speed is low, the wing works hardest to produce the lift. Thus induced drag is greatest at low speeds and reduces as speed increases. For a model in level flight, induced drag varies inversely as the square of the air speed. Doubling the speed reduces the induced drag four-fold.

## Factors affecting induced drag

Apart from air speed, the main factor affecting the amount of induced drag is the planform of the wing. For a given set of conditions and wing area, the greater the wingspan the lower the induced drag. More information is given on this in the next chapter. Furthermore, the shape of the wing and its tip also has an effect. Compared with a parallel wing, the other shapes shown in Figure 89 indicate the reduction in induced drag which can be expected.

A delta is likely to have a significantly lower aspect ratio than a conventional wing. Taking the case of a delta with only half the aspect

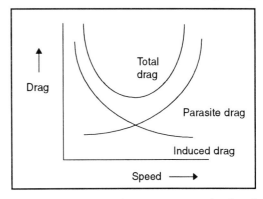

**Figure 90** *Parasite drag increases and induced drag reduces with speed. There is a clear minimum drag speed at the bottom of the total drag curve. Above and below this speed, total drag increases.*

ratio of the wings shown in the figure, the induced drag will be twenty per cent higher.

## Total drag

Having looked at the two main types of drag, parasite drag and induced drag, it is important to consider how the total drag experienced by a model alters.

### Variation of drag with speed

In level flight parasite drag increases and induced drag decreases as the square of the speed. The total drag of a model consists partly of parasite, partly of induced drag. Figure 90 shows how these two types of drag change with air speed and includes a curve for the total sum.

### Speed for minimum total drag

It is clear that the speed for minimum total drag occurs at the point where the sum of the induced and parasite drags are minimum, not

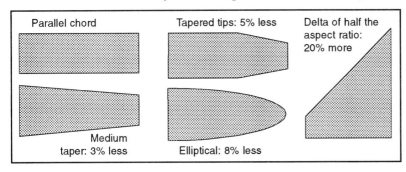

**Figure 89** *Induced drag at a constant aspect ratio will depend on the wing planform. A delta's induced drag is considerably higher than that of a conventional wing.*

at the lowest possible flying speed. At this speed, for a given amount of fuel, the maximum duration is obtained.

## Speed and speed range

Outright maximum speed can be the critical factor in the design of a racing aircraft, while speed range, the difference between the maximum and minimum, is much more important for an aerobatic model. Models can be designed and built to be fast or slow, to have a wide speed range or to have a maximum velocity not far above the stalling speed. The basic factors which affect maximum speed are the drag produced by the model and the thrust achieved from the engine/propeller combination. Therefore, to obtain maximum performance from a model, total drag should always be kept to a minimum.

The top speed is limited by the available thrust being matched by the total drag produced. We clearly don't need to worry much about skin friction at the speeds our models fly, and no mention has been made of wave drag, which didn't even affect full-sized aircraft until the Second World War, when their speeds started to approach mach 1.

So, we can minimise the other sources of drag by:

- Reducing the frontal area of the model
- Minimising the fuselage cross section
- Using fillets at major surface junctions
- Streamlining the model
- Decreasing the wing thickness
- Choosing a low drag aerofoil
- Using a V tail or tailless design
- Increasing aspect ratio

**Figure 92** *How to get it all wrong from the drag point of view. The Fokker DVIII, my first scale model, has a large frontal area and fuselage cross section, a thick, draggy aerofoil, a low aspect ratio and a conventional tail.*

### Thrust

Talk of the thrust required by an aircraft immediately leads to discussion of the power output of the engine, and of course, this is a major factor. However, the use of the correct propeller and any gearing between the engine and the propeller can have a dramatic effect, as those who fly electric models can testify. For example, a ducted fan produces dramatically less thrust from its smaller diameter, multi bladed fan for a given engine power output than a conventional propeller.

Static thrust is what you can measure on the ground by attaching a spring balance to your model and revving it at full power. This thrust affects the length of the take-off run, but is not directly connected to thrust in the air. All other things being equal, coarse pitch propellers produce more thrust at high speed than fine pitch ones. So, there are a number of ways we can increase thrust:

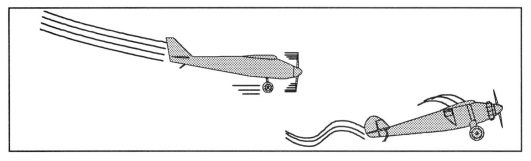

**Figure 91** *Do you want a fast flying model or a slow one?*

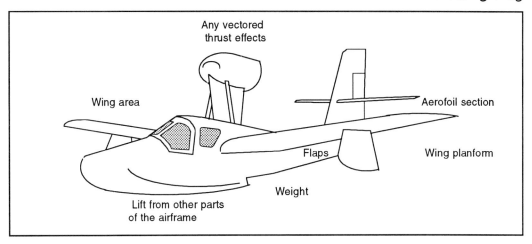

**Figure 93** *There are a number of factors which affect the lift to be generated by a new design.*

- Fitting a more powerful engine
- Fitting a silencer which increases the power output of the engine
- Using a "hotter" fuel
- Fitting a propeller better matched to the engine
- Gearing down the propeller – this will increase thrust, but reduce top speed

We have immediately created a paradox. Increasing thrust does not necessarily give us an increase in top speed. Speed is also dependent on the velocity of the air as it exits the propeller disc. This is one reason why the top speed of propeller driven full-sized aircraft is limited to around 800 kph (500 mph).

### Speed range
As well as top speed, speed range also depends on the stalling speed in straight and level flight of the model, which in itself depends on:

- The aerofoil section used
- The wing planform
- The wing area
- The weight of the model
- The use of high lift devices such as flaps or slots
- Any vectored thrust effect
- Lift generated by other parts of the aircraft

We have seen that the top speed of a model in level flight is affected only by the amount of thrust from the engine and the total drag. When these two factors balance, the only way to increase speed is to lose height in a dive. For a model, it is rare to have a never exceed speed, as there is no means of establishing when a model reaches this speed. However, many of the current fun fliers should not be flown flat-out as control flutter will quickly destroy them.

# 6. Lots of lovely lift

## Generating lift

The purpose of the wing of any model is to generate lift. It does so by using an aerofoil which deflects the air moving past it in a downward direction. A simple method of producing this downwash is to incline a flat plate in an airflow at a suitable angle to change the direction of the flow. However, it is more efficient to use a curved section in the form of one of the many familiar aerofoils.

The angle at which the air approaches the wing is known as its angle of attack, while the angle of incidence of a wing is the angle at which the aerofoil is set relative to the fuselage datum. Both are shown in Figure 96.

## Types of aerofoil

The performance of any aerofoil depends on its shape. Figure 94 shows, on three aerofoils, the position of the mean chord line which runs equidistant between the upper and lower surfaces. The more curved or cambered this line is, the more lift the aerofoil can generate.

All of the many aerofoils available can usefully be divided into three classes :

- High lift
- General purpose
- High speed

Typical examples of each of these three types are illustrated in Figure 95.

## High-lift aerofoils

A typical high-lift section has a high thickness/chord ratio, a pronounced camber and a well-rounded leading edge. Its maximum thickness lies about 25 – 30% of the chord aft of the leading edge.

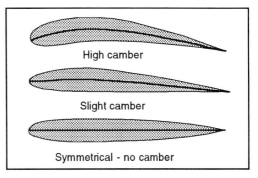

**Figure 94** *The amount of lift generated by an aerofoil depends primarily on its degree of camber*

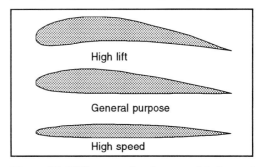

**Figure 95** *Different roles for a model demand different aerofoil shapes.*

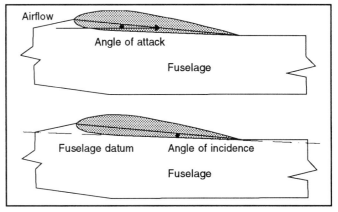

**Figure 96** *Angle of attack and angle of incidence are quite different.*

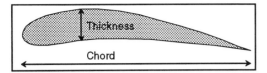

**Figure 97** *The thickness chord ratio depends on the depth and length of the aerofoil.*

The larger the camber, the greater the movement of the centre of pressure, the point through which the lift acts, with changes in the angle of attack. This movement can be decreased by reflexing the trailing edge of the wing upwards. This is often done on aerofoils for flying wings, but does result in some reduction in lift. High-lift sections are ideal for trainers and other models where a large amount of lift is more important than outright speed.

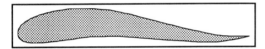

**Figure 98** *A typical high-lift aerofoil with reflex trailing edge designed for use on a flying wing.*

### General purpose aerofoils.

The average general purpose section has a lower thickness/chord ratio, less camber and a sharper leading edge than a high-lift one. The maximum thickness point is still typically about 25 – 30% of the chord aft of the leading edge. The reduced thickness results in less drag and lift than a high-lift aerofoil. This type of aerofoil is well suited to use on aircraft, such as aerobatic models, which need to combine flying reasonably fast with good manoeuvrability.

### High-speed aerofoils

A typical high-speed section has a low thickness/chord ratio, no camber and a sharp leading edge. The maximum thickness is about half-way back. Most of these sections have thickness/chord ratios less than 10% to minimise drag. Thinner sections produce the least lift but are ideal for all-out speed.

## Centre of pressure

Figure 99 shows typical pressure distributions around a wing at various angles of attack. For this particular aerofoil, no lift is produced at minus four degrees. At positive angles, there is a decrease in pressure over the first half of the upper surface which rises back to atmospheric at the trailing edge. Under the lower surface there is a pressure rise but not as large as the variation above the wing. The pressure change is most marked over the first half of the chord. The total reaction of the pressure changes over the two surfaces is represented by a single lift force. This varies in size, direction and the point where it acts on the wing. This point, the centre of pressure, moves with varying angle of attack.

### Movement of the centre of pressure

The lift produced by an aerofoil acts through its centre of pressure. Figure 100 shows how the

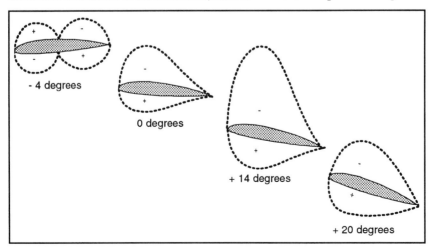

- 4 degrees

0 degrees

+ 14 degrees

+ 20 degrees

**Figure 99** *Changes in the angle of attack will alter the pressure distribution over an aerofoil.*

centre of pressure of a typical cambered aerofoil moves with angle of attack. This particular aerofoil has a large centre of pressure movement. Symmetrical aerofoils have little centre of pressure movement over the working range of angles of attack as do specialist reflex aerofoils designed for use on flying wings.

## Amounts of lift

When different aerofoils are compared at the same angle of attack and speed, the amount of lift they produce differs, depending on the aerofoil section. Generally, at any particular angle of attack, the greater the camber, the greater the lift. Changes in the shape of the leading edge also affect the maximum lift and drag as well as behaviour at the stall. A sharp leading edge stalls more readily than a well rounded one.

High-lift devices like flaps are used to increase lift, particularly at low speed, improving the performance of a wing. For any wing operating at a given angle of attack, as speed rises, lift increases in proportion to the square of the speed.

## Variation of lift with angle of attack

Figure 101 shows how the lift from a typical aerofoil varies with changing angle of attack. At zero angle cambered aerofoils still produce lift, but symmetrical aerofoils do not. Between zero and 12° the line of the graph is straight, showing a steady increase in lift. Above 12°,

although the lift still increases for a few degrees, the rate of increase reduces. Eventually a peak is reached, for the aerofoil shown at 15° angle of attack. If the angle of attack is increased further the lift starts to decrease. The angle at which the peak occurs depends on the aerofoil section.

## Stalling angle of attack

The peak of the curve in Figure 101 represents the point where maximum lift is obtained. Any increase in angle of attack results in a reduction in lift. The airflow over a wing remains smooth up to the stalling angle. Above this angle, the smooth airflow breaks down suddenly and becomes turbulent.

## Variation of drag with angle of attack

Figure 102 overleaf shows that the drag produced by a wing varies steadily with changes of angle of attack. For a cambered aerofoil, it is least at a small positive angle and increases in either direction. The rate of increase is marked at angles of attack above about 12°. After the stall it increases at an even greater rate. The sudden rise at the stall is caused by the onset of turbulent airflow over the wing.

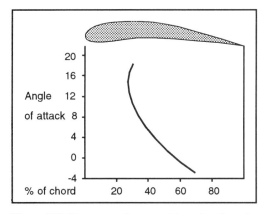

**Figure 100** *The centre of pressure (the point where the lift acts) moves along chordwise as angle of attack varies. A model's centre of gravity must be in front of the most forward position of the centre of pressure.*

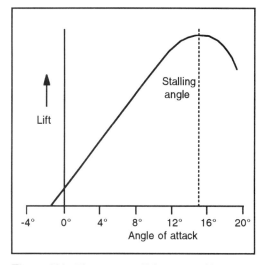

**Figure 101** *The amount of lift generated by a wing increases progressively up to the stall and then rapidly starts to reduce. The data for this graph is from a cambered aerofoil which produces no lift at - 1½° angle of attack.*

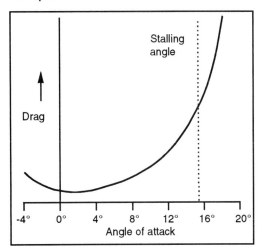

**Figure 102** *Drag also changes as the angle of attack of a wing is varied. This particular aerofoil generates minimum drag at around 2° angle of attack. The drag then rises sharply, particularly above the stalling angle.*

## Variation of lift/drag ratio with angle of attack

For a given amount of lift, the aim should be to have the lowest possible drag from the aerofoil. Typically, the greatest lift is produced at an angle of around 15°; the least drag at an angle of attack of about 1°. At both these angles the ratio of lift to drag is low. The lift/drag ratio for an aerofoil at any selected angle of attack can be calculated and a typical example is shown in Figure 103. It demonstrates that the lift/drag ratio increases rapidly up to about 4° angle of attack. At this point the lift may be 10 to 20 times the drag depending on the aerofoil used. At larger angles the ratio decreases steadily, because even though the lift is still increasing the drag rises at an even faster rate. At the stall the ratio is about 4. It is useful to know the angle of attack which gives the highest lift/drag ratio as this is where the aerofoil gives its best overall performance.

## Aerofoil sections

The aim of this section is to help decide which aerofoil to choose for any particular new design. Various aerofoils are examined and their advantages and weaknesses at model sizes reviewed.

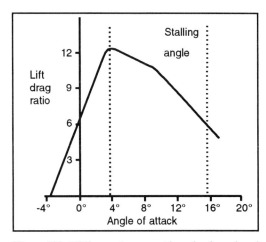

**Figure 103** *Lift/drag ratios vary with angle of attack and are important for their effect on glide angle.*

## Aerofoils

There are thousands of different aerofoils which have been developed over the ninety years since the Wright brothers first flew. They have been designed mainly to meet a range of different requirements and performance improvements for full-sized aircraft. Some have been specially produced for model aircraft and some of those designed for full-size aircraft also perform well at model sizes. The performance of any aerofoil depends on a number of selected characteristics.

- Symmetrical

Equal but low lift upright and inverted.

- Semi-symmetrical

A compromise between high lift and good inverted performance.

- Cambered or curved

Greater amounts of camber give more lift. Poor lift inverted.

- Under cambered

High lift, sudden stall, difficult to cover under surface.

- Large depth of chord

High lift at low speed, high drag at high speed.

- Small depth of chord

Low drag at high speed, low lift at low speed.

- High lift/drag ratio

Good glide angle and low power requirement.

- Small C of P movement

Small longitudinal trim changes with varying angle of attack. Ideal for flying wings.

Eleven aerofoils have been chosen to provide for most design needs and gathered into three groups. The advantages and disadvantages of each is examined to see how to select an aerofoil for a particular model. The performance of each aerofoil is compared with that of the popular Clark Y aerofoil, and, unless otherwise stated, the performance comparison assumes a chord of 250mm (10").

Details of some 200 aerofoils can be found in Martin Simons' excellent *Model Aircraft Aerodynamics*. Chapter 12 explains how to plot aerofoils from table of ordinates. Mention also needs to be made of the recent work by Michael Selig in the USA on low speed aerofoils at model sizes. Details are contained in *Aerofoils at Low Speeds* which was published in 1989. These specialist sections have proved very popular with glider and electric flight specialists looking for the ultimate in competition performance.

## Symmetrical aerofoils

The three chosen symmetrical sections are the popular flat plate, the NACA 0009 which is useful for tailplanes, fins and delta wings, and the NACA 0018 aerobatic model section. The use of symmetrical sections is most common on aerobatic models where their identical upright and inverted performance is such an advantage.

### *Flat plate*

This aerofoil is ideal for tailplanes on all sizes of model. Despite its simplicity, it is a good choice since tailplanes seldom need to produce large amounts of lift. For a wing, its limitations necessitate fast flight or a low wing loading. Its main advantage lies with its apparent lack of stall.

Figure 104 shows two curves. The vertical axis of the graph is lift and the horizontal one angle of attack. The dotted line represents the Clark Y aerofoil; the solid one shows a flat plate aerofoil. There are two main differences. First, a flat plate produces only half the lift of a Clark Y aerofoil. Secondly, while the Clark Y stalls at about 15° angle of attack, the lift from a flat plate increases up to 8°. Above that value, the lift still increases but at a lower rate.

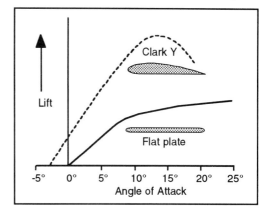

**Figure 104** *The amount of lift generated by an aerofoil depends on its angle of attack to the airstream. The flat plate is compared with the popular Clark Y section.*

This means that, in effect, a flat plate cannot be stalled.

However, as the angle of attack of a flat plate rises so does the drag. Above about 10°, the drag is far higher than for the equivalent Clark Y aerofoil. On a practical model, this means that rather than a conventional stall, the pilot has to feed on more and more power as the angle of attack increases, until level flight can no longer be maintained, when the aircraft starts a mushing descent.

This is a safer characteristic than a conventional stall on a model, where there is no practical method of monitoring either angle of attack or its related stalling speed. As a result, with a flat plate aerofoil, scale like approaches at high angles of attack can safely be accomplished with a fair amount of power. Elevator controls the angle of attack, and thus the drag and air speed, while the throttle is used to vary the rate of descent.

### *NACA 0009*

At 9% thickness chord ratio, this is a thin section, well suited for use on tailplanes and fins. It can also be used on deltas, where its thinness is compensated by the long chord. It has a gentle stall and is ideal where identical upright and inverted performance is more important than straight lift generation. Its performance improves significantly as its chord is increased.

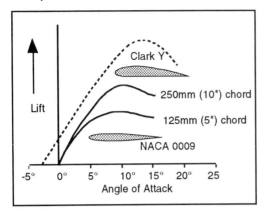

**Figure 105** *NACA 0009 does not produce a lot of lift but is ideal for tailplanes and fins.*

### NACA 0018

The NACA 0018 is an 18% thick symmetrical aerofoil that has found favour on aerobatic models. It produces slightly less lift than Clark Y, but, of course, has identical upright and inverted flight characteristics. The stall is quite sudden, particularly at larger sizes, and will readily result in a spin. As with all symmetrical aerofoils, NACA 0018 produces no lift at zero angle of attack and must be trimmed to fly at a positive angle.

NACA 0018 produces only slightly more drag than Clark Y, despite being half as thick again. Its thickness allows a really strong wing to be constructed, with plenty of room for a pair of outboard aileron servos. The aerofoil is really only suitable for larger models as

the lower curve on the graph shows a significant performance reduction at very small sizes.

## Semi-symmetrical aerofoils

This type of cambered section is, not surprisingly, popular as a compromise between fully symmetrical and the high-lift sections. It is well suited to models which need some aerobatic performance, yet still need to provide plenty of lift. Two NACA and one Eppler section offer an excellent choice of lift, drag and strength characteristics.

### NACA 2412 and 2415

These two aerofoils have 12% and 15% thickness/chord ratios together with a small amount of camber. The lift produced is similar to Clark Y, a little more than the symmetrical NACA 0018 but with a rather less sudden stall. Inverted lift is about 30% less than upright, giving worse bunting than looping performance.

The lift curve shows that, surprisingly, the thinner NACA 2412 produces more lift and, of course, less drag. There is even a 19% thick member of this aerofoil family which produces even less lift. The choice of thickness is really a question of being able to achieve the required structural strength during construction.

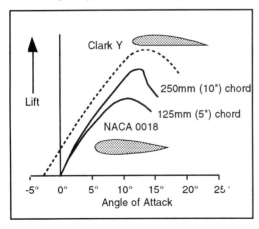

**Figure 106** *The performance of NACA 0018 is the same upright and inverted.*

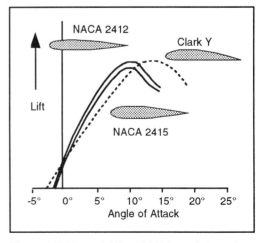

**Figure 107** *NACA 2412 and 2415 aerofoils produce more lift as the section gets thinner.*

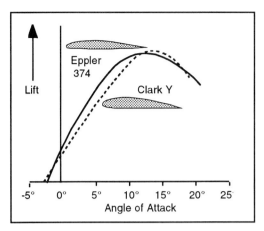

**Figure 108** *Eppler 374 has much better inverted performance than Clark Y and produces significantly less drag.*

### Eppler 374

This is a 10% semi-symmetrical aerofoil with its point of maximum thickness well aft. Both of these factors help to keep the drag very low while producing a reasonable amount of lift (about the same as Clark Y). It is well suited to faster flying models and has a gentle stall. Care is needed to ensure adequate strength is built in.

## Other cambered aerofoils

The final five aerofoils are all curved. The first is the curved plate, a surprisingly efficient section. There are then two flat bottomed aerofoils including the ever popular Clark Y. Of the final pair, one has an under camber on the bottom surface and the other is a reflex section suitable for tailless models.

### Curved plate

At first sight a curved plate aerofoil may appear too simple for use on R/C models. Figure 109 shows this is not true. A curved plate is one of the few aerofoils capable of performing well on a very small model. The performance does not alter significantly when scaled up. It does operate over a fairly narrow range of angles of attack, stalling quite suddenly at around 8°. Its use on large models will be limited by structural considerations. The aerofoil creates very low drag while

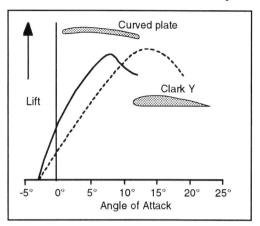

**Figure 109** *The lift characteristics of a curved plate are surprisingly good.*

producing plenty of lift, giving an efficient glide. The Gö 417a is an optimised curved plate aerofoil. Its best lift/drag ratio occurs at an angle of attack of around 4°.

### Clark Y

This aerofoil is the probably the most popular of all modellers' aerofoils. It is just over 11½% thick and its flat under surface simplifies wing construction. Variations in the chord length of this aerofoil only give a minor changes to its performance, making it suitable for most model sizes. The lift shows a steady, smooth rise to the maximum at the point of stall and a nicely rounded top giving a gentle stalling characteristic. The use of this aerofoil does

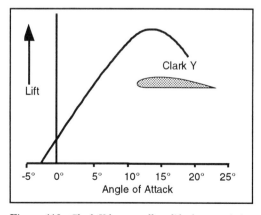

**Figure 110** *Clark Y has excellent lift characteristics matched to a gentle stall. Its inverted performance is very poor.*

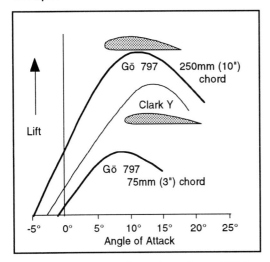

Figure 111 *Göttingen 797 produces plenty of lift, but with the penalty of a very poor inverted performance.*

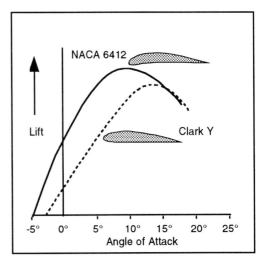

Figure 112 *NACA 6412 is a significantly better lift producer than Clark Y when operating upright.*

tend to make any model employing it balloon when rolling out of a turn.

Clark Y produces zero lift at an angle of attack of minus 3°. For any angle above this, the aerofoil will produce some lift and for any angle below it, negative lift. Clark Y operates very inefficiently when inverted and is thus unsuitable for tailplanes or aerobatic models.

### Göttingen 797

This is a thick 16% flat bottomed aerofoil and, although able to produce more lift than Clark Y, its inverted performance is even worse. Its zero-lift angle is approximately 5°. It is only suitable for use on larger models, which, even if heavily loaded will be able to fly slowly. Compared to other aerofoils able to produce the same lift, its drag is quite low. Its depth of section enables great strength to be built into the wing structure.

### NACA 6412

This 12% aerofoil is slightly under cambered and as a result produces plenty of lift but with a gentle stall. It has the added advantage of producing relatively little drag and for best efficiency should be mounted at an incidence angle of 4°. It is unsuitable for inverted flying as the low inverted lift is accompanied by a large

amount of drag. Its cambered under surface may give difficulties in getting any covering to stick to wing ribs.

### NACA 2R212 Reflex

Most reflex sections are well suited for use on tailless models such as flying wings. This aerofoil's centre of pressure does not move with changing angle of attack. It has a 12% thickness chord ratio, produces somewhat less lift than a Clark Y and has a rather more sudden stall. However, its drag is modest and the other shortcomings are well compensated by the lack of pitching problems.

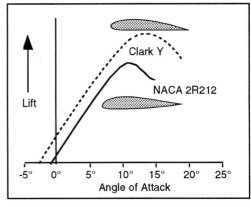

Figure 113 *Any reflex cambered aerofoil sacrifices lift in order to minimise centre of pressure movement, which in the case of this section is zero.*

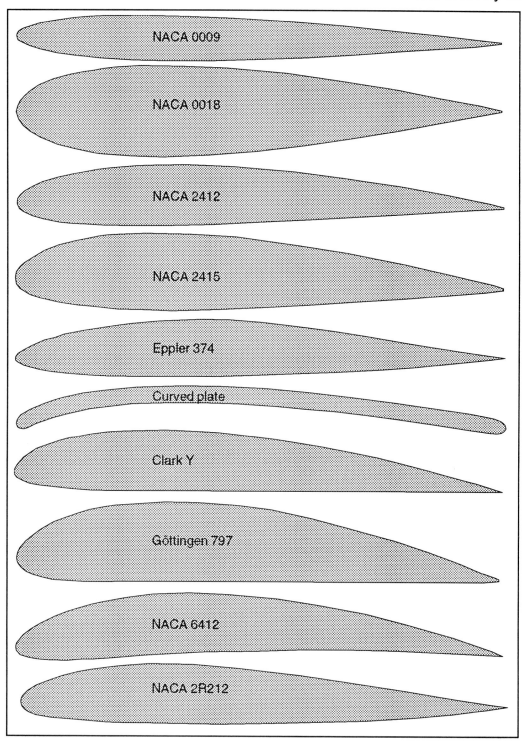

**Figure 114** *Ten popular aerofoil sections which cover almost the complete range of non-competitive model requirements. They may be photocopied and enlarged or reduced as required.*

59

Figure 115 *The classic layout that calls for a reflex aerofoil. This flying wing with a semi-symmetrical aerofoil and upswept elevons had some undesirable pitch control characteristics.*

## Your own special aerofoil

There is no reason to stick with one of the aerofoils detailed above. You can choose from a wide variety of other available sections or even design your own. Furthermore, there are many models which use one aerofoil at the root and another at the tip with a gradual change between the two. The following points should help if you decide to produce a custom aerofoil of your own for a new model.

- Symmetrical aerofoils work equally well upright and inverted.
- Camber will give an increase upright lift but reduce inverted lift. Inverted stalls can be very sudden.
- Aerofoils with a forward (15% – 33%) maximum thickness point usually give high lift. Unfortunately they often suffer from a sudden stall.

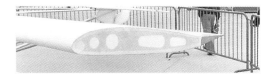

Figure 116 *A full-size microlight shows off its wing tip aerofoil at an airshow.*

- Aerofoils with an aft (33% - 50%) maximum thickness point usually give less lift. However, they mostly produce low drag, particularly if maximum thickness is near the 50% mark.
- Thin aerofoils can give excellent performance. A thickness as low as 10% should create enough lift for most models.
- Sharp leading edges can improve the slow speed performance of thin aerofoils, giving an increase in lift and a reduction in drag, but may give also result in a much more sudden stall.

## Wing planform

Having selected an aerofoil, the next important aspect of wing design is its planform or shape viewed from above. Wing planform has a dramatic impact on the amount of lift and drag for a given wing area. It also has a major effect on stalling angle.

### Wing vortices

The pressure distribution, seen from the front of a model, is roughly as shown in Figure 117. The precise shape depends on the angle of attack and the wing planform. The pressure difference

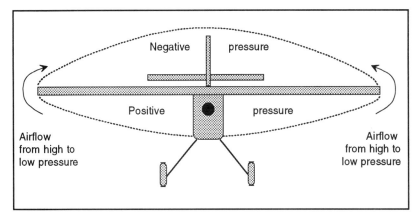

Figure 117 *Negative pressure above the wing accounts for two-thirds of the lift. The same percentage can broadly be said for the wing centre section.*

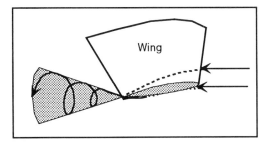

**Figure 118** *The formation of vortices is caused by air flowing around the wing tip.*

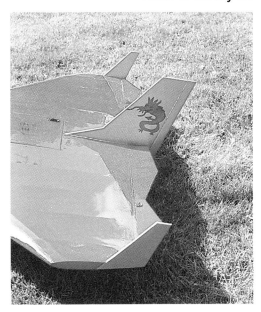

**Figure 119** *The winglets fitted to the Dragon Delta in an attempt to reduce the large amount of induced drag produced by a delta at low speeds.*

between the upper and lower surfaces of the wing causes air to flow round the tips from the high pressure region below the wing to the low pressure area above.

Because the main airflow is moving past the tips, the result is a spiral vortex forming at each tip. The direction of rotation of the vortices is in towards the fuselage when viewed from above. The greater the size and strength of the vortices the greater the induced drag.

Vortices are largest at high angles of attack and disappear at the angle for zero lift. During inverted flight, the vortices rotate in the opposite direction. As we saw in the last chapter, the induced drag produced by vortices varies inversely with the square of the speed.

Winglets on airliners have become a common feature and they certainly lessen induced drag by decreasing the size of the tip vortices. Typically, they are angled out from the wing tip at about 20° and full-size ones are swept back for high speed flight to an angle of 30°. The alternative of simple end plates can be equally effective.

## Aspect ratio

The ratio of the span of a wing to its mean chord gives an indication of its performance. Aspect ratio can be calculated by dividing the span of a wing by its mean chord. It can also be calculated by dividing the square of the wingspan by the area of the wing. The longer and thinner a wing, the higher its aspect ratio and the better its performance.

Thus a wing with a span of 1.5

metres (5 feet) and a mean chord of 150mm (6 inches) has an aspect ratio of 10. A model with a wing area of 288 square dm (3.2 sq. ft) and a span of 1.2m (4 ft) has an aspect ratio of 5.

The aspect ratio of a model has a marked effect on its manoeuvrability in the rolling plane. While in full-size aviation, high aspect ratios are used to improve efficiency, a particularly vital factor in commercial transport operations, the same is generally not as important for models. The exceptions are sailplanes and slope soarers,

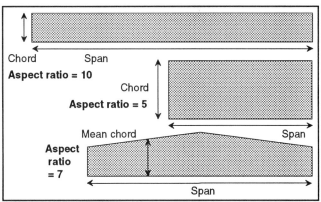

**Figure 120** *All three wings have the same wing area, but very different aspect ratios (A/R).*

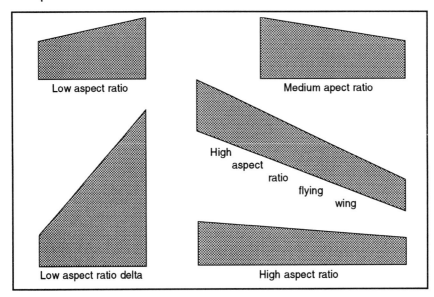

**Figure 121** *High aspect ratio wings require additional strength in the spars to achieve a rigid structure.*

where increased efficiency equals better gliding performance. Thus, the choice of aspect ratio for the sports model is a question of manoeuvrability, aesthetics and personal preferences.

By their very nature, biplanes tend to have lower aspect ratios than monoplanes. Together with interplane struts, this allows great strength to be built into the wings of these designs.

### Aspect ratio and induced drag

As explained earlier, wing tip vortices are the cause of induced drag. The size of the vortices and the resulting induced drag is inversely proportional to aspect ratio. If the aspect ratio is doubled then induced drag will be halved. Figure 122 shows two wings of the same area but different aspect ratios. The higher aspect ratio wings form smaller wing tip vortices because their narrower tips spill less air from the lower to the upper surface.

High aspect ratio wings are thus more efficient and provide a higher lift/drag ratio. Since the total drag of a wing is the sum of its parasite and induced drag, its total drag also changes with aspect ratio. Figure 123 shows how the total drag of two wings of different aspect ratios varies with angle of attack.

### Aspect ratio, lift and stalling

Changing the aspect ratio for a given wing area alters the angle of attack needed to obtain a given amount of lift. Due to changes in the downwash caused by the wing tip vortices, as the aspect ratio decreases, stalling angle increases. If a wing with an aspect ratio of 20 stalls at an angle of attack of about 12°, the same aerofoil with an aspect ratio of 8 will stall at 16°. With a very low aspect ratio of 2, the wing

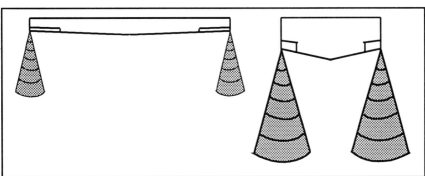

**Figure 122** *How aspect ratio affects the size of the wing tip vortices.*

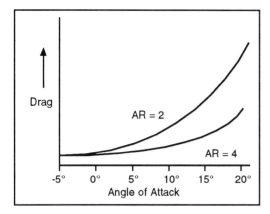

**Figure 123** *The induced drag increases quite dramatically for low aspect ratio wings at high angles of attack.*

will stall at an angle of about 25°. It is also clear from Figure 124 that the maximum lift a wing can produce, all other things being equal, reduces as aspect ratio is decreased.

## *Use of high aspect ratio*

High aspect ratio wings are found most often on low speed models, such as gliders, operating at an angle of around 4° to give the best lift/drag ratio. The total drag is low at this angle of attack but induced drag may still be fairly high with a low aspect ratio. Gliders typically have aspect ratios above 10. These figures may be compared to those of trainers with typical aspect ratios around 5.

The limiting factor in the use of high aspect ratio is the difficulty of providing sufficient strength for the wings without the excessive weight neutralising the advantages. Broadly speaking, the lower the speed of the model the higher the aspect ratio that it is practical to use.

## Sweep-back

In full-size aviation, swept-back or delta wings are commonplace on high speed aircraft. The reason for the use of sweep-back is its drag reducing properties at transonic speeds. This is hardly a problem for the modeller! Moreover, the high-speed/low-drag advantages are gained at the cost of some performance problems at low speeds. These difficulties only become apparent if sweep-back of more than about 20° is used in models, which are all low speed in full-size terms. Thus models miss the main benefits while still retaining the snags. However, swept wings are aesthetically attractive to model designers and builders alike and, as in full-sized aviation, the problems can easily be overcome once understood.

### *Effect of sweep-back on lift and drag*

Any swept-back wing suffers a marked drop in the maximum lift compared with an unswept wing of the same area and aspect ratio. Figure 125 compares typical lift curves for a straight wing, a swept-back wing, and a tailless delta wing all of the same area, aerofoil section and low aspect ratio. The stall occurs on the swept and delta wings at considerably greater angles

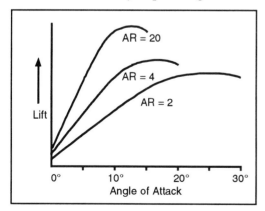

**Figure 124** *Lift increases and the stalling angle reduces as aspect ratio is increased.*

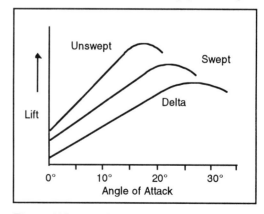

**Figure 125** *The effect on lift of varying the wing planform at a constant aspect ratio.*

of attack than those of unswept wings but the lift produced is less.

The peak of the lift curve for a delta is very flat, with little variation over a comparatively wide range of angles. This mild stall behaviour allows delta wings to be flown at angles of attack considerably higher than that for maximum lift without ill effects except a very marked increase in drag.

### Tip-stalling, aileron response and pitch up

Sweep-back causes several difficulties at low speeds. First, there is an increased tendency to tip-stalling. The second problem is reduced aileron effectiveness at high angles of attack. Comparatively large aileron movements may be necessary to manoeuvre a model at low speeds and the response may be sluggish. Inboard or strip ailerons can help as can all-moving wing tips. In addition, the exaggerated nose-up attitude of a delta at low speeds may necessitate an excessively long undercarriage.

Longitudinal instability results when the tips of a swept wing stall. The instability causes pitch up, a nose-up movement which deepens the stall as the angle of attack continues to increase. The cause of this, shown in Figure 126, is the loss of lift over the outboard sections and the resulting rapid forward movement of the centre of pressure. Figure 126 also shows the maximum downwash from an unstalled swept-back wing comes from the tip portions. When the tips stall, the maximum downwash moves

**Figure 127** *This Folland Gnat had both ailerons set slightly up at neutral to give effective washout to the wing and thus minimise the risk of tip-stalling.*

inboard over the tailplane increasing the tendency to pitch up. This effect can be reduced by vertical placing of the tailplane to avoid downwash changes.

### Alleviating tip-stalling

The three most commonly used methods on models are inboard flaps, washout and leading edge extensions. Flaps cause the inboard part of the wing to stall at a lower angle of attack, reducing the chances of tip-stalling. Washout results in a similar effect.

Extended leading edges or saw teeth are a good way to avoid the worst effects of tip stalling. As shown in Figure 129, the growth of the main vortex is reduced. A further smaller vortex, starting from the tip of the extension, affects a much smaller proportion of the tip area. Thus the severity of the tip stall is reduced and with it the pitch-up tendency. A further advantage of leading edge

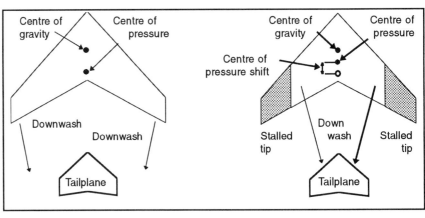

**Figure 126**
*How tip-stalling on a swept-back wing produces pitch up.*

**Figure 128** *The saw tooth leading edge is clearly visible on this swept-wing model.*

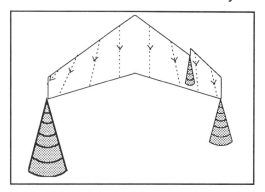

**Figure 129** *Comparison of wing vortices and span wise boundary layer flow on a swept wing (left) and one with a leading edge extension (right).*

extensions is that when the tip eventually stalls the forward shift in centre of pressure is less marked, also reducing the pitch-up effect. Sweep-back can be applied to just the leading edge of a wing or to both the leading and trailing edges. The same is true of sweep-forward. We have seen the aerodynamic dangers in having too much sweep-back. Figure 130 overleaf shows some of the possible choices open to designers but mention must be made of the main danger of sweep-forward.

When a wing tip is raised, for example when loaded during a manoeuvre, the leading edge of the wing will inherently rise more than the trailing edge, resulting in more lift at the tip giving more twist and so on until the wing is torn off. This is why sweep-forward is rare in full-size aviation and why model and full-size wings must be stiff enough to avoid this twisting tendency under load. Aerodynamically, a swept-forward wing avoids the problems associated with sweep-back.

" WHAT DO YOU THINK OF MY LATEST SAW-TOOTH LEADING EDGE? "

# Chapter 6

## Pros and cons of various planforms

The commonly used parallel chord rectangular wing invariably performs well regardless of the aerofoil employed. The less common delta is also very safe, mainly because the large degree of sweep-back provides a high degree of stability. Straight taper, elliptical, swept-back and high aspect ratio wing can all cause problems at the stall. The following are the key features, both positive and negative, of the various alternatives.

### Rectangular parallel wing

Consistent lift performance almost to the wing tip.

Tip-stalling unlikely.

Identical ribs make construction simple.

Not the most attractive visually.

### Elliptical wing

Very efficient when flying fast at low angles of attack.

Violent tip-stall likely.

Most attractive shape.

Difficult to build.

### Up to 20° swept-back parallel wing

Consistent lift performance almost to wing tip.

Tip-stalling unlikely.

Better damping to pitching gusts than rectangular wing.

Improves spiral stability requiring little or no dihedral.

Harder to build than a rectangular wing.

### Tapered wing

Can produce violent tip-stalls with small tip chord.

Fairly efficient lift and strength distribution.

Attractive shape.

Harder to build unless using foam.

### Highly swept tapered wing

Rather inefficient in relation to wing area.

Added stability useful.

Tip-stalls and pitch up possible.

Aileron effectiveness reduced at high angles of attack.

Attractive shape.

Strong but not easy to build.

### High aspect ratio wing

Potentially very efficient except on small models.

Very liable to tip-stall particularly when turning due to speed reduction of inner tip.

Thinner aerofoil tips or washout can reduce tip-stalling.

Low spiral stability needs increased dihedral angle.

Strong centre section needed.

Quite an attractive shape.

### Delta

Not efficient in relation to wing area.

Added stability useful.

Despite small tips, tip-stalls unlikely.

Stall is stable and straight.

Slow speed flight possible at very high angles of attack.

Tends to result in a nose-heavy model, particularly at larger angles of sweep.

Attractive shape.

Strong but not easy to build.

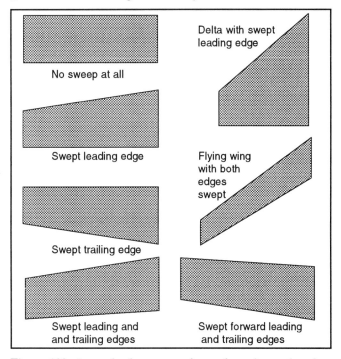

No sweep at all

Swept leading edge

Swept trailing edge

Swept leading and and trailing edges

Delta with swept leading edge

Flying wing with both edges swept

Swept forward leading and trailing edges

**Figure 130** *Sweep-back or sweep-forward can be employed on either the leading or trailing edge, or both.*

# Wing position

There are a number of wing positions that can be adopted on any model. On a monoplane these are:

- Parasol wing
- High wing
- Mid wing
- Low wing

The higher the wing position, the more pendulum stability that is imparted to a model, which tries to keep its wings level. This is a desirable feature in a trainer, but not for an aerobatic model. In fact, on a low wing design it is not uncommon to find negative pendulum stability. The reasons for this are covered in the next chapter. In addition, the vertical position of the wing in relation to the vertical location of the tailplane will affect the downwash over the tail and the changes in downwash when the wing stalls.

From a construction point of view, a parasol wing involves some form of cabane struts. High and low wings are easily attached to the fuselage and their removal provides handy access to the radio equipment. Perhaps the hardest arrangement is the mid wing location. Wings can be built in for a small one piece model. Otherwise separate plug in wings or a significant cut-out in the fuselage is necessary, with a fairing above or below the wing.

For a biplane, the two main choices are to locate the top wing in a parasol or high wing position and the lower one in a low wing position. There are also additional considerations for biplanes when it comes to looking at the separation between the wings and their fore and aft positions.

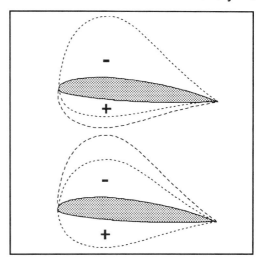

**Figure 132** *Interference between the upper and lower wing causes both to produce less lift than if they were operating in isolation.*

Not only must the distance between the wings be considered, but the stagger, if any, of the bottom wing in relation to the top wing also requires thought. While wing separation will affect the aerodynamic performance of the wing and at least one chord is recommended, stagger has more impact on the longitudinal stability and the aesthetics of the design. If stagger is used, it is important that the forward wing stalls first to pitch the nose down at the stall. For this reason the forward wing should always be set at an incidence angle one degree greater than the rear one.

## Dihedral and anhedral

The requirement for dihedral may result from the need to provide an adequate degree of lateral

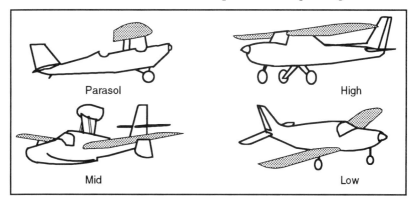

**Figure 131** *There are essentially four vertical positions where a monoplane wing may be located.*

Parasol

High

Mid

Low

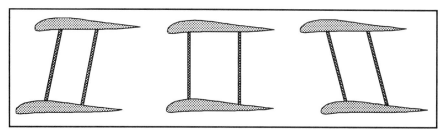

*Figure 133 Biplanes may have rear-ward stagger, no stagger or, most common of all, forward stagger.*

stability, to enable a model to turn using rudder alone or just because the designer thinks the end result is attractive. Dihedral can be applied to the whole of each wing panel or just to the outer portion.

If applied in different amounts to the inboard and outboard panels, it is referred to as polyhedral. For a four panel wing, dihedral can be applied to all panels or just to the outside ones. Either is particularly appropriate for an old timer design.

Anhedral is often required to reduce the inherent stability of a swept wing as it has the opposite effect. On the basis that 10° of sweep-back is equivalent to 1° of dihedral, the appropriate amount of anhedral can be calculated.

## Wing loading

Wing loading is one of the key factors affecting the performance of any model. The greater the loading, the higher the stalling speed, the longer the take-off run and the lower the manoeuvrability of a model, all other things being equal.

The other key consideration is that the larger a model, because of scale effects, the better it can cope with a high wing loading. This is also true to an extent for fast flying models. Figure 135

shows a range of suitable wing loading for models with varying wing-spans. It is worth noting that, since electric power inevitably results in high wing loadings due to the weight of the battery, it is normal to expect an electric design to have a wing loading towards the top of the range.

## High-lift devices

Ways of increasing the maximum lift that a wing can produce at low speeds have always been of interest to aeromodellers, particularly those

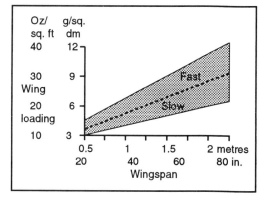

*Figure 135 Scale effects mean that wing loading can be increased as the size of the wing increases. Clearly a fast flying model can cope better with a higher wing loading than a slow flying one.*

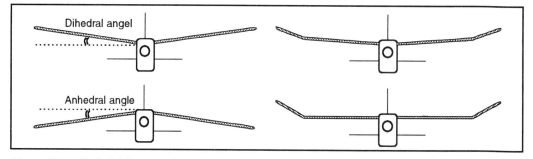

**Figure 134** *Dihedral helps to make a model look more natural. Anhedral can have the opposite effect. The model top right has polyhedral; that bottom right, tip dihedral.*

searching for high speeds. There is a wide choice of devices which improve the lift and often increase the drag of a wing. Simple flaps, split flaps and Fowler flaps (which also increase the wing area) are all feasible, as are slots and slats, the latter fixed and even movable.

## Flaps

Flaps increase the lift a wing produces, with a corresponding increase in drag. The increase in lift allows a model to fly more slowly, particularly useful when taking off or landing.

The deployment of flaps at large angles to produce drag is used to slow the model. Flaps also allow approaches with higher engine rpm, giving better engine response and slipstream over the tail surfaces to improve control at these low speeds.

Greater camber, and thus increased lift, can be obtained by deflecting a wing's leading or trailing edge, or both. Almost invariably, models fitted with flaps use the trailing edge alone. Figure 136 shows the effect of flaps on lift and stalling angle and also shows the effect of fitting slats for comparison.

## Types of flaps

Trailing edge flaps have many variations, all of which increase maximum lift. Some perform better than others. More effective flaps are generally more complex mechanically and are usually only found on true scale models.

Table 12 shows the angles of attack at which maximum lift is obtained with various high lift devices. It also indicates that the flap gives its increased lift without the excessive angles necessary with slats. A factor often forgotten is that because flaps reduce the stalling angle of a wing, their use inboard will also reduce any tip-stalling tendency.

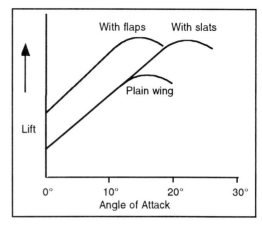

**Figure 136** *The use of flaps or slats significantly increase the maximum lift which can be generated.*

### Simple flaps

These are built and fitted in exactly the same way as outboard ailerons, but almost invariably fitted to the inboard section of the wing. The area of each flap should be around 10 – 12½% of the wing area. They will provide as much as a fifty per cent increase in the lift provided by the clean wing. It is important, when connecting them, not to forget that both flaps move in the same direction, whereas the ailerons move in opposite directions. Hinging

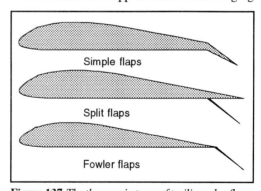

**Figure 137** *The three main types of trailing edge flaps.*

| Lift device | Stall angle | Lift increase | Lift device | Stall angle | Lift increase |
|---|---|---|---|---|---|
| Plain aerofoil | 17° | - | Fowler flap | 17° | 90% |
| Simple flap | 14° | 50% | Slat | 25° | 25% |
| Split flap | 15° | 70% | Slat and flap | 20° | 75% |

**Table 12** *The effect of flaps and slats on stalling angle and lift. An increase in stalling angle is a far from desirable feature.*

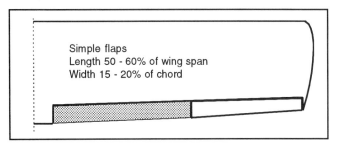

**Figure 138** *Simple flaps are normally fitted inboard of ailerons but may be full span or even mixed with ailerons to provide flaperons.*

methods are similar to those employed for ailerons.

### Split flaps

Split flaps are more effective than simple ones, but also more difficult to build into a wing structure. They need to be thin if they are to blend into the trailing edge of the wing but stiffness is paramount. Hinging can be tricky as there is not much meat in the trailing edge of a wing once a space to house the flaps flush with the under surface of the wing has been completed.

The area of split flaps should be roughly the same as simple ones, although it may be

**Figure 139** *Split flaps are particularly effective at increasing lift at small deflections and drag when fully deployed.*

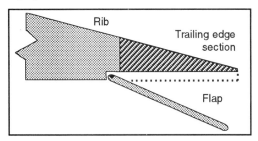

**Figure 140** *A split flap involves some clever detailed design at the trailing edge of the wing.*

advantageous structurally to use a wider chord. This will move the hinge point further from the trailing edge.

### Fowler flaps

The Fowler flap is of the area increasing type. Besides augmenting the lift by increasing the camber, it increases the wing area, thus reducing the wing loading and lowering the stalling speed still further. Construction can be quite complex, involving sliding rails as well as a hinging mechanism. It is for this reason that these type of flaps are usually found only on faithful scale models.

When flaps are lowered the lift/drag ratio is always reduced. The best ratio is obtained with flaps at angles between 5° and 30°, the exact angle depending on the wing aerofoil and the type and size of the flap. This angle should be used to shorten the take-off run and to improve manoeuvrability once airborne.

For a flap with an angular movement of 90°, the first 30° provides a steady rise in lift without much drag increase. The next 30° slightly increases the lift with drag rising significantly. The final part of the movement produces little increase in lift, but a rapid rise in drag. Since flaps are basically fitted to increase lift, the maximum angle of deflection should be limited to around 60°.

### Slats and slots

Slats are small cambered auxiliary aerofoils mounted on the leading edge of a wing along the complete span or just an outboard section of

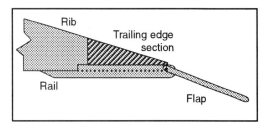

**Figure 141** *Rails are needed to allow a Fowler flap to slide back, increasing the wing area.*

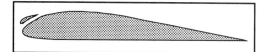

**Figure 142** *Slats are small cambered aerofoils attached to the leading edge of a wing to provide more lift at high angles of attack.*

the wing. Slats are located so that a suitable slot is formed, the shape of which should have an entry gap around twice the exit gap. If they are small their drag should be negligible and they may be fixed permanently in place.

They increase the maximum lift by as much as 70%. At the same time, the stalling angle is increased by around 10°. Outboard slats can relieve tip-stalling as well as augment lift. Figure 145 compares the performances of the same size slatted and unslatted wings.

Like flaps, slats allow the stalling speed of a given wing to be reduced. The reduction depends on the proportion of the leading edge covered by the slat and the chord of the slat.

Where the slats are fitted only to the wing tips, the increase in lift is smaller but they are an efficient way of minimising any tip-stalling tendency. However, the excessive angle of attack near the stall is likely to cause almost insuperable undercarriage design problems if

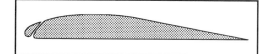

**Figure 143** *Slots are normally a structural part of a wing and can also be used to increase lift.*

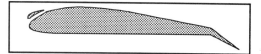

**Figure 144** *The combination of slats and flaps offers practical advantages over the use of slats in isolation.*

slats are to be of benefit during take-off and landing. This is why it is common practice to employ slats in conjunction with flaps. The combination will reduce the stalling angle of the wing to a more manageable 17 – 20°.

Figure 143 shows a variation of the classic slat arrangement, in which suitably shaped slots are built into the wing tips just behind the leading edge. Their action is the same as that of the normal slat and their shape, entry and exit slot characteristics should also be similar.

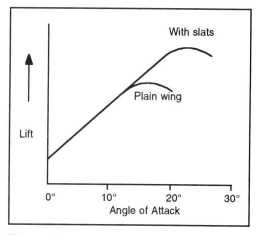

**Figure 145** *The effect of slats is to increase both lift and stalling angle of attack.*

# 7. Control characteristics

## Manoeuvrability

Manoeuvre is the ability to change the flight path of a model in pitch, roll or yaw. Stability is the enemy of manoeuvre, but is very useful to us R/C pilots who have to control our models remotely. An aerobatic model needs to be more manoeuvrable and therefore less stable than say a multi-engined toffee bomber. This is true in full-sized aviation when comparing the Tornado with the Jumbo Jet. The effects of inertia have to be overcome to manoeuvre any aircraft. Isaac Newton's laws mean the larger the model, all other things being equal, the less manoeuvrable it is.

There are, however, several other factors to be taken into consideration. The first is air speed. An aircraft flying just above its stalling speed has virtually no manoeuvre capability. The slightest attempt at a turn or climb will result in a stall. Equally, an aircraft flying flat out will have a comparatively large turning circle. Obviously the larger the wing area and more efficient the aerofoil section the more lift and the less drag, both of which are a benefit to manoeuvre.

All-up weight likewise has its impact, any increase causing a reduction in manoeuvrability.

Two factors need consideration. First, the lighter you build the model the better it will manoeuvre. Secondly, there may be a removable payload on board the model. First and foremost is the fuel, which may account for ten per cent or more of the model's weight. Next, the aircraft may carry a droppable load; anything from a parachutist to a load of toffees at a display. In both cases the model will be more manoeuvrable after it has dropped its load.

The rates of roll, pitch and yaw which a model can achieve are dependent on two factors. The first is the natural stability of the aircraft, which is in itself dependent on such factors as the position of the centre of gravity, the amount of dihedral, the size of the tailplane and fin as well as their distance from the centre of gravity. The second is the manoeuvre performance of the model which depends on the size, position and effectiveness of the control surfaces, the wing loading of the model and the excess of thrust over drag available from the engine.

We have seen that speed is dependent on the excess of thrust over drag in level flight, unless air brakes or drag producing flaps are deployed. The maximum continuous rate of turn and climb rate achievable (ignoring the effect of thermals)

**Figure 146** *My Viggen, Nexus Plan RM 242, has excellent manoeuvrability due to its unusual canard delta configuration. (**Photo Ron Dawes.**)*

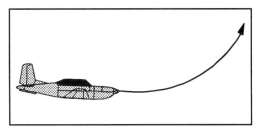

**Figure 147** *Manoeuvre in pitch demands an elevator input by the pilot, an increase of power to try to maintain speed, a wing able to provide more lift and a model strong enough to survive the manoeuvre.*

also depend on the excess thrust over drag.

The final factor worth considering is the ultimate structural strength of the model. Pylon racing afficionado's have been known to stress their aircraft to the point of structural failure and it is not unknown for wings to fold when pulling out of a steep dive close to the ground. It is beyond the realms of this book to consider how to calculate the ultimate strength of a model. Experience, both with the structure and flight manoeuvres, are the best guide but some advice is given in Chapters 8 and 9. It is worth noting that large models (those weighing over 7kg or 15lb) require serious consideration to be given to stress analysis and care taken to ensure excess strength in key structural members.

## Aerobatic capability

Aerobatics stretch both the model and its pilot to the extreme. Aerobatics demand a strong airframe to resist the high 'g' forces applied to the airframe by violent manoeuvres, plenty of power to overcome the high drag forces which result from operating at high angles of attack, and the best possible rates of roll and pitch. Furthermore, for at least some aerobatics, the ability to enter flick manoeuvres, where the aircraft is stalled at speeds above the straight and level stalling speed, spin and carry out knife-edge manoeuvres are additional requirements. Each individual type of manoeuvre requires careful consideration to visualise its effect on the aircraft design.

## Speed

A high powered engine and matching high pitch propeller are the essential prerequisites of a racer. The choice of aerofoil for any fast model also depends on the trade off between high speed and manoeuvrability. High speed requires minimum drag and a low lift aerofoil. A well streamlined fuselage with cowled engine is ideal, together with any thin aerofoil with little or no camber and low drag characteristics at low angles of attack. However, for good turning performance, the aerofoil must provide sufficient lift at high angles of attack. The initial turning ability is very dependent on how

much excess lift the wing can momentarily provide.

## Payload

At the other extreme from the aerobatic model is the aeroplane designed to carry a heavy payload. This may be just the batteries in an electric model, the fuel in an aircraft trying to establish a range or endurance record, or a load of sweets in the case of a toffee bomber. The payload carried must be added to the total aircraft weight to establish the take-off weight and the maximum wing loading. In the ultimate, an over-loaded aircraft will just stagger into the air and fly, without being able to gain height, at a speed just above the stalling speed; definitely not an attractive proposition.

## Take-off and landing characteristics

Compared with full-sized aircraft, the length of the take-off or landing run of our models is a much less important factor. Some specialist models, such as ducted fans, particularly when operating off grass, may run out of space on their take-off run. Equally, models with low drag may find an approach over trees leads to an overshoot of the landing strip, particularly when the headwind is light.

The surface quality of the landing strip is normally outside the control of the designer/pilot, although cutting the grass shorter may be a possibility. However, small wheels increase drag during the take-off run on all but bowling green quality grass surfaces. Thus the choice of wheel size can be an important factor in reducing the length of the run. Furthermore, a nosewheel configuration gives more rolling resistance than a tail dragger.

The length of the take-off run is vitally dependent on the thrust to weight ratio, the wing loading and aerofoil of the aircraft. Increasing thrust, reducing weight and enlarging the wing area all help, as do high lift aerofoils and the use of high lift devices.

## Flight duration

How long do you want to fly between re-fuelling stops? The quantity and weight of fuel can be a major consideration, and in extreme cases mean locating the fuel tank on or close to the centre of gravity. In the case of electric flight, the size of the power pack rises alarmingly. The size of the radio battery may need enlarging, particularly if it has to last for several long flights without recharging. These factors are all very similar to the payload issues mentioned above.

# Stability

Stability is a complex subject and many factors come into play. For our purposes the subject is much simplified and only factors of practical concern are covered. It is essential to have a basic understanding of the principles involved, so that any new design has the right degree of stability built in. Figure 148 shows stability in terms of a ball placed in a bowl (Stable) on a flat surface (Neutral) and on an upturned bowl (Unstable).

## The three axes

An aircraft can pitch, roll and yaw about its three axes and these are shown in Figure 149. An aircraft has to be stable about each of these axes and the three forms of stability are longitudinal stability, probably the most important, lateral stability and directional stability.

### Longitudinal axis

The longitudinal axis is a line running fore and aft through the centre of gravity and is the axis about which the aircraft rolls. Stability about this axis is known as lateral.

### Directional axis

The directional axis is a line running vertically through the centre of gravity and is the axis about which the aircraft yaws. Stability about this axis is directional.

### Lateral axis

The lateral axis is a line running span wise through the centre of gravity at right angles to the other two. Movement about this axis is termed pitching and stability about it is longitudinal.

All three axes are fixed in relation to the model and do not necessarily indicate motion relative to the ground. An aircraft may be unstable about only one or two of its axes and stable about the others or unstable about all three.

## Static and dynamic stability

The stability of an aircraft is its tendency to return to its original trimmed position after being displaced in pitch, roll or yaw.

### Static stability

If a model, trimmed in straight and level flight, is disturbed from its flight path, it is statically stable if it tries to return to its original flight condition. It is statically unstable if it tries to depart further from it. If it remains in the disturbed position it has neutral static stability.

### Dynamic stability

Although a model may be statically stable and try to return to its original position, it may overshoot and again try to correct itself, causing an oscillation to be set up. If the oscillation damps out, then the aircraft is dynamically stable. If it increases the aircraft is dynamically unstable and if it persists, without increasing or decreasing, the aircraft is neutrally stable dynamically.

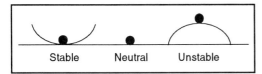

**Figure 148** *Stability is more easily understood by considering familiar objects, such as a bowl and a ball. Their relative positions give a good indication of the three possibilities for a model.*

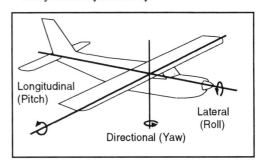

**Figure 149** *The three axes of any aircraft and the motions about them.*

### Subsidence and divergence

If a model, after disturbance, gradually regains its trimmed position without overshooting, it is statically and dynamically stable. This type of stability is called subsidence. If it continues to move away from the trimmed position it is both statically and dynamically unstable. This is known as divergence. Figure 150 illustrates the five possible forms of dynamic stability using the pitching plane as an example.

## Longitudinal stability

Stability in pitch (nose up/down) depends on the position of the centre of gravity, movement of the centre of pressure, the size of the tailplane and its fore and aft position. Moving the centre

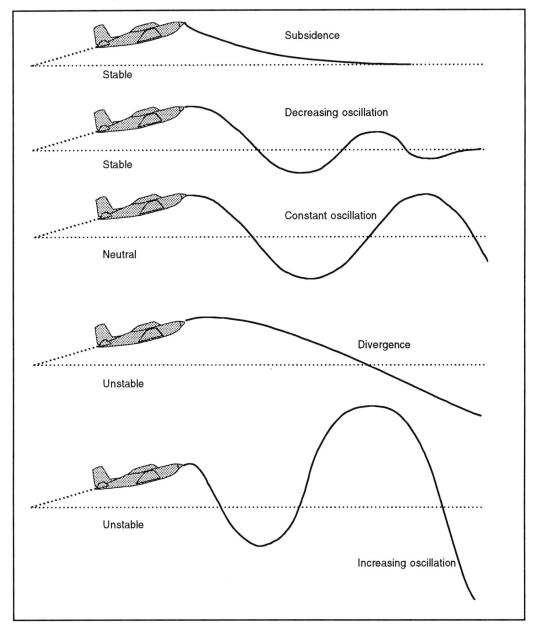

Subsidence

Stable

Decreasing oscillation

Stable

Constant oscillation

Neutral

Divergence

Unstable

Unstable

Increasing oscillation

**Figure 150** *The various paths an aircraft can take in the pitching plane after being disturbed from level flight.*

of gravity forward, the tailplane back or enlarging its size all increase longitudinal stability. These factors must be considered at the initial design stage, as, once the design is complete, only the position of the centre of gravity is easily changed.

Consideration should also be given to the required manoeuvrability of the model. A fully aerobatic model will clearly need to be less stable than, say, a trainer. For the former, a fairly short fuselage and small tailplane, with an aft centre of gravity is quite acceptable. For the latter, the opposite is true. Care must be taken with the centre of gravity position (see Chapter 3). The aft limit is clearly defined and moving any farther back will result in an uncontrollable aircraft. The forward position is less well defined. Too far forward and the model will either not lift off the runway because of lack of effective up elevator, or sink to the ground once airborne.

## Position of the centre of pressure

As the angle of attack increases, the centre of pressure tends to move forward and vice versa. As any model rotates about its centre of gravity, if the centre of pressure moves ahead of the centre of gravity a nose-up movement will result. The position of the centre of pressure depends on:

### Angle of attack

Just before a model stalls, the centre of pressure is near its most forward point. Flying fast, the centre of pressure is well aft, up to 70% on some cambered sections. The total movement depends on the aerofoil. Symmetrical sections have little movement, while the greater the camber the larger movement.

### Wing loading

The heavier a model the greater the lift its wings must provide. Thus a design with a high wing loading will operate at a higher angle of attack with a more forward centre of pressure than one with a lower wing loading.

### Looping accelerations

Any positive acceleration in the looping plane, such as a turn or loop, requires an increase in angle of attack giving a forward movement of the centre of pressure.

### Turbulence

In turbulent air any model tends to get bounced around. As a result, the angle of attack and the position of the centre of pressure fluctuate.

### Transient disturbances

Inertia may also cause the angle of attack to alter temporarily if forces acting on the model alter quickly as when lowering undercarriage or flaps.

## Degrees of longitudinal stability

Whether the right amount of longitudinal stability has been designed into the model will become clear after the first flight. The outcome can broadly be placed into one of three categories.

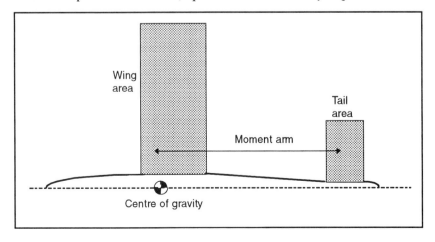

**Figure 151** *The size and distance of the tailplane from the wing both have a critical effect on a model's stability in pitch.*

# Chapter 7

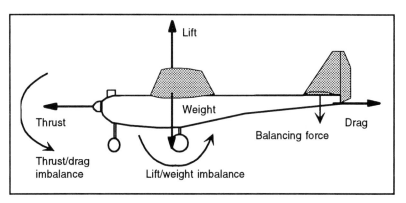

**Figure 152** *The task of the tailplane is to compensate for any out-of-balance forces caused by the weight not being exactly under the lift and the drag and thrust lines not being coaxial.*

Labels in figure: Lift, Thrust, Weight, Drag, Balancing force, Thrust/drag imbalance, Lift/weight imbalance

## Too stable

Elevator response will be sluggish and the model unlikely to spin as the elevator is incapable of inducing a sufficiently deep stall. The tailplane loads will be high for normal flying and there is likelihood of tailplane stalling.

## Not stable enough

The elevator response will be very lively and the model will stall easily when up elevator is applied, particularly at low speeds. Any stall is likely to cause a wing drop and quickly develop into a spin. There may be a noticeable trim change as fuel is consumed. Flying such a model requires great care and quick reactions.

## Unstable

This is the result of the centre of gravity being too far back. Do not try it on any of your designs! The first flight will appear something similar to a kangaroo's movements with violent manoeuvres in the looping plane quickly resulting in a dive to the ground. The elevator will over control and any application, however small, will require an immediate cancelling control. Your reactions will never be quick enough.

## Design of the tailplane

The purpose of the tailplane is to counter any imbalance existing between the four main forces and this is shown in Figure 152. Usually these forces do not all act through the same point. Furthermore both the points through which they

do act and their size vary depending on the throttle setting, speed, rate of climb or descent, weight and wing angle of attack. Thus a balancing force is necessary and is produced by the tailplane. In the United States, the tailplane is called the stabiliser. The reason for this more apt name should now be clear. The tailplane stabilises any out-of-balance forces.

If the angle of attack is reduced by a disturbance, the wing lift reduces and the centre of pressure tends to move back. This changes the balance about the centre of gravity set up by the original position and value of the lift. The result is an imbalance in the pitching plane.

The tailplane has been subjected to the same reduction in angle of attack. It should be designed so the reduction in the tailplane lift at its greater distance from the centre of gravity is larger than the imbalance caused by the reduced wing lift at its small distance from the centre of gravity. The aircraft will then return to its trimmed position.

Large movements of the centre of pressure cause greater imbalance than small ones and these movements depend on the type of aerofoil. The interaction between the centre of gravity, the centre of pressure and the tailplane governs the degree of longitudinal stability and, indeed, whether a new design will be stable.

Although a model should be stable under all conditions of flight, it should not be so stable that it is sluggish to manoeuvre. The exact amount of stability that should be designed into a model varies with its intended role. It should be highest for basic trainers and least for aerobatic models where a high degree of manoeuvrability is required.

## Lateral and directional stability

The effects of lateral and directional stability are so closely linked that they should be considered together. A disturbance which initially involves only lateral stability will also involve directional stability once the model reacts.

## Lateral stability

Lateral stability is a measure of a model's ability to keep its wings level. The main factors are the vertical position of the centre of gravity in relation to the centre of pressure, the use of dihedral or anhedral, the employment of sweep-back or forward sweep, and the size and position of the fin. Lateral stability can be positive, negative, or neutral.

### Positive lateral stability

The model comes out of a turn automatically when the controls are neutralised.

### Negative lateral stability

The model keeps starting to turn one way or the other without any control input. It needs constant control corrections to fly straight. It will tighten up in a turn, even with the controls neutralised.

### Neutral lateral stability

A neutrally stable model will stay in a turn even when the controls are subsequently neutralised after they have been used to enter the turn. The resulting bank angle is maintained as the model turns until a cancelling control is applied. This useful characteristic is the normal aim.

If an aircraft starts to roll, initially there is no restoring force. However, as the roll continues, the tilt of the lift from the wings produces a horizontal component. This causes a side-slip towards the lower wing and produces side loads on the wings and fuselage.

In a stable design these loads provide correcting forces which will roll the model level. Lateral stability is obtained by any one or a combination of the following methods:

- Inclining the wings to give dihedral.
- Sweeping the wings back.

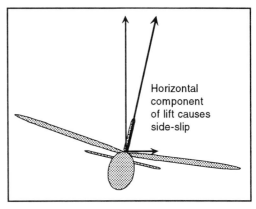

**Figure 153** *Once an aircraft starts to roll, side-slip is inevitable.*

- Placing most of the keel surface above the centre of gravity
- Using a high wing and a low centre of gravity position

### Dihedral angle

Figure 154 shows that as soon as a model with dihedral banks, it starts side-slipping towards its lower wing tip. The dihedral angle causes the airflow to meet the lower wing at a larger angle of attack than the higher wing. This increases the lift on the lower wing which levels the model. The effect may be aided by the fuselage shielding the upper wing.

The more dihedral a model uses, the greater the lateral stability and tendency to straighten up after the turning control has been released. Reduce dihedral and lateral stability will decrease or go negative, the model tending to stay in the turn or even tighten up.

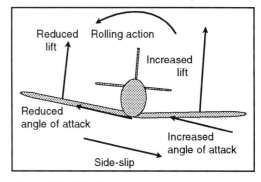

**Figure 154** *Dihedral causes an automatic correcting roll in a side-slip.*

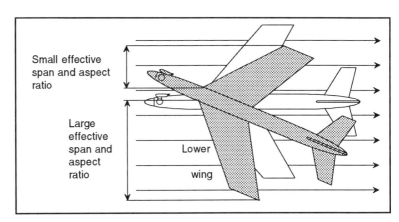

**Figure 155** *The effects of sweep-back in a side-slip are to provide correcting lift due to an increase in effective span and aspect ratio.*

Small effective span and aspect ratio

Large effective span and aspect ratio

Lower wing

## Sweep-back

When an aircraft with a swept-back wing rolls, the changed direction of the airflow due to side-slip results in the airflow over the lower wing passing over a shorter effective chord with a greater effective camber than that of the raised wing. The upper wing may also be shielded. This results in a relatively greater amount of lift from the lower wing which levels the model. The stabilising effect is also increased by the effectively higher aspect ratio of the lower wing and vice versa; the difference resulting from the change in the effective chord. This is shown diagramatically in Figure 155.

Sweep-back on a wing has a similar effect to dihedral, ten degrees of sweep-back being roughly equal to one of dihedral. Anhedral and sweep-forward have the opposite effects to dihedral and sweep-back. On aircraft with sharply swept wings the inherent lateral stability may be excessive. To counteract this stabilising effect anhedral is often used.

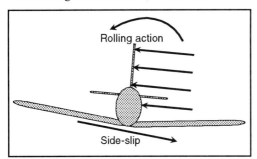

Rolling action

Side-slip

**Figure 156** *The forces on a high keel surface produce a correcting roll when in a side-slip.*

## High keel surface

During a side-slip there is a considerable force on the side or keel surfaces of a model, creating a rolling moment about the centre of gravity. If the keel surface above the centre of gravity is larger than that below it, the result will be a correcting roll which will assist in levelling the model.

## High wing and low centre of gravity

With the wing in a high position in relation to the centre of gravity, a pendulum effect occurs as the lift becomes offset from the weight, levelling the model. In addition, during side-slip the drag of the wing, acting above the centre of gravity, also helps to rotate the aircraft laterally level.

Changing the size of the fin may have unexpected results. The smaller the fin, the greater the lateral stability and the more likely the model will fly straight. Models with large fins, particularly where the fin is a long way aft, tend towards neutral lateral stability. If a new design tightens up in the turn with the controls neutralised, a reduction in fin area is often easier to implement and produces a similar effect to increasing dihedral.

## Directional stability

When a directionally stable model yaws, it will, like an arrow or dart, resume its original direction pointing into the airstream. For a given amount of yaw, size of fin and air speed, the faster the model returns to its initial heading, the greater its directional stability.

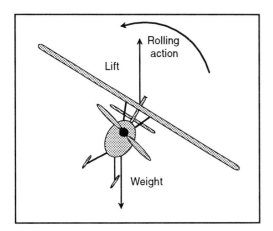

**Figure 157** *Pendulum stability provides a useful levelling reaction for a banked model.*

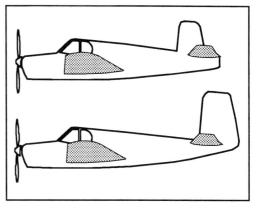

**Figure 158** *An increase in fin size and moving it farther back both affect the directional stability of a model.*

The function of the fin is to provide this stability. Without a fin most models would be unstable directionally because the centre of pressure of a typical fuselage is close to the centre of gravity. Thus a fin is necessary just to achieve neutral stability.

Directional stability depends on the relative side areas of the model forward and aft of the centre of gravity. It is the size of the fin and its distance aft which is the key factor. It is interesting to note that directional stability can be a problem at supersonic speeds for full-size aircraft, which accounts for the massive fin on the Tornado and the large twin fins on the US F15 Eagle and F18 Hornet. Fortunately, these problems do not affect us modellers.

The larger the fin and the longer the fuselage aft of the wing, the greater the directional stability. However, a model with an excessively large fin, although having great directional stability may, as has been mentioned, run into lateral stability problems. Directional stability makes a tail slide a difficult manoeuvre. Once the backward motion starts the model flips over and starts coming down nose first.

Chapter 3 suggests how large a fin should be used, but takes no account of the model side area forward and aft of the centre of gravity. In practice a small fin on most designs will provide sufficient directional stability. Moving the fin further aft can be balanced by a reduction in its area for the same degree of directional stability.

One reason why deltas need large fins is that the fin is seldom far from the centre of gravity.

### Directional stability and the spin

A model in a spin usually has the fin partly blanked by the tailplane and working at a high angle of attack. This is shown in Figure 159 overleaf, as is the tendency for a model with the weight concentrated at the ends of the fuselage, as for example in a pusher model, to act as the flyballs in a governor and try to flatten the spin.

The greater the directional stability the less likely a model is to spin. Such a design will also come out of a spin more readily, all other things being equal. Bigger fins resist the tendency to spin, and a number of full-size aircraft have had fuselage strakes added near the fin after initial flight testing to reduce this spinning disposition. It may be, of course, that the design purposely needs a quick clean entry to a spin, for aerobatic manoeuvres for example.

### Interaction between lateral and directional stability

It should now be clear that the fin affects both lateral and directional stability. However, this rarely requires compromise on fin size, as changes to provide adequate lateral stability generally leave a safe margin of directional stability. There are exceptions. When a delta

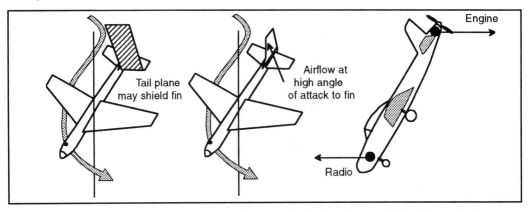

**Figure 159** *Some thought needs to be given to the potential spinning characteristics of a new design.*

stalls, the fin may become completely blanketed. The ensuing flat spin may prove difficult to stop. With a canard, there is normally a significant proportion of the fuselage forward of the centre of gravity, with only a short distance back to the fin. Both types of design need a larger than normal fin area.

There are two main combinations where lateral and directional stability interact; spiral instability and oscillatory instability.

### Spiral instability

The lateral stability of a model depends on the forces trying to level it when a wing drops. At the same time the fin tries to turn the model into the yawed airflow, in the direction of the lower wing. Once this turn has been started the higher wing on the outside of the turn travels slightly faster than the lower one, producing more lift. A roll starts which opposes, and may be greater than, the correcting effect of any dihedral or sweep-back. If the rolling effect is great enough, the angle of bank increases and the model enters a spiral dive of steadily increasing steepness. This is spiral instability.

A reduction in fin area reduces directional stability and the tendency to turn into a side-slip. This results in a smaller gain in lift from the raised wing and greater spiral stability. This form of instability is not critical and most models are to some extent spirally unstable. This characteristic on twin engined models can, however, be fatal if one engine cuts at low speed and the other is not immediately

throttled back. Excessive yaw caused by the asymmetric power and insufficient rudder control can quickly put the model into a dangerous attitude.

### Oscillatory instability

A combination of a high wing loading, sweepback and low speed are most likely to produce oscillatory instability. It is characterised by a combined rolling and yawing movement, or wallowing motion. When the rolling predominates it is called Dutch roll. If yawing is dominant it is known as snaking. When a model is disturbed laterally the subsequent motion may be either of the two extremes. In both instances the aircraft is difficult to settle down, which can be unpleasant for the R/C pilot. Dutch roll can be avoided by reducing lateral stability, while snaking can be overcome by increasing directional stability.

### Roll with yaw

When a model is yawed using rudder, the immediate effect is to roll it in the same direction as the yaw. This characteristic of all stable models is caused by the resulting side loads acting on the dihedral angle or sweep-back of the wings. The characteristic can be used to advantage to design aircraft using three channel radio on rudder, elevator and throttle only. However, a significant amount of dihedral is essential if a satisfactory turning performance to be achieved. Five degrees of dihedral is the minimum suggested, while ten degrees can produce a

**Figure 160** *A potential candidate for oscillatory instability, my fun scale Mirage 4000,* Nexus Plan R/C 1461 *never exhibited either Dutch roll or snaking.*

rapid response and allow fairly axial rolls to be performed using rudder alone.

## Degrees of stability

The amount of stability required in the three axes will depend on the type of model and the skill of the pilot. Aircraft can conveniently be placed in one of five categories.

- Difficult to fly – needs to be watched all the time.
- Reasonable – fairly frequent corrections needed.
- Satisfactory – no special vices.
- Good – generally predictable.
- Excellent – no vices whatsoever.

A second group of characteristics depend on the degree of stability as well as the effectiveness of the control surfaces.

- Insensitive – sluggish to respond to control inputs.
- Reasonable – responds well but still a bit slow.
- Satisfactory – good response but not ideal.
- Good – smooth, co-ordinated control responses.
- Oversensitive – twitchy, particularly at speed.

## Automatic stability

On some R/C helicopters, a gyroscopically operated automatic stabiliser is used on the tail rotor. It senses the yawing motion and corrects it by appropriate tail movements. Gyros can be used on fixed wing aircraft to provide stability in any or all of the three axes. They are particularly effective, when fitted to ailerons, in keeping wings level or at a constant angle of bank in bumpy conditions. Auto-pilots can provide a similar function.

## Trim

Trim affects two areas of any model design, always assuming that the design is symmetrical in planform about the fore and aft axis. This is normal in model and full-sized design practice, although the Blohm and Voss 141 was a notable deviation from this philosophy in World War 2.

## Wing and tail incidences

In the pitching plane, the designer faces two problems. The first is the correct angle to mount the wing and tailplane. The second is the amount of engine up or down thrust required.

### Wing incidence

The wing incidence is set relative to the fuselage datum line and should be chosen so that the fuselage is horizontal at normal operating angles of attack. The ideal is to ensure the fuselage is horizontal at the wing aerofoil's minimum lift/drag ratio; usually around four degrees. Thus an angle of incidence of some three to four degrees is a good starting point for a training aircraft, remembering to set the angle relative to the aerofoil's chord line.

For an aerobatic aircraft, with a symmetrical wing aerofoil, it is normal to set the wing at zero

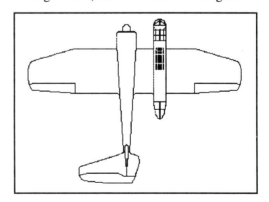

**Figure 161** *The Blohm and Voss 141 was a most unusual design that was not symmetrical about its centre line. This was an attempt to improve crew all-round vision on a single engined reconnaissance aircraft.*

**Table 13** *Suggested rigging angles for various aerofoil sections.*

| Wing aerofoil | Wing incidence | Wing aerofoil | Wing incidence |
| --- | --- | --- | --- |
| Flat plate | 3° to lower surface | Eppler 374 | 2° to centre line |
| NACA 0009 | 0° to centre line | Curved plate | 2° to lower surface |
| NACA 0018 | 0° to centre line | Clark Y | 2° to lower surface |
| NACA 2412 | 0° to centre line | Gö. 797 | 1° to lowest surface |
| NACA 2415 | 0° to centre line | NACA 6412 | 4° to lower points |

incidence, thus ensuring equal performance upright and inverted. Somewhere between these two limits may be a useful compromise, depending on the role of any other aircraft. To be avoided is the mistake made by Armstrong Whitworth with their full-size Whitley World War II bomber where they set the wing at an angle of incidence of 8°, resulting in the aircraft's characteristic nose-down attitude in flight. Table 13 suggests suitable wing setting incidences for some popular aerofoils.

### Tailplane aerofoils

The tailplane's function is as a stabiliser. Whether it produces lift in a positive or negative direction depends on the aerofoil section of the tail and its angle to the airflow. This in turn depends on the wing aerofoil and its angle of attack, together with the wing and tail's vertical positions. Downwash of the airflow behind the wing generally affects the tailplane. Thus its angle of attack is often less than appears. The downwash can even result in a flat bottomed aerofoil producing a downward force or negative lift.

Tailplanes rarely have to produce much lift and a simple symmetrical low drag aerofoil is best. A flat plate aerofoil is usually ideal and works equally well producing upright and downward forces. NACA 0009 also makes a good tailplane. An aerofoil like Clark Y is inefficient at producing negative lift which is accompanied by excess drag and is thus not a good choice.

### Downwash

When a wing moves through the air, it depresses the air downwards behind it as a result of producing lift. Almost invariably this downwash affects the tailplane, which is usually located behind the wing and thus in the area of downwash. There is a strong case for carefully considering the vertical position of the tailplane to avoid this effect. More information about the various possible tailplane positions is given in Chapter 3.

### Longitudinal dihedral

This is a measure of the angle between wing and tailplane incidences. A tailplane must be set at a suitable angle to ensure the wing produces the required lift. Some guidelines are shown in Table 14 for typical designs where the tailplane is flat plate or symmetrical, is 20% of the wing area and set two and a half wing chords behind the centre of gravity. The angles are measured from the tailplane centreline.

With a smaller tail area and/or shorter fuselage, the longitudinal dihedral angles may need to be altered somewhat. The figures are a

**Figure 162** *On some models, downwash has a major effect on the angle at which the airflow approaches the tailplane.*

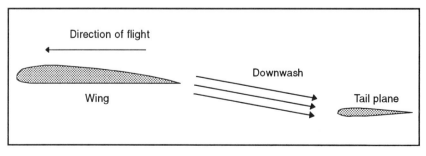

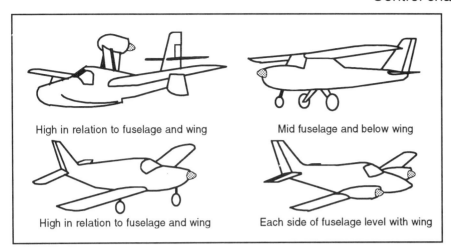

High in relation to fuselage and wing

Mid fuselage and below wing

High in relation to fuselage and wing

Each side of fuselage level with wing

**Figure 163**
*The position of the thrust line can vary considerably, depending on the layout of the model.*

guide for the designer and the final setting will become apparent during test flying.

## Engine thrust lines

In an ideal world, thrust, drag, lift and weight would all act through the centre of gravity of a model. In practice the engine may be located high above the wing and fuselage, as seen on some seaplanes, at the top, middle or bottom of the fuselage, very dependent on the needs of the particular design and the personal choice of the designer. In the case of a twin, the two engines are normally located outboard some distance from the centre line of the fuselage.

| Wing aerofoil | Angle measured from wing | Longi-tudinal dihedral |
|---|---|---|
| Flat plate | Centre line | 0 - 3° |
| NACA 0009 | Centre line | 0° |
| NACA 0018 | Centre line | 0° |
| NACA 2412 | Centre line | 0 - 1° |
| NACA 2415 | Centre line | 0 - 1° |
| Eppler 374 | Centre line | 1 - 2° |
| Curved plate | Lower points | 1 - 2° |
| Clark Y | Underside | 0 - 1½° |
| Go. 797 | Underside | 1 - 2° |
| NACA 6412 | Underside | 1° |

**Table 14**  *Longitudinal dihedral angles between wing and tailplane.*

## Up/down thrust

Down thrust gives a downward component which reduces the effect of forward thrust pulling the nose up. Up thrust does just the opposite. A good aim is to get the thrust line to pass through, or slightly above, the centre of gravity. A high wing model can still have a high thrust line if the engine is inverted. Similarly, a low wing model can still have a low thrust line if the fuselage depth is minimised. In such cases there may be little need for significant down thrust.

The high wing model in Figure 164 is typical of those with a low thrust line and may need a little down thrust to stop it climbing, due to the upward pitching action of the thrust/drag forces.

Figure 165 overleaf, on the other hand, shows how a high thrust line such as occurs with a pylon mounted engine, combined with the almost inevitable low drag line will try to push the nose down unless counteracted by a fair amount of up thrust.

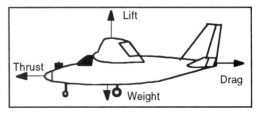

**Figure 164** *The high drag line and low thrust line on this model cause it to pitch nose up as the throttle is opened unless some down thrust is incorporated.*

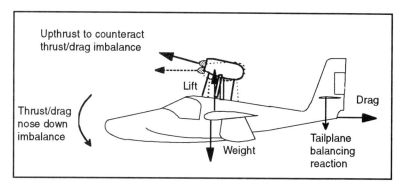

**Figure 165** *With a high thrust line, some up thrust is essential to avoid a major nose-down reaction when the throttle is opened.*

It should be noted that once a model is trimmed for level flight at a given power setting, it is only changes in power which will indicate the need for up or down thrust.

### Side thrust

The torque from the rotation of a propeller tries to roll any model in the opposite direction. The slipstream from the engine strikes the wing, fuselage and fin, adding to this roll; left for normal models with conventionally rotating engines, right for pushers. However, if the engine is located at the tail, there is no slipstream over the model.

These rolling effects can't be avoided but can be combated by offsetting the engine to correct the induced turn, which is proportional to the engine speed. The side thrust is most effective at high engine speed and the effect reduces as the engine is throttled back. Aileron or rudder trim could be used to correct the engine induced turn, but then the trim needs adjusting each time the engine speed changes. The amount of side thrust required also depends on the distance of the engine from the centre of gravity. The larger the distance, the less side thrust required.

Many models, particularly aerobatic ones, use zero-zero rigging; thrust line, wings and tail all parallel. For sports models a corrective thrust line should be built in to cure any engine induced pitch or turn. The question of how much is not easy. It depends on the relative position of the thrust and drag forces, as well as the power-to-weight ratio of the model, the flying speed and the position of the engine relative to the centre of gravity. A maximum figure for up/down thrust

of three degrees for a fuselage mounted engine, and five to ten degrees for a pylon mounted one is a good starting point. The amount of side thrust also depends on the size and distance of the fin aft of the centre of gravity. One or two degrees of side thrust is usually sufficient for a reasonable nose length, with this figure being increased to three degrees for short-nosed designs.

## Control surfaces

The control surfaces of a model aircraft enable it to manoeuvre. A conventional model has ailerons for rolling, elevators for looping and a rudder for yawing. These surfaces need to be designed and positioned to obtain the best effect at all speeds and consistent with the type of model. Differences occur in control response for elevators and rudders in the prop wash between power on and glide performance. When deciding

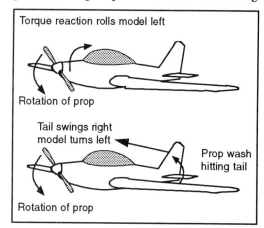

**Figure 166** *Assuming a normal direction of engine rotation, torque and prop wash on a tractor model will tend to turn a model to port.*

the size and amount of movement, this fact needs to be borne in mind.

Some more specialised designs may employ elevons in place of elevators and ailerons, or a V or butterfly tail where the functions of elevator and rudder are combined in ruddevators. Airbrakes and flaps may also be fitted.

## Effectiveness

A control surface works by producing a force which moves the model in a particular direction. This reaction is caused by the air pressure on the deflected surface. The greater the deflection the greater the control force produced, up to a certain angle.

With small movements the control force is roughly proportional to the deflection angle. The resulting drag increase is only moderate. The control force continues to increase proportionally up to an angle of 30°. Beyond this angle, the drag force becomes so large that the surface becomes an airbrake. Thus maximum movement should be restricted to 30°. The drag produced is only a problem for ailerons, as we shall see, although it does also put a load on all control surface hinges.

## Elevators

Elevators are normally hinged to the rear of the tailplane and provide control in the pitching plane. The angular movement of the elevator necessary to obtain a given change of attitude varies with speed. A low speed model will require a larger movement than a high speed one. This is

a natural effect arising from the increased effectiveness of any deflected surface as speed increases.

An area of around 5% of the wing is a good starting point for size. For an elevator running the full width of the tailplane, this results in a narrow chord. A maximum movement of around 10° up and the same down is a good baseline. Rather more may be needed for a slow flying model, say plus or minus 15°, and obviously less for a very fast flying design. The elevator movement may need adjustment after the first flight to give perfect trim, optimum manoeuvrability and also to suit the individual pilot. The movement satisfactory for normal requirements may be insufficient for manoeuvres such as spinning. Either a compromise will have to be reached or variable rates on the transmitter set for the two different requirements.

## Ailerons

Ailerons are the most difficult control surfaces to design and often fail to produce the desired performance. For example, large amounts of dihedral reduce the effectiveness of ailerons. Aileron performance progressively improves as dihedral is reduced to the point where a model becomes neutrally stable in the rolling plane. Like elevators, their effectiveness increases with speed. The rate of roll also varies with wingspan. For a given aileron size and deflection, the larger the span the lower the rate of roll at any given speed. As will be seen later, adverse drag is also a factor.

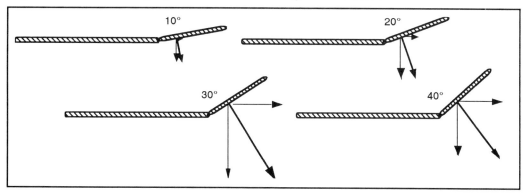

**Figure 167** *The force produced by deflecting a control surface increases in a roughly linear manner up to an angle of 30° and then reduces rapidly.*

# Chapter 7

Two types of ailerons are commonly used, the inset type where the aileron is part of the outboard wing and the strip aileron which is hinged to the whole or most of the trailing edge. The latter are simpler to design and fit. Both require the same area of around 7½ -10% of the wing area for each aileron. Both have advantages and snags.

## Inset ailerons

Inset ailerons produce two design problems. The first lies in the structural complication. The second is the fact that the downgoing aileron tends to create substantial drag which tries to yaw the model against the desired direction of turn. Fairly large movements are necessary to produce good aileron response, and this adverse drag can be counteracted by using differential movement. For example a maximum up movement of 20° could be matched by a downward one of only 10°. This can be achieved easily using offset on the aileron horns, the servo arms or any interconnecting bell cranks, or a pair of servos and the facilities of a computerised transmitter. Details are shown in Chapter 10.

Inset ailerons are more difficult to make and hinge properly than elevators. Tube and wire hinges are often preferred since they give free movement without slop. The generous up and down movement required normally calls for a short control horn. It is often possible to include the push rod within the main wing section, although this is obviously not essential.

## Adverse yaw and aileron drag

There is a phenomenon which is quite a common occurrence on early test flights of new designs using inset ailerons. It manifests itself as an attempt by the model to yaw against the direction of roll being induced by the ailerons.

When an aileron moves down its angle of attack is increased and it moves into a region of high pressure. Both increase the drag it produces. The upgoing aileron experiences the opposite effect and creates less drag. If the drag from the downgoing aileron is significantly greater than that of the upgoing one, the nose yaws in the opposite direction to the bank.

Aileron drag is usually worst at low speeds because of the large aileron movements necessary. Adverse yaw can be reduced by using differential aileron movement, so that the downgoing aileron moves through a smaller angle than the upgoing one, tending to equalise the drag from each. The alternative is to use Frise ailerons.

## Strip ailerons

Strip ailerons seem to give a smoother, more positive action with less adverse yaw than inset ones. Typical proportions are also shown in Figure 169. Equal movement up and down of around 15° is a good starting point. They require a precise neutral and a short linkage to the servo is normally practical. Very thin strip ailerons don't work well if they are mounted behind the trailing edge of a thick wing section. This is because they are operating in the wake of the wing. The best solution is to terminate the wing section in a fairly thick trailing edge and blend in thick strip ailerons.

## Spoilers as ailerons

Adverse yaw can be eliminated by replacing the ailerons with a pair of spoilers, which

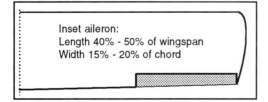

**Figure 168** *Inset ailerons are more difficult to design than strip ones.*

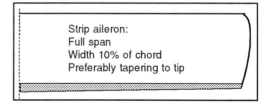

**Figure 169** *Typical dimensions for strip ailerons result in narrow chord control surfaces.*

**Figure 170** *Ailerons should blend into the wing. Very thin ailerons lie in a turbulent wake from the trailing edge.*

deploy one at a time out of the top of the downgoing wing, reducing the lift and increasing the drag on that side. Their use involves an overall loss of lift, which means that more elevator will be required in the turn than with a well balanced pair of ailerons.

### Aileron reversal.

When ailerons are moved, the downgoing aileron acts as an elevator on its wing tip and tries to twist the leading edge of the wing upwards about its torsional axis. The upgoing aileron has the opposite effect on the other wing. The wing must be sufficiently stiff to prevent any distortion. On a high speed model with very thin wings, the ailerons may be powerful enough to distort the wings. The effect of aileron reversal is to decrease aileron effectiveness as the wings are twisted, opposing the rolling movement set up by the ailerons.

### Rudders

The rudder is hinged at the rear of the fin and its effectiveness increases with speed. At large angles of yaw or side slip the fin may stall, causing a sudden reduction in rudder control and directional stability. Basically a high aspect ratio rudder is preferable, in the form of a narrow strip running the full length of the fin with the

leading edge vertical or slightly swept back. The latter is a logical shape with a swept back fin outline. A swept forward rudder leading edge should, however, be avoided. It is also desirable that the rudder should taper from base to top. A slight to moderate taper only should be employed. Excessive taper on the rudder will result in loss of efficiency and a larger area will be required for the same control force.

Rudder area is not critical but around 2 - 3% of wing area is a good starting point. Movement 20° either side of neutral should give excellent ground control and plenty of response in the air even if rudder is used as the primary directional control. Rudder size and movement may need increasing for slow flying models and vice versa.

### Options for avoiding elevator/ rudder contact

Most people find it difficult to think in three dimensions. When planning elevators and rudders, it is easy to end up with them fouling each other. Discovered before the first flight, this will demand an irritating change. Discovery in flight may well prove fatal. There are many ways of avoiding contact between the two control surfaces; either the rudder may be set forward

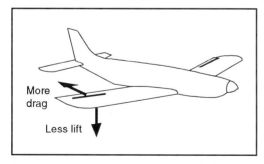

**Figure 171** *The use of spoilers instead of ailerons has much to commend it.*

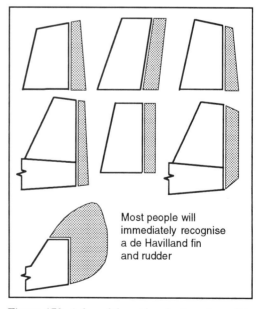

Most people will immediately recognise a de Havilland fin and rudder

**Figure 172** *A few of the wide selection of possible fin and rudder configurations.*

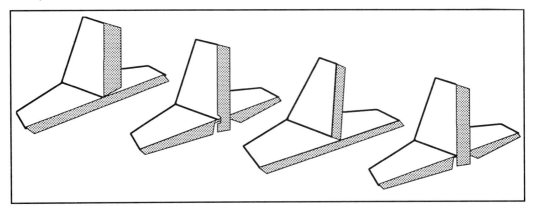

**Figure 173** *Four possible ways of preventing the elevators fouling the rudder.*

of the elevator, or the tailplane moved back so the elevator is clear of the rudder. The alternative is to cut off the corners of either the rudder or the elevator; the latter case requiring the use of an elevator joiner.

## Coupled aileron and rudder

Getting ailerons and rudders to operate in unison can significantly improve the turning performance of some models, particularly biplanes. This is because the rudder causes initial positive yaw in the direction of the turn. A connection can be designed in mechanically. It is, however, much more attractive to make use of the rudder/aileron coupling function found on most transmitters.

## Elevons

Some tailless aircraft, flying wings and deltas combine the function of the elevators and ailerons in control surfaces called elevons. These are designed to combine the two functions into a pair of control surfaces which move in unison for the elevator function and in opposition for the aileron function.

With a delta, Figure 176 shows that either elevons or separate controls are a practical solution. For a flying wing with little or no sweep-back, the same is true. However, with significant sweep-back, separate controls would not give the elevators sufficient leverage. Elevons should combine the areas of conventional ailerons and elevators; say 15% of wing area.

## Ruddevators and flaperons

On models with V or butterfly tails, the control surfaces of the tail combine the functions of elevator and rudder. The tail surfaces are normally set up at an angle of thirty degrees to the

**Figure 174** *Cut away elevators allow full rudder movement without danger of contact. In this case, the designer has used cross grained ends to the tailplane and inset the elevators.*

**Figure 175** *With a flying wing, such as the one seen here under construction, there is little option but to fit elevons to the wing tips in order to achieve sufficient elevator authority.*

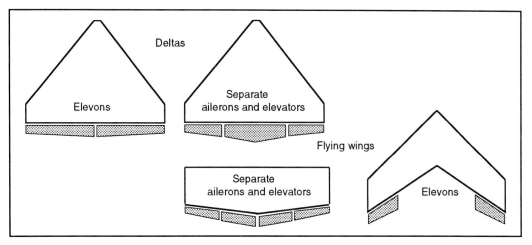

**Figure 176** *The use of separate elevators and ailerons or the combination of the two functions in elevons for tailless models depends on the particular configuration as well as the desires of the designer.*

horizontal. They are similar to elevons in terms of control connections. Their area should be around 7½% of wing area. In the same way, ailerons and flaps can be mixed in functional terms into the same control surfaces. Flaperons should be about the same size as full span ailerons.

## Airbrakes

Sleek models with low drag tend to retain their speed for some time after throttling back. Having reduced speed, any slight descent or increase in power causes an immediate increase in speed. Airbrakes can be extended to increase the drag of a model allowing speed to be decreased rapidly or controlled during a descent. Figure 177 shows two of the more popular airbrake installations. The first uses plates which either lift out of the wings on a scissors mechanism or hinge upward. The second shows the use of a split rudder as an airbrake.

Although the area of the airbrakes is small, considerable drag is produced at reasonably fast speeds. The effectiveness of an airbrake varies as the square of the speed.

Split rudders require airbrake and rudder functions to be mixed, but do provide a simple solution to construct. The most important factor to consider when incorporating airbrakes is the need to generate a significant amount of drag without causing any trim change. The area of

airbrakes should be around three per cent of the total wing area.

## Balancing

If control surfaces are hinged at their leading edge, the forces required to change the angle on all except light, slow models can be quite high. Some balance can minimise these forces, reduce servo loads and minimise the risks of control surface flutter. The two main forms of balance are mass balance and aerodynamic balance.

### Mass balancing

This is used chiefly to prevent flutter of the control surfaces, a subject covered later in this

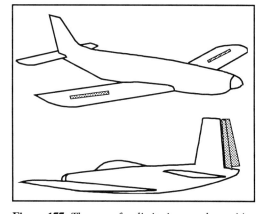

**Figure 177** *There are few limitations on the position of airbrakes on a model, apart from the need to avoid trim changes when they are operated.*

## Chapter 7

chapter. Balancing is carried out by fixing weights to the leading edge of the control surface so that the centre of gravity of the surface is brought closer to the hinge line. Figure 178 shows two typical mass-balance installations.

### Aerodynamic balancing

Aerodynamic balance can be achieved in several ways. It decreases the force that is required to move a control in flight. This form of balancing is generally done by hinging the control surface about a line set back from the leading edge. On some control surfaces, instead of an inset hinge line, aerodynamic balance is achieved by using horn balances

at the tips, as shown in the lower illustration in Figure 179.

These have the same effect as the inset hinge type, as a proportion of the total area lies ahead of the centre of pressure. Horn balances are used mostly on rudders and elevators. Horn balance is much more commonly used on models than mass balance and a good example is shown in Figure 180.

### Overbalance

If the hinge line is positioned too close to the centre of pressure, any movement of the control may cause the centre of pressure moving ahead of the hinge line. Figure 181 shows how the forces try to move the surface to full deflection.

Overbalance is unlikely to be detected by an R/C pilot. It may be mild or severe, depending

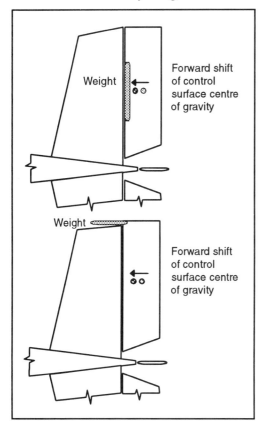

**Figure 178** *Mass balance is worth considering in designs where the chord of the control surface is large, particularly if high speeds are planned. The weight can either be fitted in the leading edge of the control surface or cantilevered forward matching full-size practice.*

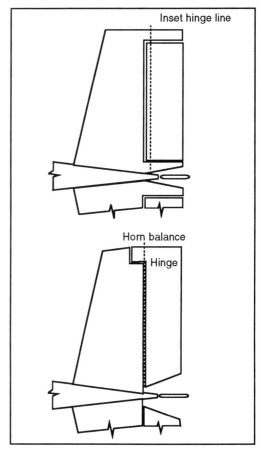

**Figure 179** *An inset hinge line or a horn balance are equally effective on any control surface.*

**Figure 180** *The Big Fun is fitted with horn balance on both elevators and rudder; an important feature for control surfaces of such a large chord. (Photo courtesy Bill-Kits.)*

on the design and flight conditions of the control surface. It should be considered and avoided at the design stage.

## All moving tails

With a flying tail, full and accurate control is retained at all speeds. First employed on some early and slow flying full-sized aircraft to provide sufficient control, it was re-employed on modern high speed jet aircraft to obviate some of the problems associated with high speed control.

As far as their use on models are concerned there is a need for considerable care in two areas. First, it is essential that the surface is aerodynamically balanced, and in practice this means the hinge point should lie with ¼ of the tail area ahead of the hinge line and ¾ behind it. The

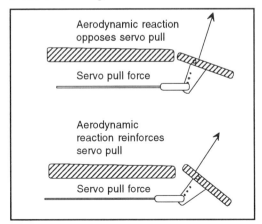

**Figure 181** *Overbalance can easily be avoided at the design stage.*

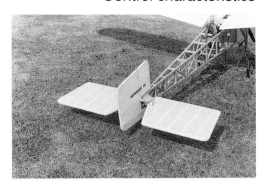

**Figure 182** *Both an all moving tailplane and fin were fitted sucessfully to my Bernhardt B2 old timer; a free give-away plan in* Radio Modeller *September 1989.*

second point is that the tail must be securely attached to the fuselage or fin. The amount of movement will depend on the speed of the model. Five degrees deflection each way will be plenty for a fast flier but as much as 10°, or occasionally even more, may be needed on a slow aircraft. Exactly the same rules apply for an all moving fin.

## Moving control surfaces

The effort to move any control surface is determined by the aerodynamic force acting through its centre of pressure and the distance from the hinge line where this force acts. This is shown in Figure 184 overleaf. The effort is provided by the push or pull force of the servo multiplied by the lever arm length of the control horn. The smaller the aerodynamic force and its distance from the hinge line, the less servo power is needed to move the control through a particular angle at a given speed.

Most servos have ample power to cope with the highest forces likely to be involved. However, micro servos are definitely limited in the output they can provide and, at the opposite

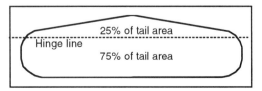

**Figure 183** *The design of all moving tails requires care if flutter is to be avoided.*

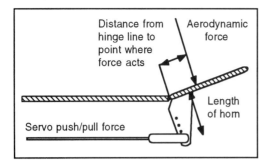

**Figure 184** *The amount of power needed from any servo depends on the size and shape of the control surface, the angle of deflection required and the speed of the model.*

extreme, large models need powerful servos to move their controls. The servo output required can be calculated, but for sports models this is really unnecessary providing the following factors are borne in mind.

The effort needed is directly proportional to the chord of the control surface. Thus for a given control force a long and narrow area will require less servo effort than a shorter, broader area. This favours the use of high aspect ratio control surfaces. The aerodynamic force is proportional to the square of the speed. Doubling the speed in a dive will quadruple the servo effort required.

High loadings can cause binding or even bending of the linkage and in some extreme cases over ride the servo force. They will also show up any slackness in the linkage and could result in flutter. Such failings mostly appear at high speeds, when the result is most critical. In an extreme case, elevators may fail to pull an aircraft out of a dive because the high hinge moment has bent the linkage. This also means that a servo pulling to give up elevator is safer than one which has to push to move the control surface in this direction. However, for a normal model using standard servos, there should be no problems. The size and speed of any model as well as the use of aerodynamic balancing should be considered before fitting micro or any other low power servos.

# Flutter

Flutter is an increasingly common problem as engine powers increase, pilots become more

skilful and models are flown faster. In common with a number of full-sized aircraft in the 1920s and 1930s, flutter on models usually has disastrous results. It is commonly experienced by those who:

- Design aircraft and do not allow for it. This is particularly a problem with fast models.
- Alter the strength, or make other minor changes when building a proven design.
- Fit a more powerful motor in an existing design so it exceeds its tested maximum speed.
- Fit sloppy linkages from the servos to the control surfaces.

Flutter is a violent vibration of the airframe and/or control surfaces caused by the interaction of their mass and aerodynamic loads. In practice, models normally experience a failure of an elevator or aileron control linkage or hinge, accompanied by a loud buzzing noise. This is usually followed by loss of control and impact with terra firma. Three main types of flutter affect the wing of an aircraft.

## Torsional flexural flutter

This type of flutter is the least likely and is caused by lack of rigidity of the wing. Figure 185 shows what happens. Torsional flexural flutter is normally avoided by having a sufficiently stiff wing to ensure that the speed above which flutter occurs is well beyond the maximum speed of the model.

## Torsional aileron flutter

This is the most common form of flutter in models. It is illustrated in Figure 187 overleaf.

The second half of the cycle is similar to the first, but in the opposite direction. Torsional aileron flutter can be prevented by:

- Mass balancing each aileron.
- Insetting the hinges, so that its centre of gravity is on or slightly ahead of the hinge line.
- Ensuring that the aileron control rigidly irreversible.

On models, inset hinges are not common and mass balancing is quite difficult. A good stiff

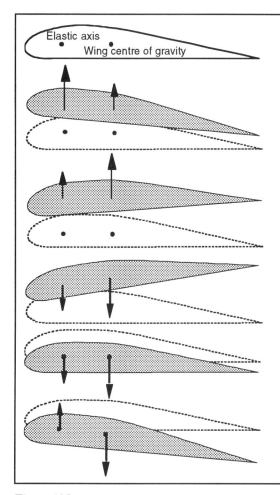

The wing is in stable level flight. The centre of gravity of the wing lies behind its elastic axis.

The wing incidence, and thus the lift, momentarily increase making the wing bend upwards. Inertia causes the wing to lag behind the elastic axis, further increasing incidence, lift and therefore deflection.

The stiffness of the wing brings the elastic axis to rest, but inertia causes the wing itself to rise further, reducing the angle of incidence.

The lift then reduces and the wing elastic axis starts descending, reducing the incidence even further.

The wing stiffness eventually halts the motion of the elastic axis at its bottom limit.

The inertia of the wing enables its C of G to exert a twisting moment which increases the angle of incidence, and restarts the flutter cycle.

**Figure 185** *It is important to understand how flutter occurs if it is to be avoided in a new design.*

linkage from the servo to the aileron will prevent this form of flutter while, conversely, sloppy linkages will encourage it.

## Flexural aileron flutter

This is similar to torsional aileron flutter and is shown in Figure 188 on page 97. It is caused by the movement of the aileron lagging behind the rise and fall of the outer portion of the wing. This type of flutter is most likely on models with high aspect ratio wings.

## Elevator and rudder flutter

So far, only wing flutter has been examined. The same problems can affect both elevators and rudders, although the stiffness of the tailplane and fin is likely to be greater than that of the wing.

All forms of flutter only occur above a particular critical speed, so that the problem is much more likely to occur on a high speed racing

**Figure 186** *The result of flutter with an all moving tail was an expensive disaster for this model.*

*The aileron is slightly down, exerting lift on the aileron hinge*

*The wing twists about its torsional axis. As the aileron's centre of gravity is behind the hinge line, the aileron lags behind, increasing the lift and twisting motion.*

*The torsional stiffness of the wing stops the twisting motion.*

*The aileron's inertia, air loads on it and slop in the control linkage cause it to overshoot, reversing the aerodynamic twisting force which now assists wing twisting in the opposite direction.*

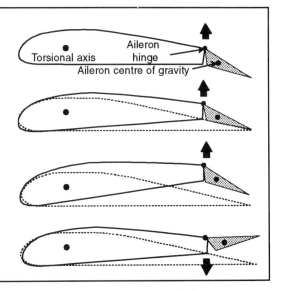

**Figure 187** *Control surfaces are vulnerable to flutter, particularly if there is slop in the linkages.*

or ducted fan model. It is still, fortunately, relatively uncommon on slower flying sports and training models. Where it does occur, it is usually caused by sloppy control linkages.

Inevitably, there are a number of ways to prevent flutter of which the most important are shown below:

- Avoid wide chord control surfaces that put the surface's centre of gravity well behind the hinge line.

I SAID " I THOUGHT I HAD FLUTTER ", NOT " I THOUGHT I'D HAVE A FLUTTER " !!

- Consider aerodynamic or mass balancing of the control surfaces.
- When designing wings, particularly high aspect ratio ones , ensure they are sufficiently stiff.
- Avoid any sloppy control linkages.
- Don't worry on a slow flying design. It is unlikely ever to reach the critical flutter speed.

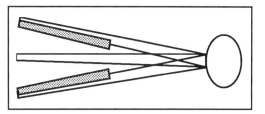

**Figure 188** *A particularly severe form of flutter occurs when the aileron and wing interact together.*

# 8 Making the most of materials

## The basic materials

Probably the two most important factors influencing the choice of materials for any new model are the preferences of the designer and the performance requirements of the model. For example, some modellers always build their wings from balsa wood and spruce, others much prefer to build foam ones. A high speed model may demand the extensive use of GRP (glass reinforced plastic or fibreglass) and carbon fibres for the fuselage while an old timer would be out of its period if it did not feature built-up construction.

From this, it must be apparent that there are no right or wrong materials. There are, however, those which are better suited to certain tasks or builders. In particular, the strength of the selected materials must be appropriate to the tasks they have to undertake. Perhaps the most important factor is that the majority of designs are inclined to end up tail heavy, unless attention is given to weight reduction at the rear end. On a conventional layout, it requires two to three times more ballast in the nose than the tail to move the centre of gravity a given distance.

### Choosing the size of material

Remembering that weight is the enemy of flight, the choice of the smallest suitable size of material is clearly an important factor. Figure 189 demonstrates the dramatic growth in material weight as size increases. Stress analysis is not a part of this book and anyway much of the strength in many parts of a model is necessary to survive the abuse it receives on the ground during transportation to and from the flying site.

In this chapter, there are a number of tables which detail the standard sizes of available material and their weights. Reference to them will help significantly in selecting the right ones for the task in hand. It is also worth considering the length in which standard pieces of wood are available.

A 1.8 metre (72") wingspan will allow the spars for each wing to be made from the UK standard 0.9 metre (36") strips of balsa or spruce. Increase that span to 2.2 metres (85") and the material cost of the spars will jump by 50%, albeit with some off-cuts going into the scrap box. However, extra long lengths are increasingly popular even though the price per unit length is

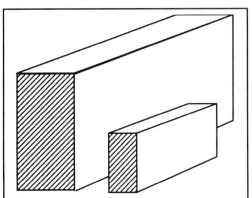

**Figure 189** *The larger item has twice the linear dimensions of the smaller one, but weighs eight times as much. This relationship holds regardless of the material used.*

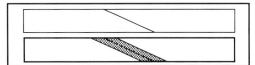

**Figure 190** *Where a sufficiently long piece of wood is unavailable, a diagonal scarf joint should be used rather than a butt joint. The addition of a reinforcing piece will further increase the strength of the joint.*

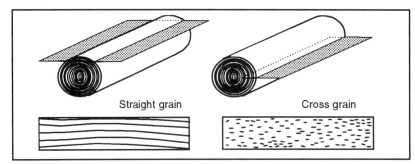

Straight grain          Cross grain

**Figure 191** *Straight grained balsa is cut differently from cross grained wood. This is clearly visible when selecting sheet wood.*

higher and it is likely that 1 metre (39") lengths will become the norm in the UK over the next few years.

## Balsa

Balsa is one of the original materials used by aeromodellers. It is lightweight, easy to cut and sand, and stronger than steel for a component of a given weight. It is, in fact, a 'hardwood', but this is allied to its close-grained structure rather than its surface hardness. It is well suited to the production of fuselage formers and wing ribs as well as tail surfaces and sheet fuselages. Strips of the wood can be used as wing spars, leading and tailing edges as well as fuselage longerons. Balsa wood is cut at the sawmill to provide straight grain and cross grain wood. Straight grain material is used in most applications, but formers and wing ribs should be made from cross grained wood, which is better able to resist splitting.

Balsa wood is supplied in a wide range of densities and selection of the correct grade of wood is important. Table 15 shows how the

| Grade | Density | Thickness and weight | | | | | | | |
|-------|---------|------|------|------|-----|------|-----|-----|------|
|       |         | .8mm | 1.5m | 2.5m | 3mm | 4.5m | 6mm | 9mm | 12mm |
|       | g/cc    | gm   | gm   | gm   | gm  | gm   | gm  | gm  | gm   |
| V. soft | .08   | 5    | 11   | 17   | 21  | 32   | 42  | 64  | 85   |
| Soft  | .11     | 7    | 14   | 22   | 28  | 42   | 57  | 85  | 113  |
| Medium | .14    | 9    | 18   | 28   | 35  | 54   | 71  | 106 | 142  |
| Medium | .17    | 11   | 21   | 33   | 42  | 64   | 85  | 127 | 170  |
| Hard  | .2      | 12   | 25   | 39   | 50  | 74   | 99  | 149 | 198  |
| V. hard | .23   | 14   | 28   | 60   | 57  | 85   | 113 | 170 | 226  |

| Grade | Density | Thickness and weight | | | | | | | |
|-------|---------|-------|-------|-------|------|-------|------|------|------|
|       |         | 1/32" | 1/16" | 3/32" | 1/8" | 3/16" | 1/4" | 3/8" | 1/2" |
|       | lb/cu ft | oz   | oz    | oz    | oz   | oz    | oz   | oz   | oz   |
| V. soft | 6     | 0.19  | 0.38  | 0.56  | 0.75 | 1.13  | 1.5  | 2.25 | 3.0  |
| Soft  | 8       | 0.25  | 0.5   | 0.75  | 1.0  | 1.5   | 2.0  | 3.0  | 4.0  |
| Medium | 10     | 0.31  | 0.63  | 0.94  | 1.25 | 1.9   | 2.5  | 3.75 | 5.0  |
| Medium | 12     | 0.38  | 0.75  | 1.13  | 1.5  | 2.25  | 3.0  | 4.5  | 6.0  |
| Hard  | 14      | 0.44  | 0.88  | 1.3   | 1.75 | 2.6   | 3.5  | 5.25 | 7.0  |
| V. hard | 16    | 0.5   | 1.0   | 1.5   | 2.0  | 3.0   | 4.0  | 6.0  | 8.0  |

**Table 15** *The weight 0.9m (36") lengths of balsa wood of varying densities highlights the importance of selecting the right grade.*

weight of balsa wood can vary. It is easy to double the weight of wood in a model by selecting the wrong grade. This can be important, not only during construction of a new design, but also when someone else builds a model from your original plans.

Typical applications of the various grades of balsa are as follows:

- Very soft – cowls, wing tips and other parts from balsa block
- Soft – wing ribs and sheet tail surfaces
- Medium – trailing edges, formers, sheet fuselages and sheet wings
- Medium hard – wing spars and longerons
- Very hard – main spars and leading edges

Balsa is supplied in a number of different cross sections. These are shown in Figure 192. The square and rectangular strip can be cut from balsa sheet, and the other specialist shapes can save considerable time during construction, particularly the shaped leading and trailing edges.

## Obechi

While not as light as balsa, Obechi (sometimes spelt Obeche) is a fairly coarse textured but soft wood. It weighs about the same as very hard balsa and has found its major application as a veneer for foam wings. It is readily available in fairly thin sheets 1.5 mm x 75 mm x 915mm ($^1$/$_{16}$" x 3" x 36") wide. Even thinner sheets or those of larger dimensions are harder to find. They are, however, available from a number of specialist foam wing manufacturers who advertise in the modelling press.

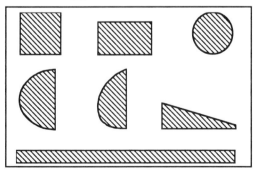

**Figure 192** *Balsa is available in square, rectangular, round, symmetrical or cambered leading edges, trailing edge and sheet forms.*

## Liteply

Liteply is a very lightweight form of imported plywood much of it coming from Spain. The 2mm (3/32") thick ply only weighs around 850 g/sq. m (3 oz per sq. ft). It has many of the characteristics of normal plywood, is quite resistant to warping, but is weaker and, of course lighter. It is ideally suited to the construction of lightweight formers. Liteply can be bought in substantial sized sheets, typically 1m x 300mm (39" x 12") which are 2mm, 3mm or 6mm ($^3$/$_{32}$", $^1$/$_8$" or ¼") thick.

Another form of 'lightply' can be home-made from layers of balsa, with the grain of alternate layers at right angles, glued together with contact adhesive to avoid the warping caused by water-based glues. In this form, the lightply will be even lighter than the commercial product.

In addition, a sandwich of balsa between two layers of thin ply can be made, or even a sandwich of ply between two layers of balsa. The main use for liteply is for fuselage formers, but it can also be used for fuselage sides, fins and tailplanes as well as wing ribs.

## Ply

There are two clearly different types of plywood on the market today; DIY quality and marine or aeromodelling quality. The latter is usually made from birch and has a more uniform strength.

Ply comes in a wide range of thickness, of which the ones most likely to be used by modellers are shown with their weights in Table 16. The thickness of ply available in

| Thickness | | Weight | |
|---|---|---|---|
| mm | inches | g/sq cm | oz/sq in |
| 0.4 | 1/64 | 0.3 | 0.08 |
| 0.8 | 1/32 | 0.6 | 0.16 |
| 1.0 | 1/24 | 0.75 | 0.2 |
| 1.5 | 1/16 | 1.1 | 0.25 |
| 3.0 | 1/8 | 2.2 | 0.5 |
| 6 | 1/4 | 4.3 | 1 |

**Table 16** *The weight of plywood of varying thickness; a material that is used in most R/C models.*

the UK is solely in metric dimensions, but the table shows the imperial equivalents.

Plywood finds its main application as highly stressed formers used around the engine, undercarriage and any cabane struts. It is also employed to make undercarriage mounting plates and dihedral braces.

Due to its weight, consideration should be given to removing material in the form of lightening holes, and it must be used sparingly towards the tail of a model.

## Spruce

Spruce strip, when used for longerons or wing spars, provides greater strength than balsa for a given size of strip. It is particularly useful for spars on high aspect ratio wings and its surface hardness makes it the ideal choice for longerons on open structure fuselages.

A range of standard metric and imperial sizes is available from most model shops and the larger sizes are also stocked by some DIY stores.

| mm | inches | mm | inches |
|---|---|---|---|
| 1.5 x 1.5 | 1/16 x 1/16 | 3 x 12 | 1/8 x 1/2 |
| 1.5 x 3 | 1/16 x 1/8 | 3 x 15 | 1/8 x 5/8 |
| 1.5 x 6 | 1/16 x 1/4 | 6 x 6 | 1/4 x 1/4 |
| 1.5 x 12 | 1/16 x 1/2 | 6 x 10 | 1/4 x 3/8 |
| 2.5 x 2.5 | 3/32 x 3/32 | 6 x 12 | 1/4 x 1/2 |
| 2.5 x 5 | 3/32 x 3/8 | 8 x 8 | 5/16 x 5/16 |
| 2.5 x 12 | 3/32 x 1/2 | 10 x 10 | 3/8 x 3/8 |
| 2.5 x 15 | 3/32 x 5/8 | 10 x 12 | 3/8 x 1/2 |
| 3 x 3 | 1/8 x 1/8 | 10 x 15 | 3/8 x 5/8 |
| 3 x 6 | 1/8 x 1/4 | 12 x 12 | 1/2 x 1/2 |
| 3 x 10 | 1/8 x 3/8 | 15 x 15 | 5/8 x 5/8 |

**Table 17** *Spruce is available in a wide range of sizes for use as spars and longerons.*

Single sheet
Single sheet with corrugations on one side
Two sheets with corrugations between them
Two sheets of unequal thickness with corrugations between them
Three sheets with two layers of corrugations

## Beech

Beech is a hard, close grained wood. Its strength makes it ideal for conventional engine bearers and also for blocks for mounting undercarriages, both in built-up wings and in foam ones. Small pieces can also make useful attachment points for the screws used to retain hatches. It is usually supplied in 300mm or 450mm (12" or 18") lengths and is tough and close grained. There seems to be little standardisation in cross sectional sizes at present, but material from 6mm to 18mm (¼" to ¾") in square and rectangular section can usually be obtained. Beech is also used to make dowel, but more often, birch is the choice for this application.

## Cardboard

Card comes in a wide range of thickness and type of construction. Plain white card, also known as cartridge paper is a thin strong material suitable for covering foam wings. Double-sided card with internal corrugations has been used for making complete models. It is available with equal thickness outside layers, with one outer layer thicker than the other, or with twin layers of corrugations. The flexibility of this material depends on the construction method used in its manufacture. Cardboard is a low cost material, often available free of charge in the form of cardboard boxes, which makes its use particularly attractive.

# The plastics

## Foam

Originally, foam was expanded polystyrene and was used to make cores for wings. Now there is white foam and blue foam, white being roughly half the weight of blue and also rather less

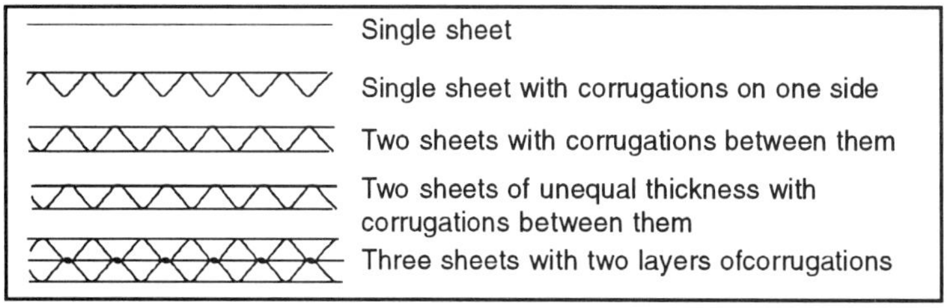

**Figure 193** *Cardboard is often corrugated. The five examples show a decrease in flexibility from top to bottom.*

expensive. Blue foam's strength is an asset in high aspect ratio wings and is also more resistant to knocks and dents. Heat shrink film can be used as a covering provided there are balsa leading and trailing edge spars to take the flight loads. This can result in a lightweight solution which is useful for electric models. Additional lightening holes can also be cut out of the foam.

Not only wings but turtle decks and other parts of fuselages can be made from the material, not to mention fins, tailplanes and ancillary items. Foam cores can be covered, in order of increasing strength, weight and cost, with heat shrink film (not necessarily the cheapest), brown paper (attached with wallpaper paste), cardboard, balsa wood or obechi veneer. Most coverings are applied with contact adhesive, such as Copydex, but a check must be made that the glue does not dissolve the foam. Blue foam is heavier than white foam, but also stronger. It should be used sparingly for applications where strength rather than weight is the critical factor. Parts such as fuselage combings can be lightened by hollowing them.

Foam is usually sold in sheets 2400mm x 1200mm (8' x 4'), and 50mm or 60mm (2" or 2½") thick is ideal. Avoid the heavier grades of foam as well as recycled material.

## Foam board

Foam board is basically an artist's material and consists of a pair of sheets of thin white card sandwiching a layer of expanded polystyrene. A popular trade name is Polyboard. It can be bought from good artist supply shops in sheets of quite substantial size, typically 1000mm x 1500mm (39" x 58") and is nominally 3mm or 5mm thick. The 5mm (¹/₅") board weights 7g/sq. cm (1.6 oz/sq. in.) and the 3mm (¹/₈") material 5g/sq. cm (1.15 oz/sq. in) It is easily cut to shape and, as well as being ideal for wing ribs and formers, can be used to build almost a complete airframe. Exposed edges can have strips of thin balsa, ply or card glued to them for protection.

## Plastics and vacuum forming

Many of the modern plastics are used to make components for R/C aircraft, such as wing bolts,

hinges, horns and clevises. They are particularly resistant to fuels and oils. However, the aim here is to examine those plastics which lend themselves to vacuum forming. Cockpit canopies are almost invariably formed over a wooden pattern as are many of the components found in kits such as cowls and spats. Furthermore, many household and food containers can be cut to provide useful pre-formed components. A good example is the use of part of a one litre lemonade bottle for a cockpit canopy.

More to the point, as often as not just heating the material and pulling it over a form will suffice, providing the form is not too deep. Mould design is important in terms of avoiding reverse curves which make it impossible to remove the finished component from the form. Gluing requires some care in the choice of adhesive and, in particular, careful degreasing of the plastic. For aircraft parts, sheet material 0.75, 1, 1.5 & 2mm (30, 40, 60 & 80 thou.) thick are useful. The key plastics are:

### ABS

ABS is widely used for components in R/C aircraft kits and with some justification. It features a fine combination of impact resistance, ability to form and low cost.

### Acetate

This plastic is widely available in a transparent form, low cost and used for many commercial canopies. It is easy to mould and the results have good optical properties.

### Acrylic

The most widely known is perspex, but there are many other forms which are popular for

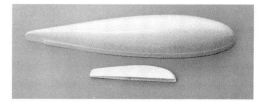

**Figure 194** *Wing tip and tailplane tip components made from ABS prove to be very lightweight.*

moulding stiff forms. Clear, translucent and opaque types can easily be obtained.

### Polycarbonate

This is the strongest of all the mouldable plastics and also the hardest to form. It is the most expensive by a factor of around two. It will withstand the highest temperatures (120°C) and is widely used for R/C helicopter canopies and model car bodies. It is a clear material and can be painted with special polycarbonate paints, widely available from model shops stocking R/C cars.

### PVC

Clear corrugated sheet has recently shown itself to be an excellent material for moulding canopies. Its cheapness and wide availability make it a good choice, as does the ease with which it can be shaped by just being heated and pulled over a form.

### Styrene

This is the material used for making small plastic aircraft kits. It is usually sold in white sheets and is cheap to buy, strong, gives excellent mould detail and is readily available in sheets of varying thickness.

## Other plastics

The other main applications of plastics are in the production of foam wings and the manufacture of iron-on covering materials. Some of the more commonly used plastics are described below.

### Expanded polystyrene

A very lightweight material in this form, the polystyrene is best cut to shape with a hot wire, though a sharp serrated knife or razor saw can also be used. It is popular for wing cores and is available in a white form and as a denser blue type, which is twice as heavy. Foam densities vary, but a typical figure for white foam is 20gm/1000cc (1.16 oz/100 cu. in.).

### Polyester

Available in a variety of forms, polyester is popular as a resin for use in GRP work, which

may be clear or coloured. It is also produced in sheet form and is the basis of many iron-on covering materials, as well as being the material used for blow moulded bottles.

### Polycarbonate

This plastic is very tough and flexible. It is used for the manufacture of a wide range of commercial and domestic items including hinges. In sheet form, it is the material from which Solarfilm is manufactured.

## Glass reinforced plastic

GRP or fibreglass has an excellent range of properties, which depend on the type and amount of reinforcement and resin. The glass reinforcement is usually in one of three forms. Chopped strand mat consists of random direction, non-woven fibres. Rovings have their fibres orientated in a single direction, while in plain weave fabric they are woven in two directions at right angles. The resin is either polyester or epoxy based. GRP has always been popular for cowls and spats, but can also be used to make whole fuselages or even complete airframes. It can also be used to add strength around engine bays, undercarriage mounts and to stiffen split flaps. While the amount of work necessary to make the plug/mould is high, the production of multiple units thereafter is quite rapid, a benefit if a pair of wheel spats is needed, or more than one model is to be built. Flat GRP laminate is also available in the form of printed

**Figure 195** *A typical GRP cowl before the air intake and outlet have been cut.*

circuit board for electronic work. Cut to shape, this material is ideal for making small items like control horns.

There are many properties which make GRP attractive for use in radio controlled aircraft.

- High strength with low weight
- High impact strength and resilience
- Suitability for anything from complete airframes to wheel spats
- Resistance to glow, diesel and petrol fuels
- Weather proof
- Dimensional stability
- Able to pass radio signals
- May be coloured as desired.
- Easy to make without expensive equipment

There are three issues facing anyone using these materials.

- The required strength
- The acceptable weight
- The mould design

Selection of the first two factors result in a decision on the thickness of the component

### *Designing in strength*

The GRP mouldings used in R/C aircraft should be relatively thin but adequate stiffness and rigidity must be provided. This can be produced in the form of the moulding itself. Thus the semi-circular, oval or curved cross sections shown in Figure 196 are inherently longitudinally stiff.

A method of increasing stiffness locally is by building up additional layers of reinforcement in the areas where more strength is required.

| Layers | gsm | oz/sq. ft | mm | inches |
|--------|-----|-----------|-----|--------|
| 1 | 300 | 1 | 0.6 | 1/40 |
|  | 450 | 1½ | 1 | 1/25 |
| 2 | 300 | 1 | 1.2 | 1/20 |
|  | 450 | 1½ | 2 | 1/12 |
| 3 | 300 | 1 | 1.8 | 1/14 |
|  | 450 | 1½ | 3 | 1/8 |

**Table 18** *The thickness of chopped strand mat laminate depends on the mat used and the number of layers. It assumes that only a reasonable amount of resin has been employed.*

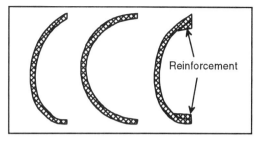

**Figure 196** *A curved or semi-circular cross section considerably increases the strength of a fuselage. Reinforcement can provide additional rigidity.*

The increase in cross section should be progressive to give a gradual change of section. Any abrupt build-up introduces weakness at the point of change of section. Figure 197 shows this as well as a good overlap design for joining two GRP mouldings. Edge-to-edge joining is not recommended.

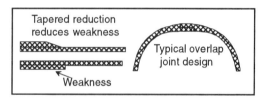

**Figure 197** *The design of joints in GRP requires careful thought if weakness is to be avoided.*

| Layers | gsm | oz/sq. ft | mm | in. |
|--------|-----|-----------|-----|-----|
| 1 | 127 | 0.4 | .4 | 1/64 |
| 2 |  |  | .75 | 1/32 |
| 3 |  |  | 1 | 1/24 |
| 4 |  |  | 1.5 | 1/16 |
| 1 | 200 | 0.7 | 0.4 | 1/64 |
| 2 |  |  | 0.8 | 1/32 |
| 3 |  |  | 1.2 | 1/20 |
| 4 |  |  | 1.6 | 1/15 |
| 1 | 300 | 1 | 0.6 | 1/48 |
| 2 |  |  | 1.2 | 1/20 |
| 3 |  |  | 1.8 | 1/14 |
| 4 |  |  | 2.5 | 3/32 |

**Table 19** *Thickness of mixed laminates is hard to estimate with great accuracy.*

| Material | gsm | oz/sq ft | 1 layer + gel coat gsm | 1 layer + gel coat oz/sq ft |
|---|---|---|---|---|
| Chopped strand mat | 300 | 1 | 1626 | 5¾ |
|  | 450 | 1½ | 2166 | 7½ |
| Plain weave fabric | 127 | 0.4 | 1006 | 3½ |
|  | 200 | 0.7 | 1191 | 4¼ |
|  | 300 | 1 | 1347 | 4¾ |
| Woven rovings | 290 | 1 | 1337 | 4¾ |
|  | 600 | 2 | 1870 | 6½ |

**Table 20** *The weight of various types of GRP laminate.*

### Estimating moulding thickness

The thickness of a proposed GRP moulding using chopped strand mat can be predicted reasonably accurately and is shown in Table 18 on page 105 for varying weights of mat.

Estimating the thickness of other laminates is not as simple, particularly when using a mixture of cloth, mat and/or rovings. The following table is a general guide.

### Estimating weight

The weight of a specific part can be calculated from Table 20, knowing the surface area of the mould and the number of layers in the finished laminate.

### Strength

The strength of a GRP laminate depends on the type of reinforcement, its directional properties and the resin/glass ratio. It is also very dependent on who actually does the work. Reinforcing materials divide into three groups.

- **Unidirectional** The fibres of rovings are oriented in one direction to give the maximum strength.
- **Bi-directional** In woven fabrics, the strands are interlaced in two different directions. Less strong than unidirectional fibres, the strength may be greater in one direction than in the other.
- **Random** Chopped strand mat fibres are oriented haphazardly, providing the weakest laminate.

### Exotic materials

Figure 198 compares strength to weight ratio, using the same resin, of GRP chopped strand mat, rovings, Kevlar and carbon fibre. The superiority of both Kevlar and carbon fibre is clear. However, the significantly higher price of these

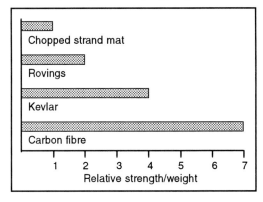

**Figure 198** *Kevlar and carbon fibre both provide marked strength improvements for a given weight of laminate.*

| Material | Relative weight | Relative tensile strength | Relative compressive strength |
|---|---|---|---|
| Woven Rovings | 1 | 2 | 1 |
| Plain Weave Fabric | 1 | 3 | 1.7 |
| Chopped Strand Mat | 1.4 | 1 | 1 |
| Aluminium | 1.93 | 0.8 | 0.6 |
| Steel | 5.58 | 4 | 2.7 |

**Table 21** *The relative weights and strengths of GRP materials compared with aluminium and steel.*

**Table 22** *The different weights of a wide range of materials used in model aircraft construction.*

| Material | Grams/cc | Ounces/cu inch | Material | Grams/cc | Ounces/cu inch |
|----------|----------|----------------|----------|----------|----------------|
| Lead | 11.4 | 6.56 | Birch ply | 0.9 | 0.528 |
| Brass | 8.3 | 4.8 | Beech | 0.83 | 0.48 |
| Steel | 7.89 | 4.56 | Spruce | 0.55 | 0.32 |
| Aluminium | 2.6 | 1.5 | Medium balsa | 0.14 | 0.08 |

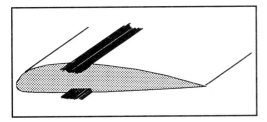

**Figure 199** *Carbon fibre tows ready to be glued into grooves in the top and bottom surfaces of a foam wing.*

two materials suggests that they should be used sparingly to provide the greatest possible strength in highly stressed areas. A typical example is the reinforcement of the wing spars of a high aspect ratio design.

Carbon fibre, Kevlar or even glass fibre tows can be glued in place to reinforce foam wings, or built-up wings for that matter. It is important, when working with foam, not to use a resin which will dissolve the foam.

## Metals

While steel has numerous uses in aeromodelling, in the form of piano wire for undercarriages, screws, nuts and bolts for mounting engines, clevises and elevator joiners, aluminium alloy is the traditional material of the full-size aircraft industry. This is not surprising in view of its remarkable strength to weight ratio. It is often employed in modelling for making engine mounting plates and undercarriage legs. Brass tube is also popular for routing fuel through formers and for undercarriage components. Lead is the usual material for moving the centre of gravity of an aircraft to the correct position once it has been built. Table 22 compares the weights of the common metals used in R/C models with a number of popular types of wood.

### Aluminium alloy

Aluminium alloy is most commonly used in sheet form. It can easily be cut and bent to shape. More complex forms can be shaped if the material is first annealed. Table 23 gives the weight of sheets of various thickness. It is popular for undercarriage legs and engine mounting plates. The alloy is also available in

| Thickness | | Weight | |
|-----------|-----|--------|---------|
| mm | SWG | kg/sq. m | oz/sq. ft |
| 3.2 | 10 | 8.3 | 27.2 |
| 2.6 | 12 | 6.7 | 22 |
| 2 | 14 | 5.2 | 17 |
| 1.6 | 16 | 4.1 | 13.6 |
| 1.2 | 18 | 3.1 | 10.2 |
| .9 | 20 | 2.3 | 7.6 |
| .7 | 22 | 1.8 | 5.9 |
| .01 | 0.004 | 0.025 | 0.08 |

**Table 23** *The weight of varying thickness of aluminium alloy.*

| Size | | Weight | |
|------|-----|--------|--------|
| mm | SWG | g/m | oz/36" |
| 5 | 6 | 147 | 4.75 |
| 4 | 8 | 102 | 3.3 |
| 3 | 10 | 66 | 2.1 |
| 2.5 | 12 | 43 | 1.4 |
| 2 | 14 | 26 | 0.85 |
| 1.5 | 16 | 16 | 0.5 |
| 1.2 | 18 | 9 | 0.25 |
| 1 | 20 | 6 | 0.2 |

**Table 24** *The weight of differing sizes of piano wire varies considerably.*

| mm | inches | mm | inches |
|------|--------|-------|--------|
| 1.5 | 1/16 | 9.5 | 3/8 |
| 2.4 | 3/32 | 10.3 | 13/32 |
| 3 | 1/8 | 11 | 7/16 |
| 4 | 5/32 | 12 | 15/32 |
| 4.75 | 3/16 | 12.5 | 1/2 |
| 5.5 | 7/32 | 13.5 | 17/32 |
| 6.4 | 1/4 | 14.25 | 9/16 |
| 7 | 9/32 | 15 | 19/32 |
| 8 | 5/16 | 16 | 5/8 |
| 8.75 | 11/32 | 16.7 | 21/32 |

**Table 25** *The available sizes of brass tube allow each to be a sliding fit in the next larger size.*

the form of litho plate, usually obtained as scrap from printers. This material is very thin, typically only 0.01mm (4 thou) thick. It is readily available in A4 sheets measuring 210 x 297mm (8¼" x 11¾") and may be used over a wooden frame to give a metallic finish.

### Piano wire

This material is the first choice for undercarriage legs. It is strong and springy, the latter being of particular importance. Joining two pieces of piano wire should avoid the use of silver soldering as the process removes the springy temper from the wire. A design of joint which is wrapped with thin wire and then soft soldered will not impair the strength of this excellent material. Piano wire is also widely used for making elevator joiners.

### Brass

The sizes of brass tube available are such that each size is a sliding fit into the size above, making the material ideal for telescopic under-carriage legs. The tube is useful for passing fuel though sealed bulkheads, making control hinges and torque rods. The material is also supplied in rectangular tube section and as thin sheet; the latter useful for making metal fuel tanks. Brass is particularly easy to solder.

## The choice of adhesives

Hardly a day seems to pass without some new and specialist adhesive appearing on the market. There is an excellent book available from Nexus Special Interests from their Workshop Practice Series: No 21 *Adhesives and Sealants* by Dave Lammas. It gives a thorough grounding for any-one wishing to study the subject in more detail.

For the purpose of this book, only a brief examination will be made of the main groups of adhesives. In each case, their strengths and weaknesses will be covered and their main uses highlighted. A key point to remember is that many adhesives depend for their adhesion on perfectly clean surfaces.

This can be a special problem with metals and plastics, where even the oils from the user's skin can prevent a successful joint. From the modeller's point of view, the key factors are strength, weight and cost and these are shown in Table 26 for the popular glues on the market in 1996.

While the purpose of tissue paste and balsa cement are obvious from their names, the

| | Acrylic | Ali-phatic | Contact | Cyano | Epoxy | Isopon | Hot glue | Polyester resin | PVA | Solvent weld |
|----------------|---------|-----------|---------|--------|----------|---------|----------|-----------------|------|--------------|
| **Drying speed** | Med | Med | Med | V fast | Med /slow | Fast | Fast | Slow | Slow | Fast |
| **Weight** | Med | Med | Med | V low | High | High | High | High | Med | V low |
| **Penetration** | Poor | Good | V poor | V good | Poor | V poor | V poor | Med | Med | Good |
| **Gap filling** | Good | Poor | Poor | Poor | Good | V good | Good | Good | Med | V poor |
| **Strength** | High | Med | High | Med. | V high | Med | Med | High | Med | Med |
| **Cost** | High | Low | Med | High | High | High | Med | Med | Low | Med |

**Table 26** *The main characteristics of the glues likely to be used for model aircraft construction.*

| Material | Acrylic | Ali-phatic | Contact | Cyano | Epoxy | Hot glue | Isopon | Polyester resin | PVA | Solvent weld |
|---|---|---|---|---|---|---|---|---|---|---|
| Paper/fabric | | ■ | ■ | ■ | | | | | ■ | |
| Balsa | | ■ | ■ | ■ | | | | ■ | ■ | |
| Hardwood | ■ | ■ | ■ | ■ | ■ | ■ | ■ | ■ | ■ | |
| GRP | ■ | | | | ■ | ■ | ■ | ■ | | |
| ABS | ■ | | | | | ■ | | | | ■ |
| Styrene | ■ | | | | | | | | | ■ |
| Acrylic | ■ | | | | | | | ■ | | ■ |
| Acetate | ■ | | | ■ | | | | | | ■ |
| PVC | ■ | | | | | ■ | ■ | ■ | | ■ |
| Metals | ■ | | ■ | ■ | ■ | ■ | | ■ | | |
| Foam | | ■ | | | | | | | | |
| Veneers | | | ■ | | | | | | | |
| Seaplanes | | ■ | ■✿ | | ■ | ■ | ■ | ■ | ■✿ | |
| Canopies | | ■ | | ■ | | | | | | |

✿ *Waterproof varieties only*

**Table 27** *The right adhesive must be chosen for gluing the wide range of materials used by modellers if a strong joint is to be obtained.*

" HAVING TROUBLE WITH YOUR SUPER-GLUE AGAIN DEAR ? "

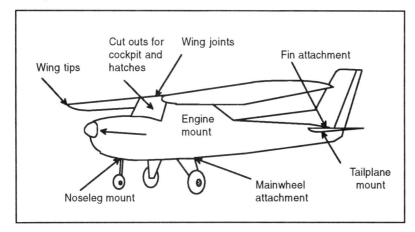

**Figure 200** *In any model, the designer must look for certain highly stressed points and ensure that sufficient strength is provided into these critical areas.*

applications to which other adhesives can be put are not so obvious. Table 27 on page 109 gives some pointers.

## Building in lightness

These are the words which must be engraved on the heart of all aircraft designers and builders, be they of the full size or model variety. A pair of scales allows every item to be weighed during the design process, as well as during construction. Their use will prove both enlightening and rewarding. They can check the weight of items such as engine mounts and wheels, as well as comparing the heaviness of various pieces of wood. They can also be invaluable in checking the finished weight of the complete model.

### The stress points

Figure 200 shows clearly where the main stresses occur on a typical R/C model. Some parts are particularly stressed on take-off and

**Figure 201** *Scales are essential to maintain a continual watch on weight. Types which are suitable for weighing small pieces of balsa as well as ones to weigh the whole model and its major components are helpful.*

landing, some during violent manoeuvres, some on a poor landing, when a wing tip may dig in or a model somersault. It is clear that special attention must be paid to the selection of the materials used at these stress points as well as the constructional detail in these areas.

# 9     Airframe alternatives

## The fuselage

The purpose of the fuselage on a model of conventional layout is to house the radio, provide a mount for the engine and fuel tank, and keep the wings and tail surfaces in their correct positions. There is a wide variety of ways in which fuselages can be built, virtually all of which depend on formers to define their cross section.

## Formers

Formers are provided to support the outer skin of the fuselage. Their position in the fuselage usually dictates the material used to make them. Formers around the engine bay are almost invariably cut from plywood. Those at the wing and undercarriage locations may be ply, any form of liteply or thick balsa, while those in the rear fuselage and tail area are normally of thin balsa. It is sometimes useful to make formers from strips of wood, as invariably those aft of the radio compartment need a hole in the middle for control runs, as well as to minimise their weight.

When considering the design of a stringered or part stringered fuselage, thought should be given to the way the stringers will attach to the formers. The left-hand former in Figure 204 shows the easiest approach. The right-hand illustration has many slots cut in it, with the risk that the wood between each will break during cutting out.

## Simple boxes

The simplest fuselage to build is the profile one. It leaves the problem of where to house the radio, particularly for internal combustion engined models where the exhaust goo may damage the radio. Easiest to design is the rectangular box cross section. It is quick to build but unfortunately it is not very aesthetically pleasing.

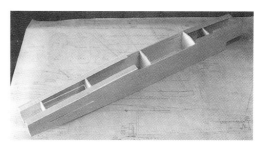

**Figure 202** *Ample triangular balsa strip will allow this fuselage to be sanded to a pleasant oval cross section. The slot for the tailplane has been accurately cut to ensure it is fitted at the correct incidence angle.*

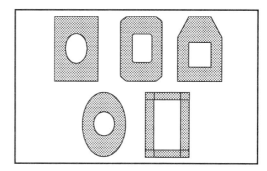

**Figure 203** *A variety of rear fuselage formers. The bottom right-hand one is built up from strip balsa.*

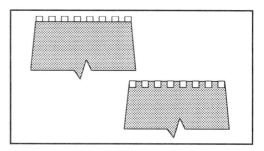

**Figure 204** *Stringers can be glued to the surface of a former or let into suitable slots.*

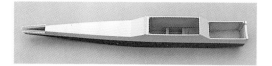

**Figure 205** *A simple sheet fuselage is quick to build and produces a strong structure.*

## All-sheet

Designing an all-sheet fuselage is very simple, but results in an uninspiring shape. To allow a more rounded effect, strips of triangular balsa can be fitted to the corners for sanding to an oval or circular cross section. For tractor configurations using internal combustion engines, it is normal to strengthen the forward part of the fuselage. Ply doublers are the usual choice, though cross grained balsa or liteply can be an adequate alternative. The other area which needs reinforcement is the wing seat. Again ply is a popular choice, but a thick grade of balsa has the advantage of increasing the area of the wing seat, thus reducing the chances of marking or damaging the wing where it sits on the fuselage.

**Figure 206** *An open frame fuselage provides atmosphere for a model with a veteran look.*

**Figure 208** *This fuselage combines a sheet forward fuselage with a box girder rear for the cabin, sides, top and bottom.*

A thinner grade of wood can be used for the fuselage sides if reinforced with balsa strip longerons and vertical members glued to the inside.

## Open frame

Strength for weight, it is hard to beat the traditional open frame layout. Providing the joints are accurately cut and glued, the structure provides strength whether it is covered or not, though covering will add to the rigidity of the finished fuselage. The structure can be built either from balsa or spruce strip depending on the size of the model and the dimensions of the individual longerons. A mix of the two materials is also quite acceptable.

A significant improvement in the strength can be achieved by putting thin plywood plates over each joint. Alternatively, balsa gussets can be

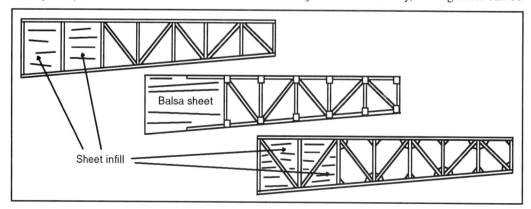

**Figure 207** *A conventional girder construction relies heavily on the fit and quality of the glued joints. These may be reinforced with small ply plates or balsa gussets.*

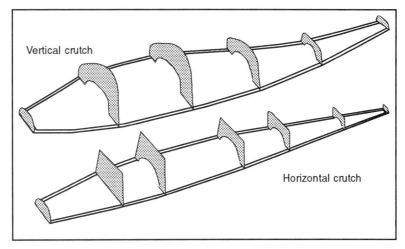

**Figure 209** *The fuse-lage formers may be divided in half and built up on a vertical or horizontal crutch. The vertical crutch has the advantage that pairs of formers are identical.*

fitted to each corner. The girder may join an all-sheet forward section or the front of the girder may have sheet in fill around the engine and radio bays. Either will keep the weight of the fuselage at the front, which is where it should be.

## Oval and circular shapes

A complex fuselage shape generally results in a much more visually pleasing appearance. There are several methods which enable double curvature fuselages to be built from wood.

### Horizontal and vertical crutches

A crutch can be used as a frame on which the fuselage is built. As can be seen from Figure 209, the fuselage may be divided vertically or horizontally into two parts and the formers added to a basic strip wood outline. The crutch can then have stringers attached to provide basic strength as well as support for the covering, or can be covered with balsa planks to provide a

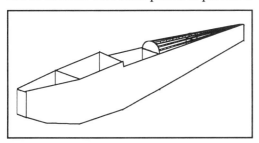

**Figure 210** *Balsa stringers can easily be used to build up a light weight yet strong rear turtle deck.*

rigid monocoque. Once each half has been built, the two are glued together to form the complete fuselage. The resulting structure will be both light and strong. If planked, access hatches can be cut out once the fuselage has been completed.

### Stringers

Not many R/C designs are likely to feature a fully stringered fuselage, but certainly parts can use stringers to advantage, as shown in Figure 210 where a rear turtle deck is built up using them. This construction method results in a very lightweight structure, with much of its strength resulting from its covering. As mentioned previously, some care is needed in the design of the formers.

### Sheeted

Sheeting can give a beautifully curved finish. The main considerations are that double curves are not feasible though a straight taper can be attractive. An adequate number of formers must be used with wood of sufficient thickness to avoid a 'starved' look. A practical minimum thickness of wood for sheeting is 1.5mm ($^1/_{16}$") with rather thicker sheet being selected where a significant amount of sanding is envisaged.

### Planked

More exotic fuselage cross sections can be achieved by planking over formers. This technique enables double curvature designs to be constructed and the resultant monocoque is immensely strong. It is also the only practical answer for a wooden fuselage where the curvature is too great for sheeting to be used. Sufficient material must be allowed for sanding down to give a smooth finish; an allowance of 1.5mm ($^1/_{16}$") being a reasonable figure on all but the smallest model. Again it is important that the fuselage formers are fairly closely spaced to avoid a 'starved' look.

### Rolled tubes

Rolled tubes can be used for pod and boom models as well as twin boom ones. The material used can be balsa sheet, thin ply, glass fibre, carbon fibre, or even standard commercial items such as a length of fishing rod or an arrow shaft.

## Advanced shapes and materials

Virtually any shape can be achieved by vacuum forming or by using GRP. In both cases, a form or mould has to be made first, normally from wood and, in the case of GRP, a female mould made from the male plug. The most common use of these materials is for just a part or the whole of the fuselage, but GRP has been employed

occasionally to make complete models. Any GRP fuselage will be tough, with an excellent surface finish. Chapter 8 gives more details of how to design in this excellent material.

### Metal

The main areas where metal is employed in fuselage construction is in the area of cowls, undercarriages and engine mounts. As most R/C modellers have fairly limited metal working facilities, designs requiring much more than piano wire to be bent to shape or aluminium sheet cut and formed as an undercarriage mount are rare. Lithoplate can be glued to finished structures to give a realistic metal finish. It is readily available in A4 sheets and can be cut with scissors.

### GRP and wooden cowls

GRP is almost the ideal material for an engine cowl. It is strong, lightweight and totally fuel resistant. As indicated in Chapter 8, a mould does have to be made first and, in the time taken to make a mould, a wooden cowl can be built. Often, the right shape can be achieved by fitting blocks of soft balsa between a pair of ply formers and cutting/sanding to the desired shape. Circular aluminium cowls of various diameters are available commercially and can form the starting point for a new model.

A key design factor for a cowl is the cooling air for the engine. The path for the airflow must be as unobstructed as possible. Conventional

**Figure 211** *A wooden cowl, built up from balsa, completely hides this engine/silencer combination, yet provides adequate cooling air.*

**Figure 212** *Thought must be given to the amount of material which requires removing to fit it around the selected engine/silencer.*

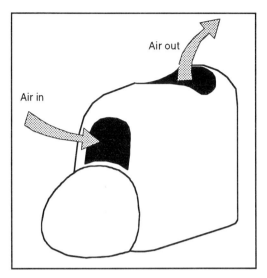

**Figure 213** *Any cowl must have adequately sized air intake and exit holes to avoid engine overheating.*

wisdom is that the air outlet area should be twice the inlet area. This is fine unless the inlet area is large. Perhaps a better guideline is to ensure that the outlet area is at least the size of the top of the cylinder head, and that the inlet area is at least two-thirds of this size.

Clearly, the current generation of four stroke engines run significantly hotter than two strokes, but if the silencer of the latter is included within the cowl, there is little difference in the total heat.

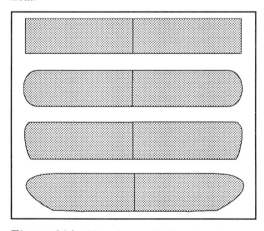

**Figure 214** *The shape of the wing tip can considerably improve the look of a parallel chord wing.*

# Wings

The wing is undoubtedly the most important part of any model aeroplane. This is not surprising since the wing sustains the model in flight and to a large extent governs its performance. There are many choices when it comes to wing construction; the wing planform, the aerofoil section, the method of construction and the way it is attached to the fuselage. Having already examined the aerodynamic factors, we will now consider the structural details.

## Parallel chord

Without any doubt, parallel chord wings are the easiest to build, but Chapter 6 has shown their aerodynamic shortcomings. However, the benefit of identical wing ribs is an attractive proposition and washout is unlikely to be needed with most shapes as the chances of tip-stalling are slight. For many designers the least attractive feature of parallel chord wings is an aesthetic one. They look rather utilitarian. This can, to some extent, be overcome by the design of the wing tips which may be anything from square through to semi-circular.

## Tapered

Tapered wings are only slightly more difficult to construct than parallel chord ones, but not significantly so. In the case of built up construction, each rib will be different, but unless the taper is large, the ribs can be formed from master root and tip ribs using the bread and butter technique. For a foam wing, the taper makes little difference when the core is cut. A factor to consider, however is that tapered wings are more prone to tip-stalling than parallel chord ones, so that designing in some washout is a sensible precaution.

## Elliptical

If you choose to use an elliptical wing planform, you must put up with the consequences. Construction will not be easy and tip-stalling a near certainty without plenty of washout. One compromise is to use a straight leading and trailing edge and end up with a close approximation to an elliptical wing without many

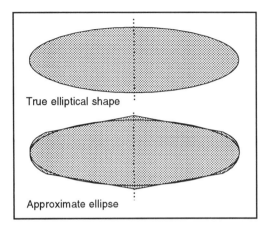

True elliptical shape

Approximate ellipse

**Figure 215** *An approximation to an elliptical wing is possible using straight leading and trailing edges.*

of the constructional difficulties. Despite the optical illusion, the near elliptical wing shape in the bottom drawing of Figure 215 is virtually the same size and shape as the true ellipse also shown in the top drawing.

## Wing tips

There is a wide choice of shapes for any wing tip. Factors to consider are aerodynamic efficiency, ease of construction, strength and vulnerability to damage if a wing tip digs in. Figure 216 shows a range of possibilities starting from the left with square and diagonal tips and moving right to more pleasing curved ones.

Despite the range of choice, by far the most popular type of wing tips are those which are square or almost square; ease of construction being their key advantage. Square tips can either

use a strong tip rib, thicker balsa or ply, or employ balsa block.

The latter can also be used for a slightly curved tip. A semi circular or circular tip is usually either built up from pieces of balsa sheet or, to provide greater strength, laminated from strips of balsa or thin ply.

## Biplanes and triplanes

The wings used in multi wing models are different from those used in monoplanes. All

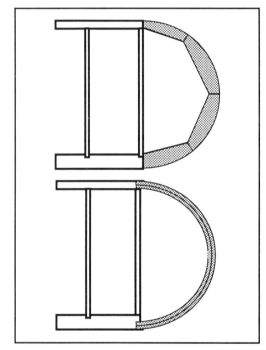

**Figure 217** *Circular tips can either be built up from sheet balsa or laminated from strips.*

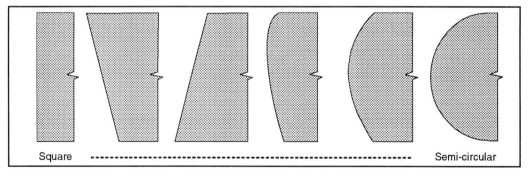

Square — — — — — — — — — — — — — — — — — Semi-circular

**Figure 216** *There is a wide variety of possible wing tip shapes with varying degrees of constructional difficulty.*

**Figure 218** *The popularity of square or near square wing tips is clear, as this illustration of the tips of three popular kit designs show.*

things being equal, they are smaller, of lower aspect ratio and usually provided with struts, sometimes bracing wires, which can help to take the loads imposed on them. This does enable lighter wings to be designed for such aircraft, which is a good thing bearing in mind the end result. Two or three wings are likely to be heavier than a single one of the same wing area. Even worse, the interaction between closely mounted wings means that for an equivalent monoplane area, 1.3 times the total wing area will be needed for such designs.

### Multi engined aircraft

The major difference in most multi engined models is that engine nacelles have to be built into the wings. It is useful to consider the nacelle as a mini forward fuselage where the firewall

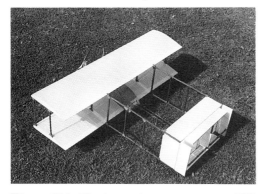

**Figure 219** *The inter-plane struts on my JH2 play an important part in ensuring the structure is sufficiently strong.*

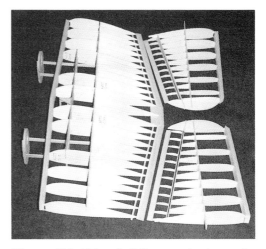

**Figure 220** *When building a twin, it may be convenient to build the wing in three parts, rather than the more conventional two-part construction.*

formers are integrated with the main spars. Thus the use of plywood inboard main spars is popular for this type of layout. Nacelles are normally covered with balsa planks or sheeting to meld them into the wing.

When foam wings are used, a simple rectangular cut-out in the leading edge of the wing allows a built up nacelle to be glued straight into the wing. A typical example of this is shown in Figure 38 in Chapter 2.

## Aerofoils

Chapter 6 looked at selecting an aerofoil for aerodynamic reasons. We will now examine the choice from a constructional point of view.

### Flat plates

There are some constructional advantages to the use of flat plates. First, there is the speed of construction: just cut out the wing outline and glue the sheets together. No ribs to cut out! Second, a sheet balsa wing is significantly lighter than an equivalent foam/veneer one. Third is the resistance to crash damage and the ease of repair.

As a comment on the ultimate strength of an all-sheet wing, one of my 4cc (0.25) powered fun-jet's wings supported a total of 22kg (40 lb)

Chapter 9

**Figure 221** *My F15 Eagle (Nexus Plan RC/1412) has a wing built from a single thickness of 3/16" (4.75mm) balsa.*

before covering, equivalent to a loading of 10G. The wing covering and the lift generated by the fuselage provide a further considerable safety factor.

It should be clear that flat plate, all-sheet wings are well suited to the needs of small, sports scale, modern jet fighters. The wings of these aircraft are all characterised by low aspect ratio and low thickness chord ratio. The first of these enables a sheet wing to be used without too much flexing or twisting, and the second is realistically met by the very thinness of the sheet.

### Curved plates
The curved sheet wing maintains many of the advantages of the flat plate in constructional terms but provides significantly more lift.

Against it is its lamentable inverted performance. However, it can be used for simple models when simulating an under cambered wing section and when construction speed is important. Some form of under wing ribbing is usually required to maintain the curved shape.

### Flat bottomed aerofoils
Flat bottomed aerofoils, like the widely used Clark Y, are very straightforward to construct. Having a flat underside, they are easily assembled on a flat building board which is why they are so popular. Most pre-shaped leading and trailing edges are designed to fit these type of aerofoils.

### Symmetrical and semi-symmetrical aerofoils
The fact that these aerofoils are not flat bottomed is the root of their construction problems. One of the easiest solutions is to design a tab into each rib, so that the wing can be built on a flat board and the tabs then removed. However, the difficulties don't end here. Many pre-shaped leading or trailing edges are not symmetrical in shape, and thus other solutions, such as square or rectangular strip may be necessary for the leading edge, with a pair of strips of sheet for the trailing edge.

### Under cambered aerofoils
These aerofoils present a few constructional problems. The leading and trailing edge strips

**Figure 222** *The use of tabs on symmetrical ribs is a great boon to construction.*

**Figure 223** *Packing strips will support the leading and trailing edges of under cambered wings at the right angle.*

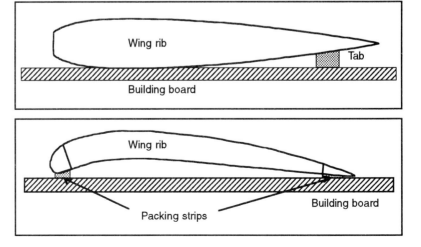

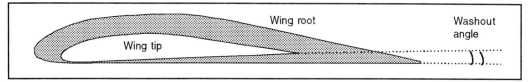

**Figure 224** *Washout is the angle between the root and tip ribs. It is positive if the tip is at a lower angle of incidence than the root, thus reducing the chances of tip-stalling.*

may need wedging at an angle on the building board. The real difficulty is attaching the covering material to the concave under surface. This is because the tautening effect when shrinking the material in place tries to pull it away from the ribs.

### Washout

A primary method of reducing tip-stalling is to employ washout. Figure 224 shows the relative incidences of the wing root and wing tip. Effective washout requires only a few degrees, otherwise, the outer section of the wing will provide insufficient lift. Somewhere between one and three degrees is recommended, the former figure on a slightly tapered wing, the latter applying to a steeply tapered or elliptical wing form.

Building in washout is straightforward with foam wings; the root and tip master ribs being attached to the foam at the appropriate angles. Built up wings require some thought about the problem at the design stage. One of the easiest methods is to prop up the trailing edge with a tapered strip. This is shown in Figure 225.

The amount of washout to be included depends on the design of the wing and on two key factors; the aspect ratio and the wing taper. As a guideline, add 1° of washout for any wing where the span is more than eight times the chord, 2° if more than twelve. Add 1° if the tip chord is less that three-quarters of the root chord and 2° for an elliptical wing shape.

A neat way of producing a tapered wing with washout is to use a single aerofoil and cut increasingly large wedges from the underside as the ribs progress from root to tip. This is shown for a wing with seven ribs in Figure 226. A final alternative is to raise the trailing edge of both outboard ailerons at their neutral position so that they provide the desired degree of washout.

## Wing construction

### Leading and trailing edges

Generally, it is easiest to use specially shaped balsa strip for these tasks, provided the wing does not taper in the vertical plane. A number of standard sizes and shapes are available, and these are shown in Table 28 overleaf.

For leading edges, square or rectangular balsa strip can also be employed and then sanded to shape; the latter working particularly well where there is a vertical wing taper. Leading edges can even employ square strip installed diagonally or a dowel, although the former may tend to split the ribs in the case of an impact with a solid object.

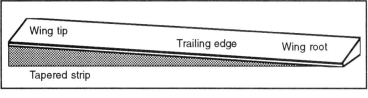

**Figure 225** *Accurate washout can be built in by propping up the trailing edge with a tapered strip during construction.*

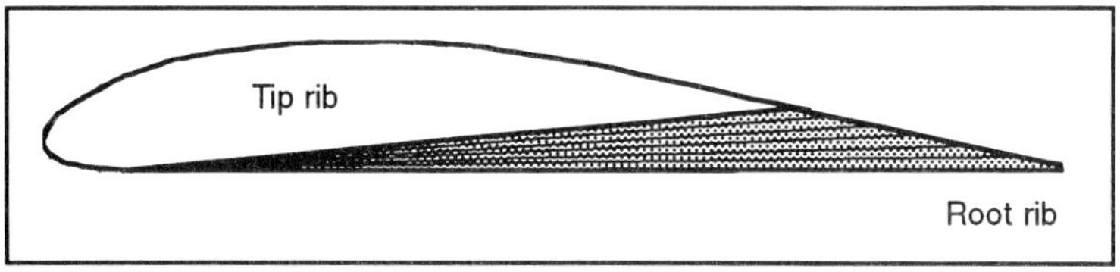

**Figure 226** *Cutting a set of ribs from a single aerofoil section.*

119

| Leading edge | | Trailing edge | | | |
|---|---|---|---|---|---|
| mm | inches | mm | inches | mm | inches |
| 6 | ¼ | 3 x 9.5 | 1/8 x 3/8 | 6 x 25 | ¼ x 1 |
| 9.5 | 3/8 | 3 x 12.5 | 1/8 x ½ | 8 x 31 | 5/16 x 1¼ |
| 12.5 | ½ | 4.5 x 12.5 | 3/16 x ½ | 9.5 x 38 | 3/8 x 1½ |
| 19 | ¾ | 4.5 x 19 | 3/16 x ¾ | 12.5 x 38 | ½ x 1½ |
| 25 | 1 | 6 x 19 | ¼ x ¾ | 12.5 x 50 | ½ x 2 |

**Table 28** *Leading and trailing edges are available in a wide range of standard sizes.*

Trailing edges can be built from pairs of strips of balsa sheet with the bottom one sanded to a taper. Vertical webbing can considerably strengthen this solution. Equally a rectangular balsa strip or even a dowel can form a satisfactory trailing edge. The overall strength of a wing can be increased by the use of strategically placed gussets glued into vulnerable corners.

## Spars

Good design practice calls for a pair of mainspars, located at the top and bottom of the wing ribs. The use of a web to join the spars adds significantly to their strength in the vertical plane. This strength has to resist the upward lift of the model in flight and the downward load experienced when landing. The latter can, on occasions, cause very high shock loadings.

The spar does not provide all the strength of a wing. The leading and trailing edges, the wing ribs and the covering all contribute to the strength of the wing in the vertical direction. The choice of actual wing spar configuration will depend on the wing planform and depth of chord, the strength required and the acceptable constructional complexity. Figure 229 shows various popular spar configurations.

Table 29 indicates that the vertical extent of the spar and the addition of webs, if two spars are used, are the key to strength in the vertical

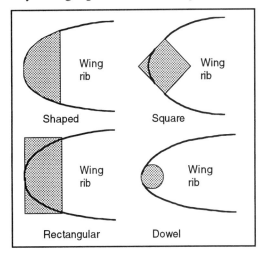

**Figure 227** *A number of alternative solutions to the construction of leading edges.*

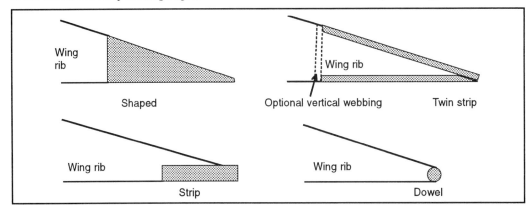

**Figure 228** *There is a wide variety of ways of constructing wing trailing edges.*

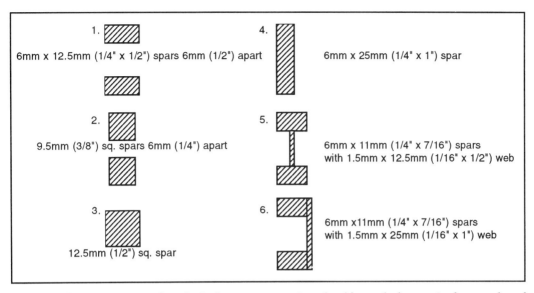

**Figure 229** *The choice of method of spar construction should match the required strength and speed of construction of the model.*

plane. Thus a single square spar has four times the strength of a pair of spars, each of half the depth. Even more impressive, a pair of spars with a web are as much as twenty four times stronger than a pair without a web, and only marginally heavier. For best results, the grain of the web should be vertical. It should also be noted that doubling the depth of the wing and its mainspar multiplies the strength in the vertical plane eight-fold. Thus the strongest wing construction usually requires a thick aerofoil.

If two balsa spars are used with foam wings, the foam itself acts as a web. However, since the foam is relatively soft the spar must be wider than for a built-up wing, so that the foam 'web' area is as wide as possible. 25mm x 2.5mm (1" x 3/32") is a realistic size for such a spar.

Alternatively carbon or glass fibre spars could be used to advantage.

On any normal wing, regardless of planform, the stress is greatest at the root and reduces to zero at the tip. For this reason, a tapered spar is commonly used to reduce weight without compromising the strength of the wing. The main reasons for a stiff main spar and a rigid wing are to maintain the design angle of incidence across the span and to minimise the risk of flutter at speed.

The D box spar is a particularly strong solution, relying on spreading the load between the leading edge and the mainspar. This is the main reason for the popularity of sheeting between the leading edge and the main spar, a secondary benefit being that this is the area of

| Type of mainspar | Strength |
|---|---|
| 1. Pair of 6mm x 12.5mm (1/4" x 1/2" spars) | 1 |
| 2. Pair of 9.5mm (3/8") square spars | 2 |
| 3. Single 12.5mm (1/2") square spar | 4 |
| 4. Single 25mm x 12.5mm (1" x 1/2") spar | 16 |
| 5. Pair of 6mm x 11mm (1/4" x 7/16") spars with a 1.5mm (1/16") web | 24 |
| 6. Pair of 6mm x 11mm (1/4" x 7/16") spars with a full depth 1.5 mm (1/16") web | 24 |

**Table 29** *The strength of a mainspar is very dependent on the type of construction used.*

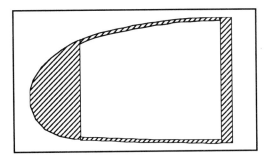

**Figure 230** *Sheeting the top and bottom of the wing from the leading edge to the mainspar provides an immensely strong D box shape.*

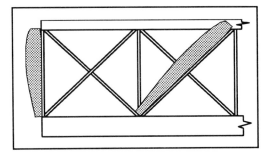

**Figure 233** *Geodetic ribs are inevitably very different shapes to the normally located ones.*

greatest curvature of the wing's aerofoil and the sheeting will help to maintain the accuracy of the section.

## Ribs

The purpose of wing ribs is to hold the various spars in position and to ensure the surface of the wing has the desired aerofoil section. This means that strength is not the key factor. For rectangular wings, all ribs will be identical and only a single one needs to be designed.

For built-up tapered wings, every wing rib needs to be drawn separately. This is not difficult using a reducing photocopier or a CAD program on a computer. Alternatively, of course, the sandwich method requires only a master root and tip rib to be drawn. For more exotic wing planforms, every single rib is different, and requires careful dimensioning in the design stage.

An even more complex situation occurs should a geodetic wing structure be selected; usually for high aspect ratio wings and tailplanes. The diagonal wing ribs will be of the original aerofoil section, but stretched along the chord axis only. The structure itself will be immensely strong for a given weight as well as being extremely warp resistant.

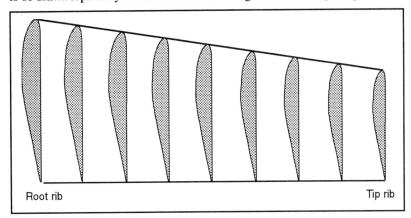

Root rib

Tip rib

**Figure 231** *Every rib on a tapered wing is different both in length and depth.*

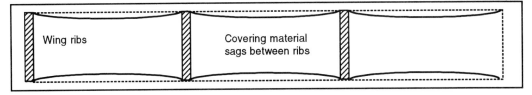

Wing ribs

Covering material sags between ribs

**Figure 232** *The ribs must be close enough together to support the covering material, with minimum sagging to maintain the aerofoil section.*

### Rib thickness and spacing

Ribs are normally made from cross grained balsa 1.5mm - 3mm (1/16" – 1/8") thick. The required spacing between ribs depends on their ability to support the material that forms the wing surface. Clearly ribs should be closer together for a wing covered with film or fabric than for a balsa sheeted one. Somewhere between 50 and 75 mm (2" and 3") should provide adequate support; the wider spacing being suitable for larger wings.

### Capping strips

Capping strips serve two important purposes. The first is to improve the vertical strength of the rib, in a similar manner to a mainspar. The second is to provide a wider surface to support the material used for the wing covering. Capping strips can also be used on foam wings to make them look like built-up ones after they have been covered.

### Sheeting

For a built up wing, sheeting over the complete upper and lower surfaces of the wing to provide a double skin will produce an excellent surface and accurately replicate the aerofoil section. It is not, however, a cheap solution with the current price of balsa. The strength of the spars can be reduced as the sheeting itself acts as a monocoque, giving excellent stiffness to the wing structure.

## Foam wings

Foam wings are easy to design provided the shape is a relatively simple one. An elliptical

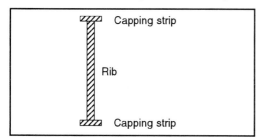

**Figure 234** *Capping strips add strength to thin ribs and provide better support for the covering.*

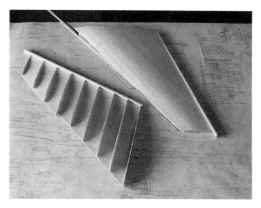

**Figure 235** *A wing with saw tooth leading edges, under construction. The top and bottom surfaces are skinned with 1.5mm (1/16") balsa.*

wing would be very difficult to cut from foam. For other shapes, just establish the root and tip aerofoil sections and decide on any degree of washout. Normally, leading and trailing edge spars are added to the core to give improved strength. Cutting out the cores with the right tools is a quick task. Alternatively, there are a number of companies which will do the job, including veneering the cores.

The two popular veneers are obechi and balsa. Obechi gives a somewhat stronger result and is rather more ding proof. Cores can also be covered with brown wrapping paper or cardboard, the latter providing a more substantial surface finish. In all cases, the end result can be covered and painted as usual, but GRP resin will provide an outstanding and long lasting finish. Small wings can just have the bare foam covered with iron on film or fabric.

### Cut-outs in foam wings

It is essential to be able to run snakes through foam wings, and make cut-outs for servos and undercarriage mounts. Unfortunately, all cut-outs weaken a foam wing. Strengthening is usually provided by plywood or balsa inserts.

## Joining wing panels

Dihedral braces have been the traditional way of joining built up wings. They should be glued to the leading edge, mainspar and trailing edge. For the lightest models they can be made from

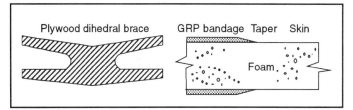

**Figure 236** *Avoid sudden changes in section at the wing joint to prevent potential areas of weakness from stress concentration.*

hard balsa wood, but almost invariably, plywood is preferred. Foam wings can be joined with a bandage and GRP resin across the centre section and extending just beyond the sides of the fuselage.

### Sweep-back

Typical examples of the use of sweep-back are model deltas and flying wings. Some care is necessary to ensure that all the slots for spars as well as the leading and trailing edges are cut to the correct angle. Joining at the centre also requires some thought as simple dihedral braces cannot usually be employed. A good solution is to use centre section spars as can be seen in Figure 237. The 'main' spars can then be matched to the sweep-back angle of the wing. Fortunately, swept-back wings rarely need dihedral so that the construction and joining of both wings on a flat building board is usually a practical proposition.

A saw tooth leading edge is not difficult to construct, as Figure 238 demonstrates. It is one of the simplest ways of improving the performance of swept-back wings at model sizes. It does involve cutting the leading edge into two pieces and splicing it together. With modern adhesives and a leading edge of reasonable cross section, strength should not be a problem.

**Figure 237** *Whether this delta model should be considered a fuselage or wing is debatable.*

## Attachment of wings to the fuselage

There are two popular methods of allowing the wings to be removed from a model. The first is the use of dowels through the fuselage, together with elastic bands. The second involves a forward pointing pair of dowels in the leading edge with wing bolts at the trailing edge. Perhaps more common on gliders than powered models are plug in wings employing metal rods and tubes, or metal or wooden strips and slots. Finally the tongue and groove system has retained its following, offering an easy knock off solution without damage.

### Cabane struts

For a monoplane with a parasol layout, for a biplane or a triplane, cabane struts are necessary. These can be made from piano wire, metal strip or tubing. The methods of attaching them to both the wing and fuselage are many and varied. A number of these are illustrated in Figure 240. Their shape in three dimensions needs to be worked out carefully before their construction commences.

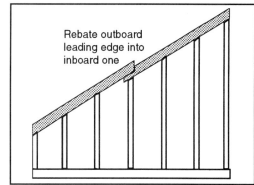

**Figure 238** *The joint in the leading edge of a swept wing with a saw tooth leading edge is unlikely to cause any structural weakness.*

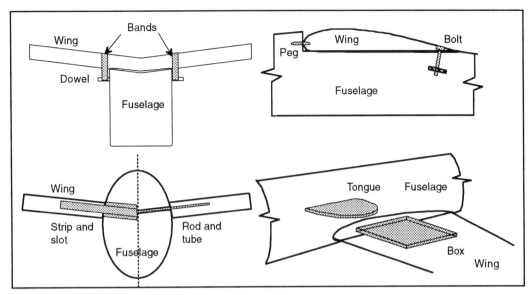

**Figure 239** *There are a number of ways of attaching wings to fuselages. The most common are elastic bands and dowels or pegs and wing bolts.*

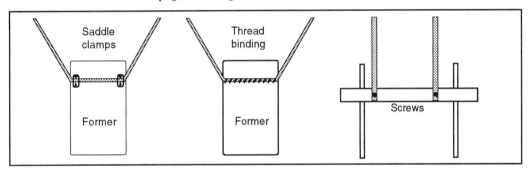

**Figure 240** *Wire cabane struts can be clamped or bound to formers. Metal strip can be screwed to hardwood longerons – often engine bearers.*

Wood can also be used to make cabanes, either hardwood or ply. The advantage of wooden cabanes is that they can easily be designed as part of, and glued into, the fuselage. Whichever method is employed, accuracy of construction and attachment to the fuselage is essential if the correct wing angle of incidence is to be maintained.

## Wing struts and rigging.

Many biplanes and some monoplanes use wing struts and the construction of these requires careful thought. The factors to be considered are whether these struts are for show, or are going to carry loads in flight, or on landing for that

matter. There is also the question of whether rigging wires will be added, just for show or to take real loads.

**Figure 241** *A typical cabane system built from aluminium strips.*

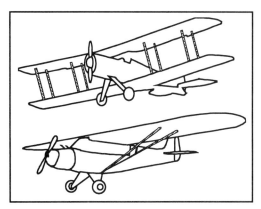

**Figure 242** *Typical biplane and monoplane struts may be very different in size and construction.*

The choice of material for any strut depends on the loading it is likely to have to withstand. Decorative struts can be built from balsa, but load carrying ones are better made from hardwood, ply or metal. If made from wood, consideration needs to be given to the end attachment. Metal strip or wire, drilled and epoxied into the end of the strut, can produce a neat attachment.

Rigging can be functional and make use of nylon covered fishing trace, which consists of a number of twisted steel wires with a rustproof covering. It is available in a wide range of strengths from a few to many tens of kilograms (pounds).

Decorative rigging can make use of shirring elastic, a mono filament elastic covered with a

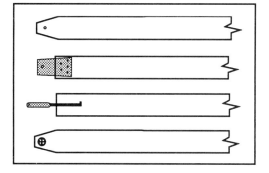

**Figure 243** *The attachment hole may be in the wooden strut itself or a metal plate epoxied into the strut. Alternatively, a clevis and rod may be built in or press stud attachment used.*

**Figure 244** *Many biplanes have a mass of struts and rigging wires, often adding essential strength to the airframe.*

cotton sheath and available from drapery stores. In either case, fittings will be required to attach the rigging wires to the wing and fuselage. These can be made from small pieces of ply or metal sheet, cut to the appropriate shape and drilled. Alternatively, small metal screw eyes can be purchased or even fabricated from wire.

## Tailplanes and fins

Fins and tailplanes are generally placed a long way aft of the centre of gravity, so their construction needs to be light weight. They must also be warp resistant and securely attached to the fuselage; normally at right angles to each other with the elevator and rudder at their trailing edges.

The tail surfaces can be glued directly to the fuselage, in which case they will often need additional support in the form of triangular balsa strip. This has the advantage that any sort of fairing will reduce interference drag. The alternative is to cut slots in the fuselage to give the surfaces greater support.

It is important to consider the way the control surfaces are going to be attached to the tailplane and fin. Many hinging systems, when used with built up surfaces, require a meaty rear spar or balsa blocks in front of the spar to house the hinges. In fact, the construction method may well be influenced by the choice of hinges and vice versa.

### All sheet

Undoubtedly the most popular way of building a tailplane or fin is to cut it from balsa sheet, but

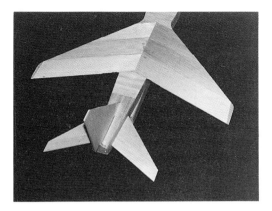

**Figure 245** *All sheet tail surfaces with cross grain tips are quick to build.*

such a solution is prone to warp. Better is to fit tips with the balsa grain across, as shown in Figure 246.

The thickness of the sheet will vary from 3mm (1/8") for small models up to 9mm (3/8") for 10cc (0.60) powered ones. Holes can be cut in the sheet to reduce the overall weight. This also gives an attractive effect when a translucent covering material is employed.

## Built up

To build even lighter surfaces, a balsa framework provides one of the best solutions of all. A tailplane can easily be constructed entirely from lightweight balsa strip, though ribs will be necessary if an aerofoil section is chosen. The tips, if shaped, can be cut from pieces of balsa sheet or even formed in the same way as wing tips.

**Figure 247** *The tail surfaces of this model feature built-up construction with lightening holes in the all sheet control surfaces.*

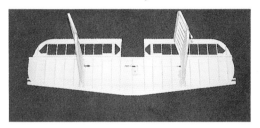

**Figure 248** *Twin fins and tailplane using sheet and rib construction for the main surfaces and open structures for the control surfaces.*

### Sheet cored

For a lightweight structure with each rib clearly apparent, a 1.5mm (1/16") balsa sheet core can be sandwiched between two frameworks. This is shown in Figure 249 overleaf. Complex aerofoil sections can be incorporated, though each rib will have to be cut in half longitudinally.

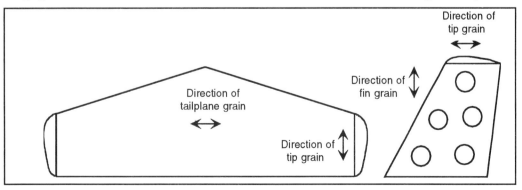

**Figure 246** *Tail surfaces resist warping better if fitted with cross grain tips. Lightening holes are optional.*

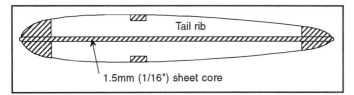

**Figure 249** *Tail surfaces built around a thin balsa sheet core provide strong lightweight structures and can involve complex shapes if desired.*

## Foam

Sheet covered foam cores provide a rapid building solution but, due to their weight, are less than ideal from a balance point of view if the model has a long fuselage. However, if constructed with lightening holes and a lightweight skinning, they can provide a rapid and low cost solution.

## V or butterfly tails

From a constructional point of view, the only difference in building a V or butterfly tail is the need to provide some method of mounting the two surfaces at an angle to each other and the fuselage. This may involve the use of lightweight 'dihedral' braces and a V groove in the top of the fuselage, or just the provision of suitably angled slots in the fuselage sides.

## Attachment to the fuselage

The main reason for even considering attachment of the tailplane to the fuselage is the paramount requirement for accuracy relative to the fuselage datum line or, more importantly, to the angle of incidence of the wing. All the work on design in this area can come to nought if constructional accuracy is not attained. Placing the tail on the top surface of fuselage, or on the underside are the easiest options from a constructional point of view and are the most reliable in getting the tailplane setting correct. A tail mid mounted in the fuselage is somewhat harder, while mounting it half way up or on the top of the fin presents the greatest difficulties.

In the latter two cases, the leverage on the fin can be large, fitting in the control runs to the elevator function difficult, and engine vibration a problem if the fin is insufficiently rigid. Nevertheless, given a stout fin (not all sheet) a satisfactory solution is not hard to attain.

The past practice of attaching the tailplane to the fuselage by rubber bands is not a good one,

since any movement of this surface will affect the neutral of the elevator due to an increase or reduction in the length of the control run.

All moving tailplanes produce installation problems all of their own. They need to be mounted with a pivot point through the fuselage; the pivot lying at around 25 % mean chord back from the leading edge. How this may be achieved is covered in the next chapter.

# Types of undercarriage

The function of an undercarriage is to enable a model to take-off from the ground and arrive back safely again. During flight, the weight and drag it produces are entirely unproductive. Both of these factors need consideration when selecting the type of undercarriage to be fitted to a new model. Later in this chapter, details are given of floats and hulls for water planes as well as skis for use when flying off snow.

## Fixed

The simplest solution for a model is to land on its belly or a skid. A ply under surface, or strip of spruce in the case of a skid, are easy to construct and may be reinforced with GRP if the landing area is rough. A fixed undercarriage should be as light as possible and is usually made

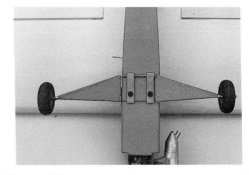

**Figure 250** *A pair of aluminium clamps hold this undercarriage in place. The strut fairings are made from iron-on film.*

**Figure 251** *Aluminium alloy mounts provide stylish undercarriages which are really very simple to construct.*

from piano wire. Unfortunately, it is likely to produce a lot of drag. For this reason, it is not uncommon to find some sort of streamlining applied to such a design, although spatted wheels can give problems when operating off less than bowling green smooth grass. A wire frame can be folded from piano wire and covered with iron on film to reduce drag.

Mainwheels can be fixed to a shaped aluminium plate with nuts and bolts or a length of piano wire bent to match the aluminium plate. This provides a practical but unsprung undercarriage mount.

GRP mounts of a similar shape also provide some degree of springing and can be made very light. They can also be reinforced with carbon fibres to increase strength or reduce weight. Both aluminium and GRP mounts result in realistic looking legs similar to those found on the ubiquitous Piper Cub and other light aircraft.

## Sprung

Some sort of springing is almost essential to help absorb the impact of a less than perfect landing.

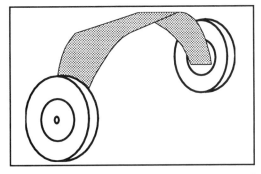

**Figure 252** *A GRP mount usually has curved legs to avoid stress build up.*

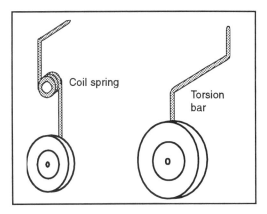

**Figure 253** *Sprung undercarriage legs can either use a coil spring or a torsion bar.*

Many fixed undercarriages rely simply on the springing of the leg material, but coil springs are now the norm for noselegs, and torsion bar springing is common on mainlegs.

This does not rule out any other form of suspension. Coil springs, particularly when housed in telescopic brass tubes can simulate realistic oleo operation. To locate and maintain the undercarriage in position, swinging struts can be fabricated from piano wire, which is heavy, brass tube that is surprisingly strong and easily replaced if damaged, or even lengths of hardwood strip.

For a more complex design, a cardboard cut-out of the various struts, hinged with pins, will ensure that the correct geometry has been achieved before metal is cut. All the extra constructional effort of a working system

**Figure 254** *A bird's nest of struts and wires, together with vertical springs add authenticity to this old timer.*

**Figure 255** *A torsion bar sprung undercarriage assisted by coil springs mounted in telescopic brass tubes. This undercarriage is fitted to an autogyro which can have a high vertical rate of descent at touchdown.*

becomes worthwhile when you are finally able to watch the vertical movement of the undercarriage struts on take-off and landing.

## Retracts

A retractable undercarriage may not be the prime consideration for your average model, but they are commonly found on aerobatic models and, of course, scale ones. The important factors to consider are the retraction mechanism, mounting, wheel wells and doors.

### Retraction mechanism

Commercial retracts are normally raised and lowered by one of three systems. First and most popular are those operated by air pressure. Second come the ones moved by a powerful retract servo and third are those with a built-in electric motor, usually operating the legs by a screw jack mechanism.

### Mounting

Blocks fitted in foam wings or plywood pieces glued to the ribs and main spars are by far the easiest way of locating the undercarriage legs. They can easily be tailored to suit the mounting lugs found on each retract leg. As with fixed undercarriages, it is essential that the mounting system spreads the loads evenly through the airframe, either by careful structural design or by judicious GRP reinforcement.

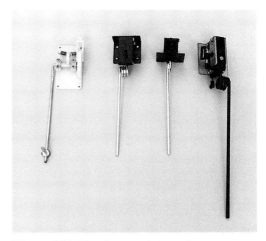

**Figure 256** *The shape and sizes of retracts vary considerably, as does the position of the mounting lugs.*

### Wheel wells

Wheel wells need to be larger than those necessary just to house the wheels. This is because during take-off and landing, the undercarriage legs will be subjected to quite a pounding and the legs may well bend or the wheels get clogged up with dirt.

If the size of the wheel well is insufficient to take this into account, the wheels may well foul the sides of the wells or at worse jam in the up position. This can cause embarrassment when trying to land, and is also likely to run the undercarriage battery flat in the case of electrically operated systems.

### Undercarriage doors

Doors that close over the undercarriage reduce drag in flight and add to the attractiveness of the model. However, serious consideration needs to be given both to their hinging and to the method by which they are operated. Connection to the undercarriage leg by wire or thread is feasible, while a separate servo is yet another possibility.

## Tricycle or tail dragger

### Noselegs

The majority of R/C trainers use a noseleg configuration because of its advantages.

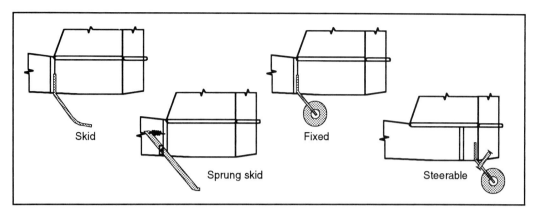

**Figure 257** *Either a skid or a tailwheel can be used, the latter with or without steering. Castoring tailwheels can cause ground looping difficulties.*

Steerable nosewheels provide excellent control on the ground, particularly when taxying at low speeds. A snake is a convenient way of running the connection down from the rudder servo to the noseleg and can be used to provide a degree of bump protection for the rudder servo (or aileron servo if rudder control is not fitted).

### Tail draggers

A tailwheel configuration provides a lighter weight, lower drag form of undercarriage. Once the difficulties of managing to keep straight on take-off have been mastered, it is generally preferred to a nosewheel solution.

Clearly a simple skid can be employed at the rear in a tail dragger configuration, made from wood or piano wire. In either case some springing is possible. The next stage up is to use a tailwheel. This may be fixed, or a steerable unit connected either to the rudder or directly to the servo to provide the ultimate solution for ground steering.

Free castoring tailwheels can cause problems in ground handling, with a particular propensity to ground looping if the throttle is opened too fast. All tailwheels need a substantial tail post or rear former for attachment, but great care is needed to avoid a build up of weight in this area.

## Wheels

Having looked at the undercarriage layout, consideration must now be given to the wheels themselves. First, what size should they be? The smoother the take-off strip, the smaller the acceptable diameter and, of course, with smaller size comes a weight and drag reduction. Obviously, the larger the wheels, the better they will be able to cope with the bumpiness and grass tussocks found on the average club strip.

Wheels should be selected to suit the model from the wide range of commercially available items. The key factors to bear in mind are:

- The size of the model
- The weight of the model
- The type of model
- The surface of the flying strip
- Whether the wheel will be a mainwheel, nosewheel or tailwheel

For a fast model, the drag of the wheels and the undercarriage legs is a factor. Thin section wheels can be an advantage here, and spats should also be considered.

**Figure 258** *Closed loop control of the rudder with tailwheel steering and a flexible connection to prevent jolts being transmitted to the servo.*

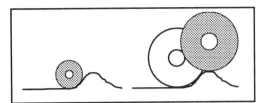

**Figure 259** *A large wheel will ride over the bumps found on the average flying field which may well completely stop a small one.*

## Wheel spats

Wheel spats can look very attractive and do reduce the drag caused by the wheels. They can be built up from a mixture of ply and balsa wood or formed from plastics such as ABS or GRP. Consideration needs to be given to their durability in relation to the roughness of the strip from which the model is to fly. More important is their method of attachment to the undercarriage legs and the ease with which they can be removed for repairs. The best solution is to build a small framework of metal wire into the spat and then solder it to the undercarriage leg.

## Installation

Noselegs are normally attached to the engine firewall. Many commercial engine mounts include facilities to trap the leg between the mount and the firewall. The best alternative is to fix the leg to the firewall with saddle clamps.

Mainwheel legs can be attached to hardwood blocks with saddle clamps or secured in grooves in the blocks by straps. Drilled vertical blocks are necessary to anchor the end of the torque rods.

**Figure 260** *A selection of different sizes and types of wheels.*

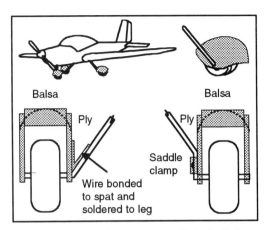

**Figure 261** *Wheel spats can easily be built from ply and balsa as an alternative to ABS or GRP.*

These block can be attached to wing ribs, which may need to be reinforced. In the case of foam wings, the blocks can be glued into suitable cut outs. Equally common are fuselage mounted main legs. These are installed in the same way as the wing mounted ones, except that it is usual to place one torque rod behind the other as shown in Figure 263.

Where the mainwheels are fitted to an aluminium mount or piano wire frame, there are several ways of fixing the mount to the fuselage of a model. It can be held on with elastic bands and dowels, clamped at the rear, with bands and a dowel at the front, screwed in place, or even plugged in. The choice much depends on the landing skill of the pilot, the roughness of the

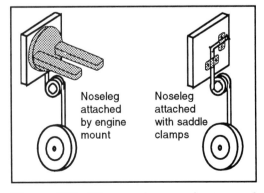

**Figure 262** *The noseleg can be trapped behind a purpose-designed commercial engine mount or attached to the firewall using saddle clamps.*

**Figure 263** *Saddle clamps hold both mainwheels in place with the torsion bars running the width of the fuselage.*

flight field and the desire to build in a degree of bouncability.

Regardless of the method of installation selected, mainwheels should be located some 20% to 25% of the wing span apart to ensure adequate lateral stability on the ground.

## Operating off water

There are three main problems for any model which flies off water. The first is the need to make the model waterproof. The second is the requirement that it floats correctly in the water and does not try to dig its nose in as soon as it starts to move. Finally, spray thrown up by a hull or floats can get into the propeller disc and stop the engine during take-off. The subject of float planes and seaplanes could easily occupy

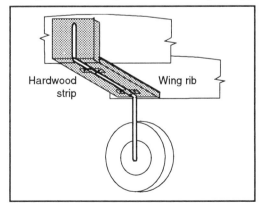

**Figure 264** *Torque rod mainleg attachments use a pair of saddle clamps or a grooved slot and retaining strips.*

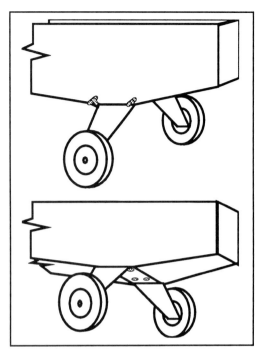

**Figure 265** *Typical methods of attaching the main undercarriage using dowels and elastic bands (top) and nuts and bolts (bottom).*

a whole book. The aim here is solely to show how to produce a working pair of floats or a seaplane hull.

### Floats

A pair of floats can easily be built to replace an existing wheeled undercarriage. They need to displace around twice the all-up weight of the model. This is simple in the metric system. For each kilogram of model weight (including the weight of the floats), the volume of each float must be 1,000 cc. In imperial units, for each pound of weight, the volume of each float needs to be 27 cu in.

Figure 267 overleaf indicates suitable proportions for a pair of floats. The dimensions are related to the length of the fuselage and should be increased if the fuselage is particularly short and vice versa. They can be cut from foam or built up from balsa and ply.

Anti-spray strips can be fitted to the chines, the corners formed between the V bottom and sides of the hull, to reduce the spray thrown up

**Figure 266** *A model fitted with old timer floats. Behind is a more modern design of float.*

by the floats. A small water rudder, connected by a link to the air rudder, will significantly improve the ability to turn on the water, particularly if there is any significant wind blowing.

Any model needs to have its floats fitted so that the centre of gravity lies over the step. Remember that the weight of the floats themselves may well move the centre of gravity of the whole model.

The purpose of the step is to prevent porpoising on take-off and landing. Hard points will allow piano wire struts to be attached to the floats with saddle clamps. Care must be taken to ensure that the floats are parallel to the fuselage datum to avoid excessive drag in the air.

The sit of the model on the water must be such that the wing is at a small angle of incidence, otherwise the model will be unable to lift off the water. For operation off damp grass,

it may be necessary to reinforce the underside of the floats.

## Seaplanes

While there are many similarities between float planes and seaplanes, the hull design of the latter needs special examination. Fundamentally, the hull can be designed to the same basic layout as a float. Lateral stability on the water is normally provided by the provision of wing tip floats. The use of a waterproof glue in construction is obviously essential.

Again, the centre of gravity should lie on or just forward of the step and a V hull is the norm. The angle of the V should be steepest at the nose or bows of the seaplane and reduce aft of the step in a natural blend. Anti-spray strakes can be fitted and a water rudder is also a good idea.

## Wing tip floats

To keep the model on a level keel on the water, some form of wing floats are necessary. Two different types are popular. The first are floats attached to the wings by struts, while the other type are in the form of a solid structure attached to the wing. Typical dimensions for both are shown in Figure 269.

The floats should be mounted so that they are both just touching the water when the model is floating wings level. Their volume is defined in terms of the width or beam of the fuselage.

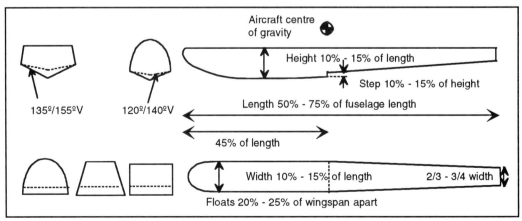

**Figure 267** *Floats are not difficult to design and produce. They can provide additional pleasure flying off water or even damp grass.*

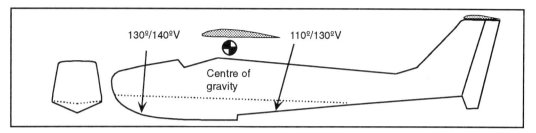

**Figure 268** *The typical proportions of a seaplane hull to ensure a new design can smoothly take-off.*

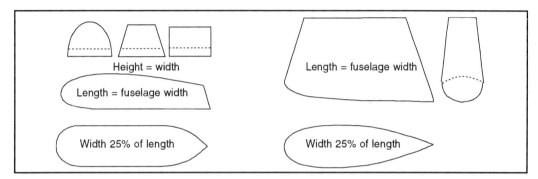

**Figure 269** *Two entirely different types of float. That on the left is attached to the wing by wood or wire struts, that on the right attaches directly onto the wing.*

Clearly the nearer to the wing tips they are mounted the smaller and lighter they should be and vice versa.

To avoid water loops, tip floats should be attached to the wing at roughly the half span point. Their under surfaces should be sloped outwards by around 3° to 5° and, for the right-hand design, the bottom of the underside should slope down 3° from front to rear.

## Operating off snow

Skis, like floats, can be fitted to most models. For those in the UK, the number of occasions when they can be used is fairly limited, so the ability to remove them is an essential requisite. As with floats, they must be mounted parallel to the fuselage datum.

**Figure 270** *An old seaplane hull, which has seen much use, shows a typical profile.*

The size of skis can easily be determined from the graph in Figure 271, which relates individual ski size to total aircraft weight. Avoid the trap of skis which are too small and sink into the snow. Skis are best made from several laminations of good quality ply, bent up at the front, and painted or varnished. The under surface should be waxed each time they are used.

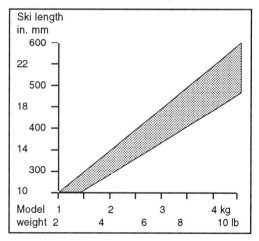

**Figure 271** *The length of skis required is directly related to the weight of the model.*

The width of the skis is directly related to their length and they should be mounted parallel to the fuselage datum with the centre of gravity half way along their length. The distance between skis should be the same as the distance between the wheels of a conventional undercarriage to ensure adequate lateral stability on the ground.

Some form of springing is also a good idea to absorb the bumps below what appears to be a smooth surface of snow. A typical solution is illustrated in Figure 273. These particular skis are a direct plug-in replacement for an existing wheeled undercarriage and can be fitted in minutes.

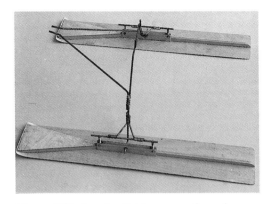

**Figure 273** *A pair of skis can easily replace an existing undercarriage at the first sign of snow.*

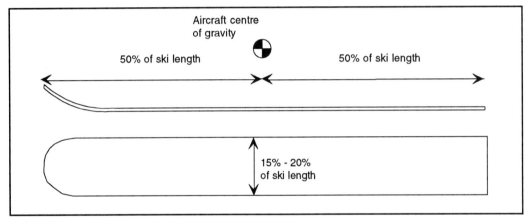

**Figure 272** *While snow is not common in much of the UK, a pair of skis that can be fitted in place of the mainwheels can provide a great thrill when it does arrive.*

# 10 Control configurations

## Primary controls

Any conventional model will use three primary controls; elevator, ailerons and rudder. Some more specialised designs may employ elevons in place of elevators and ailerons, or a V or butterfly tail where the functions of elevator and rudder are combined in ruddevators. Airbrakes and flaps may also form part of the model.

It is comparatively rare to find control surfaces built from anything other than sheet balsa or shaped balsa trailing edge. Often during the design process, an important point that is missed is the need to provide a secure method of hinging. How this is achieved is very dependent on the construction method employed.

## Elevators

Elevators are normally hinged to the rear of the tailplane and provide control in the pitching plane. The angular movement of the elevator necessary to obtain a given change of attitude varies with speed. A low speed model will require a larger movement than a high speed one. This is a natural effect arising from the increased effectiveness of any deflected surface as speed increases.

The four common methods of construction involve

- Cutting the required shape from sheet balsa
- Cutting the required shape from trailing edge section
- Building up the elevators from balsa strip and sheet
- Using a balsa core with balsa strip leading edge, trailing edge and ribs either side

Often, separate elevator halves offer an attractive design solution and joining them together requires careful thought. The two halves may be connected

**Figure 274** *This particular biplane features twin tailplanes and elevators and triple fins and rudders.*

by a bifurcated elevator pushrod from the servo, or with a strip of plywood, spruce or dowel. Metal joiners provide a secure method but do increase tail weight.

## Ailerons

Two types of ailerons are commonly used, inset ones where the aileron is part of the outboard wing and strip ailerons which are hinged to the trailing edge of the wing. Both are usually made from strips of trailing edge section, although inset ailerons are frequently built-up structures similar to those used in wings. Differential movement can be achieved easily using:

- Offset aileron horns
- Offset servo arms
- Offset interconnecting bell cranks
- A pair of servos and the facilities of a computerised transmitter

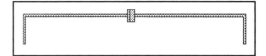

**Figure 275** *A commercially available elevator joiner provides a simple yet strong way of joining two halves of an elevator to a single servo.*

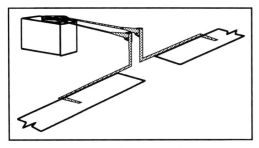

**Figure 276** *The simplicity of the linkage to strip ailerons from a central wing mounted servo.*

Inset ailerons are more difficult to make and hinge properly than elevators. Tube and wire hinges are often preferred since they give free movement without slop. The generous up and down movement required normally calls for a short control horn. It is often possible to include the push rod within the main wing section, although this is obviously not essential.

Strip ailerons are hinged directly to the wing trailing edge in the same manner as rudders or elevators and the necessary linkage can be simplified to a degree, as shown in Figure 276.

### Aileron hinges

Ailerons can be hinged at the top, in the middle, and occasionally at the bottom. They are also often built with inset hinges. Consideration also needs to be given to using a sealed type of hinge, which can significantly improve the performance of inset ailerons.

### Differential and Frise ailerons

To avoid adverse yaw, and the consequent reduction of effectiveness when ailerons are used, either differential or Frise ailerons should be used. Differential is simple to design into the linkage and Figure 278 shows a number of alternatives. Whichever solution is chosen, it is important that a decision is

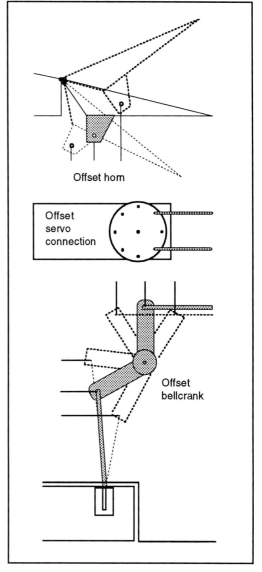

**Figure 278** *Aileron differential can be built into a model with offset horns or an offset bell crank. Alternatively it can be introduced at the servo arm.*

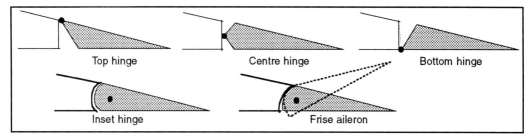

**Figure 277** *There are various options when selecting the position of the hinges of any aileron.*

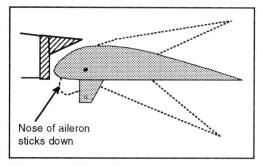

**Figure 279** *When a Frise aileron is moved up, its nose sticks down into the airstream, creating drag in the direction of the required turn.*

made before construction starts, rather than when the radio is finally being installed.

Frise (pronounced freeze) ailerons call for inset hinges, allowing the nose of the aileron to project down into the airstream when the aileron is raised. This requires careful thought about the cross section of the aileron and wing around the hinge point. A typical Frise aileron installation is shown in Figure 279.

There is a need for some form of triangular strip to fair in the top of the aileron to the upper wing surface. The complexity of a Frise aileron is rarely justified, when compared with the relative simplicity of aileron differential.

### Spoilers as ailerons

The construction of spoilers for use as ailerons is exactly the same as for wing mounted airbrakes, although they may well be located further outboard. Naturally they are connected up so that only one is deployed at a time. Details of how to make them is given shortly in the section of this chapter dealing with airbrakes.

### Elevons

The construction of elevons is virtually identical to that of elevators and ailerons. The use of elevons, however, requires some form of mixer, now a common option on most transmitters. For those without this facility, an on board electronic or mechanical mixer is a relatively straightforward solution. Both of these items are easily obtained from model shops, but the

"THEY'RE MY FREEZE AILERONS !!!"

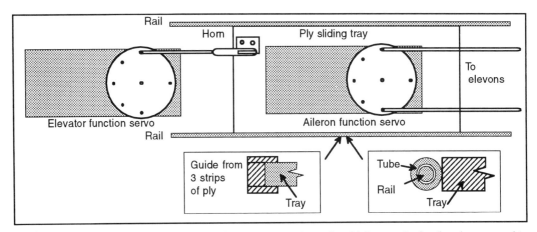

**Figure 280** *A sliding tray can easily be made using piano wire rails with brass tube fixed to the tray or thin plywood grooves in which the tray slides.*

economic alternative is to make the sliding tray shown in Figure 280.

## Rudders

Rudders need to be light as they are invariably fitted at the rear of the aircraft. They are a simple control and usually made from balsa sheet.

A built-up balsa framework, or any of the four methods used for building elevators may be employed. Again, some thought is needed with a built-up rudder when selecting the type and positioning of the hinges and the control horn.

## All moving tails

All moving tails tend to be made in two halves joined by a pair of steel rods. One is the pivot; the other fixed to the actuating arm. The tail must always be securely attached to the fuselage or fin. Exactly the same rules apply when building an all moving fin.

## Airbrakes

Figure 282 shows two of the more popular types of wing mounted airbrake installations. The first uses plates which hinge out of the wings. The second features a scissors mechanism to lift the airbrake. The airbrakes themselves can be made from balsa sheet or ply, but must be sufficiently stiff not to distort when deployed in the air-stream.

Figure 283 shows the use of a split rudder as an airbrake, requiring the use of two mixed channels for correct operation. Two rudders are built, usually from sheet balsa, and hinged side by side at the rear of the fin. They operate in unison for the rudder function and in opposite directions to give an airbrake effect. There is not much room for hinging and it is essential that the rudders do not foul each other when working together in rudder mode.

Airbrakes are still a fairly unusual item on any powered aircraft, but they can prove necessary

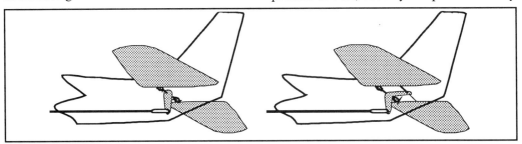

**Figure 281** *All moving tails are either operated by an elevator joiner or incorporate a pair of rods, one acting as the pivot and the other as the operating arm.*

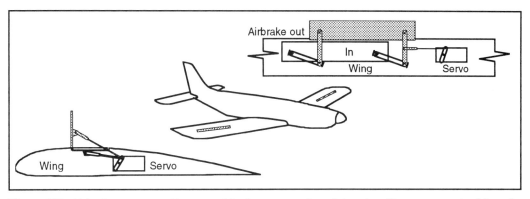

**Figure 282** *Airbrakes are normally mounted in the outer section of the wing. The power required from the servo is a major consideration when deciding whether to use a system operating on a scissors mechanism (top diagram) or one involving hinging up the airbrake (bottom sketch).*

with any high powered low drag design, as well as providing some interesting design and construction points. Spoilers used to provide aileron control are built in exactly the same way as airbrakes.

**Figure 283** *A split rudder airbrake can help to avoid trim changes when the airbrake is operated.*

## Simple and split flaps

Simple flaps can be constructed and hinged in a very similar way to ailerons. There is only one possible problem and that concerns the use of torque rods for both flaps and ailerons. In this case, a concentric tube-based system is usually the best. The alternative is to use snakes to the outboard ailerons or to use strip ailerons with a mixed aileron/flap function.

Split flaps, on the other hand, need to be thin to recess smoothly into the under surface of the wing. The use of ply or Liteply, possibly with thin reinforcing strips to prevent warping, will provide a quick and easy solution.

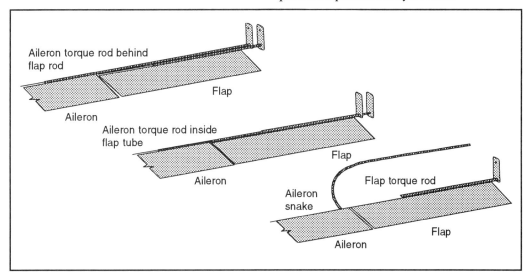

**Figure 284** *Three alternative ways of designing the control connections to outboard ailerons with inboard flaps.*

**Figure 285** *Split flaps made from 0.8mm (1/32")
balsa faced on each side with 0.4mm (1/64") ply.*

## Hinging

The hinges of any control surface need to be:

- Easy to fit
- Simple to align
- Secure
- Strong
- Free to move
- Light weight

There is a wide range of choice and each type has clear advantages and snags. A choice of preferred type must often be made at the design stage.

To reduce the effort required by the servo, the hinge line can be moved back from the leading

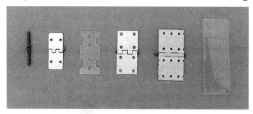

**Figure 286** *Different types of hinges to meet a variety of requirements. From left to right, a point hinge, small leaf and pin, moulded flexible, medium and large leaf and pin, and mylar strip.*

edge, as mentioned in Chapter 7. This is fairly straightforward if point or wire and tube hinges are adopted. However, a hinge line on the leading edge is satisfactory on most designs.

## The radio equipment

The radio is the heart of any R/C model and care is required to ensure it provides positive slop-free control. All parts need to be protected from vibration and the possibility of an unplanned impact with the ground.

### Planning the installation

It's no use designing and building a model without giving early thought to the installation of the radio equipment. For a small model, this may, in any case, involve a fair amount of shoe horning in of the various radio components.

The radio, particularly the battery, should be used to balance the model, rather than adding lead ballast. A larger battery can also be useful if long flights are planned or if the model needs ballast to bring the centre of gravity to the correct position.

For larger models, routes for the control linkages are important. If all the radio equipment is currently installed in an existing model, it can be useful to make up space models of servos, battery packs and receivers. Typical examples are shown in Figure 287.

One thing that often gets forgotten is where to put the receiver aerial. This is not normally a problem, except with small models and unconventional ones. Careful planning is

| Type | Cost | Ease of fitting | Air leaks | Flexibility | Strength |
|------|------|-----------------|-----------|-------------|----------|
| Leaf and pin | High | Moderate | Yes | Excellent | High |
| Point hinge | High | Easy | Yes | Excellent | High |
| Moulded flexible | High | Moderate | Yes | Good | Medium |
| Mylar strip | Medium | Moderate | Possible | Good | Medium |
| Tube and wire | Medium | Difficult | Yes | Excellent | High |
| Film covering | Low | Moderate | No | Good | Medium |
| Stitched material | High | Easy | No | Good | High |
| Thread | Low | Difficult | Yes | Excellent | Medium |

**Table 30** *The main characteristics of the various types of hinges, that will affect the choice made for any particular application.*

| Item | Wt g | Wt oz | Item | Wt g | Wt oz |
|---|---|---|---|---|---|
| Club receiver | 60 | 2 | 150 mAh Nicad | 32 | 1.2 |
| Lightweight receiver | 30 | 1 | 225 mAh Nicad | 45 | 1.6 |
| Standard servo | 50 | 1¾ | 500 mAh Nicad | 76 | 2.7 |
| Mini servo | 25 - 30 | 1 | 850 mAh Nicad | 100 | 3.6 |
| Micro servo | 15 | ½ | 1200 mAh Nicad | 112 | 4 |
| High power servo | 90 | 3 | Electric flight switch | 60 | 2 |
| Retract servo | 50 | 1¾ | Speed controller | 90 | 3 |

**Table 31** *Typical weights of the various parts of a typical airborne pack.*

necessary, particularly with a pusher layout where the propeller is ideally placed to cut through the aerial wire if it is left to trail. A route out to a wing tip can be made using a snake outer or drinking straws.

### Number and positioning of servos

Thinking about a four channel model, it is common sense to mount the elevator, rudder and throttle servos in the fuselage, but what about the aileron servos? One in the wing centre section is usual, though care must be taken to ensure it doesn't foul any items in the fuselage when the wing is fixed in place. The alternative is a pair of servos, each located behind the aileron itself, if the wing is thick enough to house them. This does ensure short slop-free connections.

Servo arms come in a wide variety of shapes and sizes. They should be selected to suit the size of the model and the power required to move the appropriate control. When designing the servo installations and control linkages, thought must be given to the most suitable type of output arm. It must be long enough to give the desired movement and have a selection of holes in the required positions if offset movement is to be incorporated. Where space is tight, removing one side of the servo arm often solves the problem.

## Control runs

Whatever method is employed for connecting the servos to the controls, it must provide a

**Figure 288** *On some models, there is sufficient space to install four servos abreast.*

**Figure 289** *Seven servo arms from two different manufacturers illustrate the wide range of different configurations available.*

**Figure 287** *The receiver and servo space models are empty plastic housings. The battery flat pack is balsa wrapped in masking tape, while the square pack is an old empty case.*

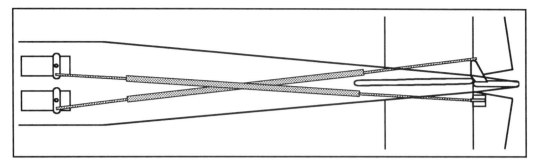

**Figure 290** *Crossing push rods provide a neat solution to the connection of elevator and rudder to a pair of servos mounted side by side in the fuselage.*

lightweight, free movement without slop or parts touching or rubbing.

### Push rods

The main requirement is that any linkage should be rigid and not able to flex. It should also be as light as possible. This is why the normal preference is push rods of hard 6mm (¼") to 12mm (½") square balsa, depending on the size of model, with wire end fittings bound on. However, alternative materials such as birch dowels or GRP arrow shafts are equally acceptable providing they do not increase the rear end weight of the model.

### Bell cranks

When designing control linkages, particularly to ailerons, the use of bell cranks can be invaluable. Where corners have to be turned or where differential control movement is needed, their employment is all but essential. They are normally supplied with angles of 180°, 90° or 60°. Mounted on a small piece of ply, they can be installed in any convenient corner.

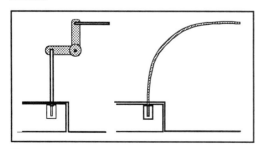

**Figure 291** *Either a bell crank or a snake can be used turn a control linkage through 90°.*

### Snakes

Snakes are popular for awkward linkages, such as those to inset ailerons, but any substantial curve will involve slop in the linkage, resulting in a sloppy neutral and the possibility of flutter. Consideration of this slop should be balanced against the same phenomenon found if a pair of push rods and a bell crank are employed to turn the control run through ninety degrees.

### Closed loop controls

The use of wire fishing trace, or commercially available specialist wire, to provide closed loop controls provides a light, positive method of operating the controls without any slop. It can, however, cause wear to the servo main bearing if not a ball raced one.

An intermediate arm can be employed to overcome this difficulty and also make trim adjustments simple. In addition, commercial closed loop systems can be purchased with a built-in tension adjuster. Figure 294 shows just such a solution.

**Figure 292** *It is essential to anchor snakes where they pass through formers to minimise slop and avoid the possibility of flutter.*

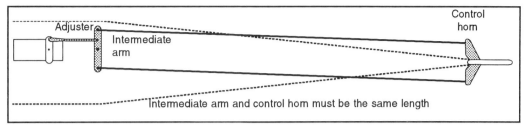

**Figure 293** *Closed loop controls are the least sloppy, giving positive control and minimising the risks of control surface flutter.*

Some thought is necessary to ensure that the wires can run straight to the control surfaces without fouling any part of the airframe, particularly at the point where they emerge from the fuselage.

Closed loop controls do minimise the weight of the control connections at the rear of the model and this alone can be justification for their use.

## Horns

There are really only three factors to consider when thinking about control horns. The first is their length, the second is their position and the last is the amount of offset, if any, from the hinge line.

There is a wide range of proprietary horns available on the market, of which a selection is shown in Figure 297. They come in a variety of sizes, with different amounts of offset and a number of different attachment methods. Alternatively, horns can be home-made from good quality plywood or plastic sheet and glued into the material of the control surface.

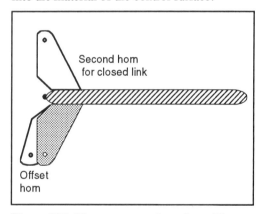

**Figure 296** *There are a number of possible configurations for any control horn.*

**Figure 294** *Three different control surfaces are to be connected by closed loop in this installation.*

**Figure 295** *Typical closed loop connections to rudder and elevator.*

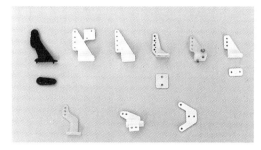

**Figure 297** *Nine different control horns. The one, bottom right, is specially designed for closed loop controls.*

## Clevises

Linkages will need to have a screwed on fitting at one end to allow fine adjustment. This is true even for use with computerised transmitters with neutral adjustment, since it is important to maintain the correct control geometry at the neutral position to avoid undesired differential movement. Z bends can be formed to connect the other end of the control linkage.

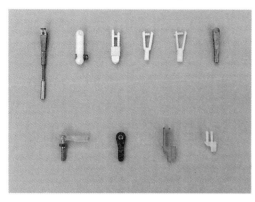

**Figure 298** *Clevises may be metal or plastic. There are ball joints and wire keepers in the bottom row.*

## All moving tails

The control connections to all moving surfaces differ from those required for conventional control surfaces in several ways. First, it is even more important that they are slop free. Secondly, they often make use of a special type of horn, shown in Figure 299. The tail is attached to the fuselage by two steel rods which pass through the two holes in the bell crank.

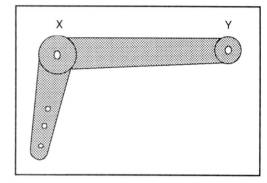

**Figure 299** *For an all moving tail, the surface pivots about a rod passed through X with a second rod through Y transmitting the movement from the servo.*

# 11 Final finishing off

## Cockpits

### Canopies

A canopy may be decorative rather than functional, but unless a suitable commercial one is available, this item will have to be home made. Clear plastic sheet can be formed in a variety of ways, all involving heat, some also involving vacuum forming, over a plug. Household mouldings, such as the Easter egg covering shown in Figure 300, can also provide excellent cockpit canopies.

Commercial canopies are available in a wide range of shapes and sizes and may be used as they are or cropped to provide a different shape and size. Their use will increase the realism of any model for a negligible increase in weight and only a small increase in drag.

### Open cockpits

Any opening in the structure of the fuselage will weaken it. An open cockpit will do just this but may be very desirable as a means of improving the look of a model. Strengthening pieces should be considered around this and any other openings in the fuselage.

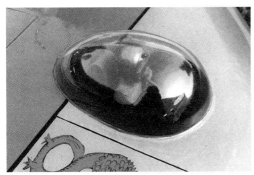

**Figure 300** *An interesting shape of canopy made from one half of the covering of an Easter egg.*

### Pilots

Many people feel a model aircraft without a pilot has something missing. If you are of this view, then the key factor to remember is that apart from adding visual appeal, a pilot also adds unproductive weight to the model.

Fortunately, pilots made from balsa wood or, even better, silicon rubber are very light. The proportions of a simple head and upper torso are shown in Figure 303 overleaf. A full-bodied pilot is rarely visible or needed. Roughly carved

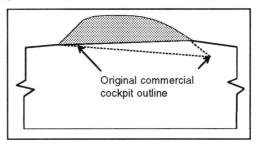

**Figure 301** *Any commercially available canopy can be modified and cut to size.*

**Figure 302** *The pilot and his lady friend add terrific atmosphere to this model of Al's Autogyro.*

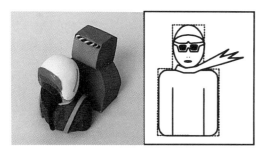

**Figure 303** *A simple head and shoulders jet jockey with ejection seat adds atmosphere to a model. A pilot can be made from two balsa rectangles and a length of coloured material for a scarf.*

and painted, it is surprising how convincing the simplest replica can look. Another alternative is to find a doll, such as Action Man, but here, weight may well prove a stumbling block.

## Hatches

Without any doubt, on most models the opening where the wing attaches to the fuselage provides the best form of access to the radio equipment. There are, however, a number of reasons why this solution will not always work and one or more hatches may be necessary. You may build a one piece model or the configuration of the model may not result in the radio being sited below the wing.

There may, in any case, be a need to get access to the fuel tank and the engine. Hatches always seem to provide some awkward design and

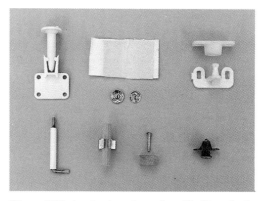

**Figure 305** *A selection of catches. Working clockwise from top left, a commercial catch, Velcro with press studs below, a cupboard catch, a Dzus fastener, a screw and block, a dowel and clip, a spring loaded rod and tube.*

construction problems. Providing lightweight, tidy, easy to operate hatch catches can be far from easy, but provides an interesting challenge.

## Stores

A range of items can add interest to a model and make it look more realistic. Typical are machine guns, bombs and guided missiles, all of which add to the character of almost any design. They can usually be made from bits of balsa and plastic gleaned from the scrap box. Figure 306 shows air-to-air missiles simply made from balsa and card. Their weight is negligible and construction time minimal.

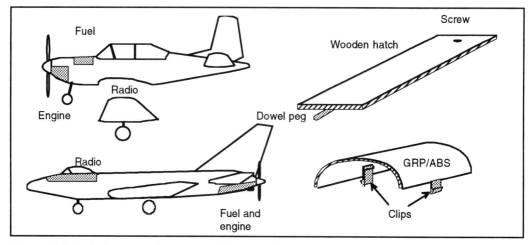

**Figure 304** *Typical access points on two different model layouts. Hatches can be retained with a peg and screw, clips, Velcro, commercial hatch catches or even plastic kitchen cupboard catches.*

**Figure 306** *A pair of missiles adds to the reality of a fun scale jet fighter.*

# Types of covering

The aims of the covering of a model are several and varied. First, the material may be required to make an open structure airtight. Second, it may be needed to aid structural strength or resist dings. Finally, it may form part or all of the final colour scheme and/or fuel-proofer. There is a large choice of covering systems available to today's modeller and thought should be given to the final choice of covering at the design stage.

- Is it required to aid structural strength?
- Are fumes a problem when applying the covering?
- Must it provide the final colouring
- Must it be fuel-proof. If so, to what type of fuel?
- How much strength must it add to the surfaces covered?
- Must it be relatively puncture-proof?
- What weight is acceptable?

Table 32 looks at some of these characteristics for all the more popular covering systems.

## Tissue

As a covering material, tissue may appear to have little place on modern R/C aircraft, but it does offer a cheap and well proven method of strengthening any part of a model which has an all-sheet finish. It is a good medium for covering fuselages and, where wings are covered with heat shrink film, matching paint colours are available. On small models, it may even be the appropriate material for the whole structure, although the ease with which it is punctured makes it an unattractive covering for open structures.

## Nylon

Nylon is much stronger than most other available fabrics or materials for covering a model, be it sheeted or an open structure. What needs to be borne in mind is that nylon shrinks considerably and will distort or warp any inadequately strong structure. Furthermore, the material absorbs a great deal of clear dope (fortunately fairly light) and can also absorb a lot of coloured paint (not so light). However, for longevity, it is only bettered by GRP.

## Heat shrink fabric and film

By far the most popular coverings are the heat shrink, usually self-adhesive, iron-on materials. Their weights and strengths vary considerable, and the following information refers to the popular range made by Solarfilm. Similar materials are produced by other companies under other names. Table 33 compares them with more traditional covering materials.

|  | Tissue | Nylon | Ht shrink film | Ht shrink fabric | Glass skin | GRP |
|---|---|---|---|---|---|---|
| **Structural strength** | Low | High | Medium | High | High | V high |
| **Smell** | High | High | Nil | Nil | Medium | Med/high |
| **Colour** | Some | Some | Excellent | Excellent | None | Good |
| **Fuel proof** | No | No | Excellent | Good | Excellent | Excellent |
| **Strength** | Low | High | Medium | High | High | V high |
| **Puncture resistance** | Low | High | Medium | High | High | V high |
| **Weight** | Low | Medium | Medium | Medium | Med/high | High |

**Table 32** *The characteristics of a number of different covering materials vary considerably.*

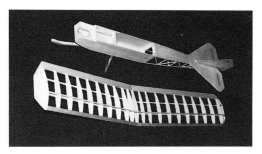

**Figure 307** *All ready for covering, the choice of material to use will depend on the structure of the model and the type of field from which it will be flown.*

Note that where a range of weights is given, paler colours such as yellow and white are heavier than dark colours, with transparent colours the lightest of all.

For those iron on materials which do not have an adhesive backing, Balsaloc may be used as an adhesive, applied to the wooden structure before covering. It contains 50% water, which evaporates and 50% resin, so that even a thin coat will weigh 40gsm (1½ oz per sq. ft).

## Glass skinning

One of the best ways of producing a perfect finish on a wing is to skin it with resin. There are several proprietary types and, with care, they need not add too much weight to a wing. They do provide a really strong solution and, with a little elbow grease, probably the smoothest and glossiest one.

## Painting

The pigments used in any coloured paint are heavy. When the solvent has dried, there is still a major weight penalty to consider. Thus the choice of covering of any model can be dominated by this single factor. Visibility in the air may also be a factor, particularly with unusual configurations. Reds, oranges and yellows give the best contrast with the sky and dayglo colours are particularly visible.

## Decoration

Even the final decoration of a model requires some forethought. It may add a little weight

| Name | Type | Self adhesive | Wt gsm | Wt oz/ sq yd |
|------|------|---------------|--------|--------------|
| Modelspan | Lightweight tissue | No | 12 | ½ |
| Modelspan | Mediumweight tissue | No | 17 | 2/3 |
| Modelspan | Heavyweight tissue | No | 21 | ¾ |
| Japanese silk | Silk | No | 15 | ½ |
| Nylon | Nylon | No | 30 | 1 |
| Airspan | Polyester tissue (needs a light coat of dope) | No | 24 | 1 |
| Litespan | Tough synthetic material to replace tissue /dope | No | 30 | 1 |
| Fibafilm | Super light, fibre reinforced polyester film | No | 42 | 1½ |
| Solarfilm | Iron on plastic film with smooth glossy surface | Yes | 55 - 70 | 2 - 2¾ |
| Solarspan 2000 | Multi layer, heavy duty iron on film, 50% stronger than Solarfilm | Yes | 65 - 75 | 2½ - 3 |
| Solartex | Iron on fabric | Yes | 85 - 95 | 3½ |
| Glosstex | Iron on fabric with high gloss fuel proof paint finish | Yes | 120 - 130 | 4¾ - 5 |
| Solarkote | Iron on polyester film | Yes | 70 - 80 | 2¾ - 3 |

*The weight of pale coloured pigments, used in iron-on materials, is greater than those used in darker colours. Transparent materials are lightest of all.*

**Table 33** *Weights of various covering materials, excluding the weight of any dope, paint or fuel-proofer needed.*

and, with a bit of luck, attractiveness. For a gifted few it can convert a dull looking model to a truly memorable one. Transfers or decals, whether self adhesive or water slide can add interest and lettering can be found in both these forms as well as on sheets of dry rub letters and numbers. Thin self adhesive stripes can be purchase from car accessory shops and used to emphasise the lines and speed potential of a model as well as providing a good divider between different coloured areas of the model.

## Fuel-proofing

For any model which is powered by an internal combustion engine, some sort of fuel-proofing will be essential. The weight of one or two coats of a suitable varnish must be considered when arriving at an estimate of the final all-up weight. The engine and fuel tank bay may benefit

**Figure 308** *My fun scale F20 Tigershark, a free plan given away with* Radio Modeller *June 1984, covered in red and white Solarfilm with thin black stripes is a startling yet scale colour scheme.*

from additional coats. Clearly, this is quite unnecessary on any electric powered model, unless used to provide a more durable finish to the aircraft.

# 12 Drawing the design

## Manual methods

Perhaps the most popular paper for drawing the design a new model is the back of a cigarette packet. However, once the design has been sketched out, a full-size drawing is almost essential to enable the model to be built accurately. For the economically minded, the back of an old roll of wallpaper (not the embossed or pre-glued type) is a cheap solution, but is limited in width to 530 mm or 21". A better solution is to buy some tracing paper as this is tough, allowing many changes to be made with an eraser. It also has some advantages when the time comes to make copies. Mounted on a sheet of white paper, it is the ideal medium and still used by professional drafting staff.

### Making copies

The two main sources of copies are first copy shops with large photocopiers. These will normally

I THOUGHT I'D FLY IT ON MY COMPUTER TOO !

handle sheets up to A0 size. The alternative, if the drawing has been done on tracing paper, is to get a dyeline copy. Shops providing this type of service are usually located close to local council offices, where they provide prints of house plans requiring planning permission.

### Drawing instruments

You will need a good straight edge, or ruler if you like, preferably at least one metre (36") long, as well as a square and protractor. A set of French curves, or a bendy curve is a great help. People seem either to be able to get on only with the former or only with the latter. You will need several pencils from around HB to 2H and a good quality eraser.

### Drawing boards

The drawing board can be the kitchen table, providing it's clean, flat and available. A better proposition is a sheet of hardboard, to which the drawing can be attached with masking tape. Best of all is a real drawing board. New ones are very expensive, but there are many available second-hand, now that professional drawing offices have largely switched to computer aided drawing.

## Computer Aided Drawing (CAD)

If you are fortunate enough to own a personal computer, the world is your oyster as far as computer aided drawing is concerned. CAD is to the drawing board as a word processor is to handwriting. Corrections, copying repeated features like wing ribs, even drawing one wing and repeating it as a mirror image is a trivial task and great time saver. Indeed moving a completed part of the drawing to another part of the paper to avoid crowding is easy.

There are, however, two shortcomings to CAD. The first is that to view the whole drawing shrinks it down to the size of the monitor screen, typically 250 x 200mm (10" x 8"). At this scale, the detail is hidden. You have to get used to working with only part of the drawing visible at any one time; not as difficult as it sounds. The second problem is getting a full-sized print of

**Figure 309** *Drawing up a scale model using a CAD package on a PC. On the screen is the start of a new design for a three engined, electric powered model.*

the drawing. Virtually all CAD packages allow the drawing to be transformed to the universally accepted AutoCad format. There are many organisations which run this professional program together with A0 plotters. They will be able to provide a print from your drawing saved on a floppy disk.

You need to recognise that modern CAD packages give different facilities and set different speed and memory requirements for their host computer. Starting with AutoCad, it is expensive – several thousand pounds – and requires almost daily use to keep familiar with its facilities.

Coming down to the real world, there is AutoCad Light, still several hundred pounds. Then there a number of good low cost programs such as DraftChoice, AutoSketch, EasyCad, DesignCad, ModelCad, TurboCad, and Tommysoft Cad, not to mention the special aeromodelling ones such as Airfoil Plot Pro, Model Design Pro, Afedit and for the specialist, Electro Flight Designer and Soaring Edge. The choice of program may well be influenced by other tasks the user wishes to undertake, such as designing a house extension or new garden layout, drawing electronic circuits or making printed circuit boards.

## Detailed design

Every component of the aircraft must be drawn in two dimensions and, for three dimensional items, a three-view may be necessary. It is a good

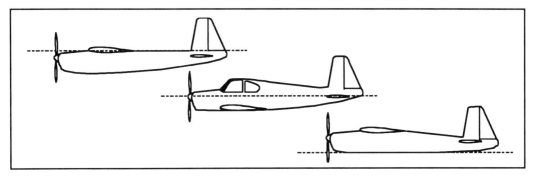

**Figure 310** *Three different fuselages with top, centre and bottom datum lines shown dotted.*

idea to start by choosing an aerofoil as this is essential before either the wing or fuselage outlines are drawn. Drawing the fuselage demands the use of a datum line. This is an arbitrary straight line drawn across the plan and is usually the centre line, but may also be the top or bottom of the fuselage if either are straight lines through a significant part of their length.

For the wing, start with the leading and trailing edges. Then add the ribs and mainspar, followed by other details such as tips, attachment to fuselage, ailerons and control linkages.

## Indicating different materials

There are conventions which are used on professional plans to show the types of material being used. It is as well to stick to these conventions, particularly if anyone else wants to build from your plans or you wish to get the plan published. The main ways of indicating various materials and construction points are

shown overleaf in Figure 312. An examination of Figure 313 will show how these appear on a published plan.

Where there are several layers of materials to show, as for example in a fuselage side view, it can be beneficial to cut away part of the fuselage with a pair of solid wavy lines. This then allows a better idea of the internal structure between these lines to be drawn.

## Drawing aerofoils

Basically there are three ways of obtaining aerofoils of a size suitable for a new design. They can be found in specialist aerofoil computer programs, they can be enlarged or reduced from a single outline using a photocopier or overhead projector, or they can be plotted from a table of co-ordinates.

The first alternative includes programs such as Aerofoil Plot Pro which contain a library of aerofoils. Run on a PC, the program enables them to be printed out to any required chord length.

The second alternative is very straightforward. Obtain a single drawing of the chosen aerofoil (there are a number shown in Figure 114) and then use a photocopier to enlarge or reduce it to the sizes chosen for each individual rib. This requires the production of a table. Supposing we have a 150 mm (6") drawing of our aerofoil and want ribs from 150 - 190

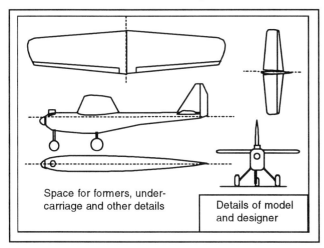

Space for formers, under-carriage and other details

Details of model and designer

**Figure 311** *Laying out the components of a new model requires a little forethought.*

155

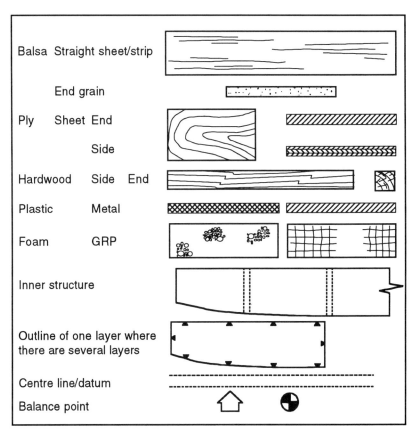

**Figure 312** *The correct way to indicate the various materials when drawing a plan for a model.*

mm (6" - 8") long in increments of 5mm (¼"), Table 34 shows how the results should turn out.

The last method is the most time consuming and involves drawing the aerofoils using French curves or a bendy curve and a ruler. The co-ordinates defining aerofoil outlines are listed as percentages along the chord length and are available from, among others, Martin Simons' book *Model Aircraft Aerodynamics*. A pocket

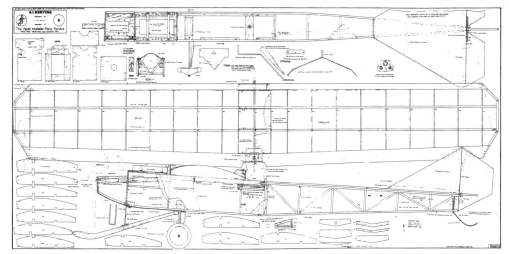

**Figure 313** *This drawing of my Albertine shows how a professional plan should look.*

| Rib size mm | 150 | 155 | 160 | 165 | 170 | 175 | 180 | 185 | 190 |
|---|---|---|---|---|---|---|---|---|---|
| % increase | 100 | 103 | 107 | 110 | 113 | 117 | 120 | 123 | 127 |
| Rib size ins | 6 | 6¼ | 6½ | 6¾ | 7 | 7¼ | 7½ | 7¾ | 8 |
| % increase | 100 | 104 | 108 | 112 | 117 | 121 | 125 | 129 | 133 |

**Table 34** *Examples of percentage increases for photocopying aerofoils, using metric or imperial units.*

calculator can be used to convert the percentages to the required sizes.

### Transferring the information

Once the plan has been completed, the information can be transferred to wood for cutting out by pinning through, ironing the image onto the wood if the plan has been photocopied, or by cutting out the components from the plan and gluing them to the wood. Cutting out your own kit allows a baseline check of total weight to be made before construction commences.

## Getting it published

The key factors involved in getting a design published are an original model which flies well and some good photographs of it. A tidy and comprehensive plan must be produced, though it need not be drawn to professional standards. Finally, an article of about 2,500 words needs to be written, typed double space, preferably on a word processor and ideally with a copy on a floppy disk. It is also essential to remember to take some photographs of the model during the construction phase.

Figures 317 and 318 overleaf show some of the classic mistakes made when taking photographs. You will really need access to a single lens reflex (SLR) camera to enable satisfactory

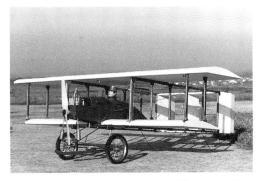

**Figure 315** *When someone else builds a model from your plan, it is very rewarding. A Frenchman, D. Lancelot, was kind enough to send me this illustration of his version of my JH2 Stringbox.*

close-up photographs to be taken. You should also take a selection of pictures showing construction detail, as such information is always of interest to budding builders of your new design.

Editors of magazines are busy people and you should not expect an instant reply, nor early publication in your favourite journal. Backlogs of articles range from several months to well over a year, so be patient. Most magazines only publish one or two new plans a month.

Do not forget to enclose a stamped addressed envelope if you want a reply and your article back should it prove unsuitable. Then sit and wait for a positive response.

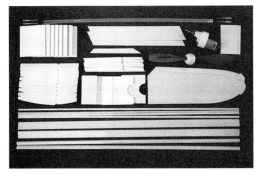

**Figure 314** *Cutting out a kit of all the parts can make building a new model a more enjoyable process.*

**Figure 316** *Ready for covering, my Flintstone Flier clearly shows off the internal structure.*

**Figure 317** *Four classic failures when trying to get a publishable airborne shot. From top left clockwise, underexposed due to the bright sky; too far away; part of the model cut off; and finally, hopelessly out of focus, due in part to fast panning.*

**Figure 318** *Failures on the ground are common too. From top left, clockwise, pity about the water butt and garden door; so under-exposed it's hard to see the installation details; what is it? Only the photographer knows it's an aileron; and finally, a snapshot which shows the people, pity about the models and the background.*

# 13  The first flight

## Before the first flight

Before the maiden flight of any entirely new model, and particularly one which is an original design, it is vital that a number of checks are made to minimise the risk of problems on that nerve wracking first flight. You could even feed the key parameters of the model into a computer program like the NHP/CSM R/C Flight Simulator and check out the theoretical performance without any risk of damage. However, you will not be able to cover every single variable, though you may get a good indication of any potential problem.

## Balance

The most important single factor in ensuring the safe first flight of a new model is to locate the centre of gravity in the correct position. Chapter 3 shows how to find the right place. Too far back and the model will be uncontrollable, reacting so rapidly to any control input that a crash is only seconds away from lift off/launch. Too far forward and the model may refuse to take-off or sink into the ground after launch despite full up elevator. In less severe cases, lots of up elevator may be needed for level flight, with a sluggish response in the pitching plane.

CENTRE OF GRAVITY TOO FAR AFT! . . .

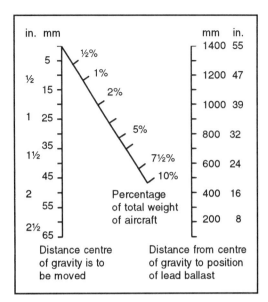

in. mm                          mm  in.
                               ┌ 1400  55
  5        ½%
 ½         1%                   ┌ 1200  47
 15              2%
                               ┌ 1000  39
 1   25
                               ┌ 800   32
     35          5%
 1½             7½%             ┌ 600   24
     45          10%
 2            Percentage        ┌ 400   16
     55       of total weight
              of aircraft       ┌ 200    8
 2½  65

Distance centre        Distance from centre
of gravity is to       of gravity to position
be moved               of lead ballast

**Figure 319** *The amount of lead required, as a percentage of the total model weight, depends on the distance the centre of gravity has to be moved and the distance of the lead from the centre of gravity.*

Of the two, a centre of gravity that is too far forward is an inconvenience; too far back is fatal. Ballasting the model to achieve the correct centre of gravity may increase the wing loading, but without the ballast, the chances of a successful first flight are low. The nomograph in Figure 319 shows how much weight (as a percentage of the total model weight) must be added to any model to move the centre of gravity a given distance. Many people forget to balance a model laterally as well. A small amount of lead in the wing tip, if required, can avoid lateral balance problems such as crooked loops.

### Rigging

It is all too easy to end up with the wing or tail not parallel or at right angles to each other. The rigging of any new model should be checked carefully in all three dimensions. In addition, ensure the wing and tail incidence are correct and the angle the model sits on the ground is right. Finally, the up/down and side thrust of the engine should be checked as should all the controls to see that they are neutral with respect to their main surfaces.

### Checking the weight

Once the model has been completed, a final check of the all-up weight should be made. Kitchen scales are ideal for smaller models, normally coping with up to 2.5 kg (5½lb). Above this weight, a spring balance or bathroom scales both offer a capability up to maximum likely weights. This check will confirm:

• How close the model is to the original weight budget
• The actual wing loading

Note that if the weight is over 7kg (15.4lb), a

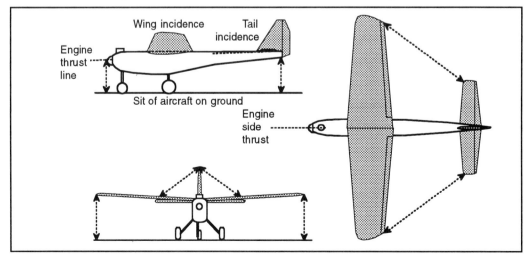

**Figure 320** *It is essential on any model, particularly a new design, to check the wing and tail are square to the fuselage, and the fin and tailplane are at right angles to each other.*

fail safe and a CAA exemption certificate are legal requirements.

## Control throws

All controls must be checked to ensure that they move in the correct sense, with aileron the most likely to be accidentally connected up in reverse. The amount of movement required is more problematic. It should be obvious that a slow model requires larger control throws than a fast moving one, large control surfaces need less movement than small ones and all moving tails require the least. Don't forget the prop wash over some controls and their likely change of effectiveness if the engine stops half-way through the maiden flight.

In trying to decide the amount of control movement for a new design, it is useful to look at the throws on similar types of aircraft. Suitable models may exist at your club, but if not, examine plans such as those given away free in *RCM&E* or *Radio Modeller*. The following throws are suggested as a good baseline in the absence of a better alternative:

- Elevator 10° up and down. Too much movement rather than too little is useful if the pitch trim proves to be incorrect.
- Inset ailerons 20° up and 10° down, strip ailerons 10° up and down
- Rudder 20° either way even if rudder is the primary directional control. On a twin, a little more rudder deflection is never a bad idea.

## The use of rates

Probably the best way of overcoming the difficulty in selecting the right control throws is to use the rate switches now fitted to most transmitters. A large throw with the ability to reduce it after take-off if the control proves to be too effective can both calm the nerves and prevent catastrophe on that heart-stopping first flight.

## Choosing the propeller

To find the best propeller to suit your new model, the first thing to do is to try to estimate the maximum speed of the model. This is not as hard as it sounds. Figure 322 provides some useful

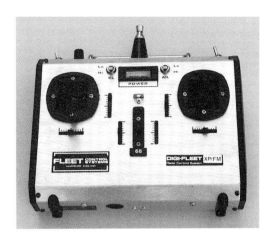

**Figure 321** *Most modern transmitters, such as this British one by Fleet, feature elevator and aileron rate switches, which fall easily to hand and are invaluable during the first flight of a new model.*

speed pointers. It should not be too difficult to fit a new design onto the vertical scale.

Having arrived at a maximum speed, it is important to choose a propeller pitch to achieve that maximum speed, and this is done from Figure 323 overleaf. The propeller diameter should then be chosen to give maximum power revs in the air. These revs are usually quoted by the manufacturer, or can be obtained from the engine test articles which regularly appear in a number of modelling magazines.

Maximum static revolutions should be set at some 500 rpm below the optimum, since the engine will speed up a little in the air as it unloads.

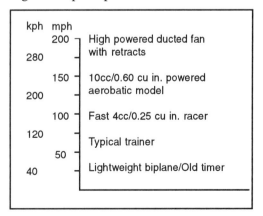

**Figure 322** *An estimate of the maximum speed of a new model can be made by comparison with the baseline figures quoted.*

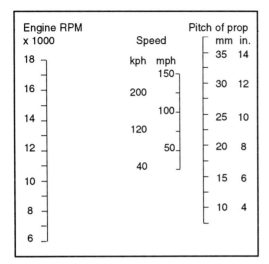

**Figure 323** *The pitch of the propeller can be selected once the maximum speed of the model has been estimated and the maximum engine rpm established.*

If you don't own a tachometer, try to borrow one to see the effectiveness of your chosen propeller. The best take-off and climb performance is achieved at the cost of top speed. A fine pitch propeller, say 10cm (4") pitch, with the diameter increased to maintain the same revs, will be much more efficient at low speeds and therefore provide a better acceleration. A larger diameter, finer pitch propeller also has its place on models with large cowls. A final important point to remember is that a large propeller turning at low revs is much more efficient than a small one turning at high speed.

### Taxying trials

Opening up the motor and taxying your brand new model around the flying field can give a first indication of some of the handling characteristics. For a tail dragger in particular, it will immediately highlight any tendency to nose over or ground loop, either of which may suggest a change in location of the mainwheels before the first flight. It will also give some indication of the effectiveness of the rudder and the elevator.

### The video

If you are fortunate enough to own a video camera, or you have a friend who does, a video of

**Figure 324** *A first flight is always nerve wracking. Here I have the engine mixture on my Albertine set on the rich side to minimise the risk of an engine cut in the air.*

the first flight can be invaluable. Not only is it a good memento, but it will remind you of what actually happened during the flight and help you to make any necessary changes to the model before flight testing continues. Clearly, you will need an experienced hand to operate it while you concentrate on flying.

### A first hop

If you are in any doubt about the position of the centre of gravity and the model is fitted with an undercarriage, then a short hop into the air can quickly show up any pitch instability, or lack of sufficient elevator power. A little lead in the nose or tail can then rectify a potential disaster before it happens.

## The first flight

If possible, try to make the first flight when the weather is fine and there is a light to moderate wind blowing down the runway, if your flying field boasts such a thing. It is also preferable that no-one else is flying at the time, since this will make it easier to hear and subsequently deal with any engine cut.

### Flaps on take-off and landing

When flaps are used for the first time on take-off, they should be set to a maximum angle of 30°. At this setting the lift/drag ratio is such that the maximum advantage is obtained. For landings, however, the high drag of fully lowered flaps

**Figure 325** *Safely airborne at last. Do not let the euphoria stop you carrying out the necessary handling checks before the first landing.*

(like airbrakes) is useful since it permits a steeper approach without the speed becoming excessive. The increased lift allows a lower approach and touch-down speed. The high drag has another advantage in causing a rapid deceleration during any float after round out and before touch down.

### Raising flaps in flight

After take-off when a model is climbing, raising flaps rapidly causes an immediate reduction in lift and the model may sink unless up elevator is fed in. When countering the sink, the attitude of the model becomes noticeably more nose-up as the angle of attack is increased.

It is best to raise flaps slowly to avoid the need for exaggerated corrections. The opposite is true of lowering flaps, when some degree of ballooning can be expected. Unfortunately it is impossible to predict with any accuracy whether raising and lowering flaps will cause a nose-up or-nose down trim change.

## Controllability

From the pilot's point of view, variation in the centre of gravity position is apparent from the amount of stick movement necessary to displace the aircraft from its trimmed attitude. With a forward centre of gravity, elevator stick movements will need to be fairly large. With an aft position, stick movements must be much more gentle. Level flight may be impossible to maintain. The

centre of gravity is in roughly the right position when the elevator can be used to change the attitude of the model, centralised and the aircraft remains in this new attitude.

If you have the misfortune to experience flutter in flight, close the throttle immediately, level the model and land. Any delay is likely to lead to a catastrophic structural failure, should this not have already occurred. Chapter 7 gives details of how to avoid a recurrence of flutter.

## Stall characteristics

The stall characteristics of a new model should be checked early in the flight test programme. The inability to enter a stall may indicate too far forward a centre of gravity or simply a lack of elevator power.

The type of stall, sudden and sharp or just a mushy descent will depend on the aerofoil section used, the wing planform and the degree of longitudinal stability. A sudden wing drop at the stall may be indicative of an unmatched pair of wings, an aircraft which is poorly rigged, a lack of lateral balance or one which has a low margin of stability. It may also result in the model entering a spin.

## Spinning and spin recovery

Eventually, entry to a spin and spin recovery should be checked. Entry should be possible with full up elevator, full rudder and the engine at tick over, unless the model is very stable.

Recovery by releasing the controls is usually effective, but opposite rudder and down elevator may be needed on a relatively unstable design. In such cases, a burst of power to increase the slipstream over the controls may also prove helpful.

## The first landing

This is where the adrenaline starts pumping. Assuming that a stall has been tried, you will have a warning of any unpleasant vices, as well as an indication of the stalling speed. Keep the speed above the stall and plan to land in the middle of the strip, holding off just above the ground and then lowering the model to a safe touch down.

**Figure 326** *The Albertine (Nexus Plan RM 273) about to touch down, with a Flair Fokker triplane in the foreground.*

## Assessing flight performance

Once safely on the ground, nerves take over. While you are relaxing and congratulating yourself, run through the following points in your mind.

| | |
|---|---|
| **Take-off** | Swing direction |
| | Length of run |
| **Stability in** | Pitch |
| | Roll |
| | Yaw |
| **Control in** | Pitch |
| | Roll |
| | Yaw |
| **Any use of rates** | Elevator |
| | Aileron |
| **Trim positions** | Elevator |
| | Aileron |
| | Rudder |
| **As engine is throttled** | Change in pitch |
| | Change in yaw |

| | |
|---|---|
| **Characteristics of** | Stall |
| | Spin |
| **Handling** | On take-off |
| | On finals |
| | On the round out |

### What changes to make

After making an assessment, and only then, consider making changes to the centre of gravity and control neutrals/throws before undertaking a second flight. For many aircraft, it will take several flights to try a full range of manoeuvres and get all the characteristics sorted out.

The basic rule is only to make one change at a time to correct any particular problem. Otherwise, it becomes very difficult to establish which change affected the improvement and a lot of time can be wasted.

### Side and down thrust

If the elevator or rudder trims need adjusting with throttle changes, the thrust line of the engine should be altered. Adding down thrust to an upright or inverted motor presents no problem using washers.

Side thrust changes necessitate modifying the engine bearer plate or bearers themselves if these are used. The latter is very difficult. Alterations to side-winder engine installations are, of course, opposite in such a procedure (i.e. washers for sidethrust). If using a radial mount, it's plain sailing; washers in the appropriate corner will do the trick.

| Flight characteristic | Change required | Remedy |
|---|---|---|
| Very light on the controls, drops a wing at the stall and spins very readily | Less responsive and less inclined to drop a wing | Move centre of gravity forward slightly |
| Sluggish in response to the elevator and requires plenty of up trim | More responsive to elevator | Move centre of gravity back slightly |
| Rapidly rolls out of turn when control released. Aileron rolls, particularly slow ones, hesitant/jerky. | Remain in turn after releasing control, opposite control needed to roll out of turn. | Increase fin area or reduce dihedral |
| Remains steadily in a turn after the control is released | Come out of the turn without need for opposite control. | Reduce fin size or increase dihedral |
| Won't fly straight and will spiral dive without control corrections. | Come out of the turn easily on its own. | Reduce size of fin or increase dihedral |

**Table 35** *How to change the stability of a model by examining its control response in flight.*

## Stability characteristics

The stability of the model in one or more planes may not be quite right. Table 35 shows a list of characteristics, the change in characteristics required and the remedy. A reduction in fin size or increased dihedral may mean that less engine side thrust is required and vice versa.

Table 36 looks at the impact of changes to lateral stability for models without ailerons, where the rudder is the primary turning control.

Having finally completed any necessary changes to improve the handling of your new

| Change to design (Constant rudder area/deflection) | Effect of rudder |
|---|---|
| Reduce fin area        Increase dihedral | More effective |
| Reduce dihedral | Less effective. Ground steering unaffected. |
| Increase fin area | Less effective |

**Table 36** *Changes to the flight characteristics of models without ailerons.*

model, you can now approach a second design with increased confidence and maybe get plans of your model published in one of the modelling magazines. Good luck!

# Glossary of terms and abbreviations

**A**

*ABS* A plastic used for moulding fuselages and other components.

*Aerodynamic mean chord* The chord line at the aerodynamic mid point of a wing, along which the centre of gravity is positioned.

*Adverse yaw* The effect of aileron drag causing the opposite turn to that demanded.

*Aerofoil* The cross-sectional shape of a wing.

*Ailerons* Moveable surfaces at the trailing edge of wings giving control about the roll axis.

*Airbrakes* Controls used to increase the drag of a model.

*All moving tail* A tailplane, the whole of which moves to give an elevator effect.

*AMC* Aerodynamic mean chord.

*Angle of attack* The angle between the chord line of an aerofoil and the airflow.

*Angle of incidence* The angle between an aerofoil's chord line and the fore/aft datum line of the fuselage.

*Anhedral* The angle by which a wing is inclined downwards from the lateral axis.

*Aspect ratio* The ratio of the span to the average chord of a wing.

**B**

*Balanced surface* A control surface with part of its area in front of the hinge line.

*Ballast* Weight carried to adjust the position of the centre of gravity of a model.

*Beam* The maximum width of the hull of a seaplane.

*BEC* Battery elimination circuit.

*Bell crank* A device for transferring control linkages through a sharp angle.

*Blue foam* A blue polystyrene foam with a stronger, more consistent structure than white foam.

*Boundary layer* The layer of air next to the surface of a model flying through the air.

*Bunt* An outside loop achieved by the use of down elevator.

*Butterfly tail* Tail surfaces set in the form of a V to provide both the fin and tailplane functions.

**C**

*Cabane struts* An arrangement of struts for supporting a parasol wing or the top wing of a biplane or triplane above a fuselage

*CAD* Computer aided design

*Capstrip* A thin strip glued to the top and bottom of a wing rib to form an 'I' section.

*Camber* An unsymmetrical aerofoil section with more camber on top than underneath.

*Canard* A model with its tailplane (foreplane) in front of the wing. Also the forward winglets either on a model with wing and tailplane in their conventional locations or on a delta.

*Carbon fibre* A very strong composite material.

*cc* Cubic centimetre.

*Centre of gravity* The balance point or the point through which the total weight of the model acts.

*Centre of pressure* The point through which the lift of a flying surface acts. Its position varies with angle of attack.

*Chines* Corners between the sides and bottom of a float or seaplane hull.

*Chopped strand mat* A material used in GRP consisting of random direction, non-woven fibres.

*Chord* The width of an aerofoil, wing or tail surface from leading to trailing edge.

*Clevis* An adjustable connection between any control surface and its linkage.

*Closed loop* A control linkage using thin wire to both sides of a control surface in a push/pull mode.

*cm* Centimetre.

*cu.* Cubic.

*Cyano* Instant glue.

**D**

*Dihedral* The angle by which a wing is inclined upwards from the lateral axis.

*dm* Decimetre.

*Doubler* A reinforcing thickness of balsa or ply laminated onto a flat component, e.g. a fuselage side.

*Dowel* A cylindrical section of wood or metal.

*Drag* The total retarding force which occurs when a flying model moves through the air.

**E**

*Elevator* A control surface normally hinged to a tailplane and used for control in the pitch axis.

*Elevons* Surfaces combining the functions of elevators and ailerons.

*Epoxy* A two-part adhesive or laminating resin.

*Expanded polystyrene* White (or blue) polystyrene foam used mainly for making wing cores.

**F**

*Fibreglass* See GRP.

*Fin* The fixed vertical tail surface of a model.

*Flaperons* Wing mounted control surfaces combining the functions of flaps & ailerons.

*Flaps* Wing mounted surfaces which produce extra lift and drag depending on their deflection angle.

*Flat bottomed section* An aerofoil with a straight, flat underside.

*Flutter* Continuous vibration of flying or control surfaces, usually occurring at high speed and resulting in structural failure.

*Former* A fuselage cross sectional member.

*Frise ailerons* A special design of aileron which avoids adverse drag by equalising the drag produced by the up going and down going ailerons.

*ft* Foot.

**G**

*Galloping ghost* An early form of proportional control where the rudder and elevator flapped continuously.

*Geodetic* A form of structure involving diagonally crossing members for torsional rigidity.

*Gravity, centre of* The balance point or the point through which the total weight of the model acts.

*GRP* Glass reinforced plastic, sometimes called glass fibre. A material made from glass fibres laminated with a resin to form a structure or provide reinforcement.

*Gsm* Grams per square metre.

**H**

*Heat shrink film* Plastic covering material with built-in heat sensitive adhesive and high gloss finish.

*Horn* Structure projecting from a control surface to provide leverage for the control linkage.

**I**

*in.* Inch.

*Incidence* The angle between the chord line of an aerofoil and the fore/aft datum line of the fuselage.

*Induced drag* That part of total drag caused by a wing producing lift.

**K**

*Kevlar* A high strength organic fibre used as a composite material.

**L**

*Laminar flow* Non-turbulent boundary layer flow.

*Lateral axis* The axis about which a model rolls.

*lb* Pound.

*Leading edge* The first part of a wing to meet the airflow.

*Lift* The upward force produced by a wing which supports the model and balances the weight in straight and level flight.

*Lift/drag ratio* The ratio of the amount of lift to the amount of drag produced at a given angle of attack.

*Longeron* A strip of wood used as a length wise fuselage constructional member.

*Longitudinal axis* The axis about which a model pitches or loops.

*Longitudinal dihedral* The angular difference between wing and tailplane angles of incidence.

**M**

*Mean camber line* A line joining the leading and trailing edges of an aerofoil, equidistant from its upper and lower surfaces. If the line is curved, the aerofoil is cambered.

*Mean chord* The average chord of a tapered wing.

*Mixer* An electronic or mechanical device which

mixes two control functions together to operate one pair of surfaces e.g. elevons, flaperons, ruddervators.

*mm* Millimetre.

*Monocoque* A structure where its strength is derived from its outer skin.

*Mylar* A flexible plastic material used to make heat shrink materials and hinges.

**N**

*Nicad* Nickel-cadmium re-chargeable battery.

**O**

*oz* Ounce.

**P**

*Parasite drag* That part of the drag produced by the shape of the model as it flies though the air.

*Parasol wing* A wing mounted above the fuselage using cabane struts.

*PC* Personal computer.

*Pitch* Movement about the longitudinal axis of a model.

*Polyboard* A material consisting of a sandwich of expanded polystyrene between two layers of card.

*Polyester resin* Two-part resin, used to make GRP laminates.

*Polyhedral* A dihedral layout with an additional amount added to the outer panels of a wing.

*Porpoising* Seaplane hull planing instability characterised by sometimes severe longitudinal rocking.

*Pressure, centre of* The point through which the lift of a flying surface acts. Its position varies with angle of attack.

*Push rod* A rigid control link from a servo to a control surface.

*PVA glue* A slow drying, flexible glue used for general wood construction.

*Pylon mounting* An engine mounted above the fuselage on a streamlined pylon.

**R**

*Reynolds no.* A scale effect that varies with the speed and size of a model.

*Rib* A chordwise constructional member in a wing which replicates the aerofoil section.

*Roll* Movement about the lateral axis of a model.

*Rovings* Material used in GRP construction where the fibres are orientated in one direction.

*Rudder* The control surface which controls yaw.

*Ruddervators* Control surfaces on butterfly or V tail models combining rudder and elevator functions.

**S**

*Semi-symmetrical* An aerofoil with a small amount of camber and convex upper and lower surfaces.

*Sliding servo* A type of mechanical mixer.

*Slop* Undesirable free movement in any control linkage.

*Snake* A type of control link comprising a Bowden cable or plastic rod in a plastic tube.

*Span* The wing tip to wing tip size of a model.

*Spar* A major component which lies along the span of a wing.

*Spoiler* A control used to reduce lift by spoiling the airflow over part of a wing's upper surface.

*Spray strips* Strips on forward chines to reduce the spray from floats and seaplane hulls.

*Sq.* Square.

*Straight and level flight* Flight in a constant direction, with the model neither climbing nor descending.

*Stall* The condition where a model reaches its lowest speed in straight and level flight. At the stall there is a marked loss of lift, an increase in drag and a loss of height. Stalling speed is affected by manoeuvring and using high lift devices.

*Step* A vertical discontinuity in a float or seaplane hull bottom, used to resist porpoising.

*Symmetrical section* An aerofoil with no camber.

**T**

*Tailplane* The horizontal stabilising surface of a model.

*Taper ratio* The length of the chord at the wing root divided by its length at the tip.

*Thickness/chord ratio* A measure of the aerodynamic thickness of an aerofoil, normally quoted as a percentage. It is the ratio of the depth to the length of the chord.

*Tip* The outboard end of wing or tailplane.

*Tip-stall* A wing drop caused by a stall on the outboard portion of only one wing.

*Torsional stiffness* The ability of a structure to resist twisting.

*Trailing edge* The rear edge of a flying surface.

**V**

*Variable camber* Use of moveable parts of the wing section to change its camber in flight, usually by means of trailing edge flaps.

*Veneer* Thin wood sheet used as a skin for foam wings.

*Vortex* A twisting stream of turbulent air created in the wake of a wing. A pair trail behind wing tips in flight, rotating in opposite directions such that the air between them is descending.

**W**

*Washout* A built-in twist in a wing where the tip is at a lower angle of incidence than the root.

*Web* A structural part between two others, typically spars, to increase strength.

*Wing area* The span of a wing multiplied by the mean chord.

*Wing floats* Small floats fitted to a seaplane to provide lateral stability on the water.

*Wing loading* The weight of a model divided by its wing area.

*Wing thickness* The maximum thickness of the wing, divided by the chord at that point, as a percentage.

*Wt* Weight.

**Y**

*Yaw* Movement about the directional axis of a model.

**Z**

*Zero lift angle* The angle of attack at which an aerofoil section produces no lift.

# Bibliography

Boddington, David 1996 *Building and Flying R/C Model Aircraft* Hemel Hempstead: Nexus Special Interests

Cain, Tubal 1996 *Model Engineer's Handbook* Hemel Hempstead: Nexus Special Interests

Chinery, David 1995 *Fly Electric* Hemel Hempstead: Nexus Special Interests

Greenwood, D.P. 1980 *Plastics (Craftwork & Technology)* London: John Murray

Miller, Peter 1995 *Designing Model Aircraft* Upton-upon-Severn: Traplet Publications Ltd.

Lammas, David 1991 *Adhesives and Sealants* Hemel Hempstead: Nexus Special Interests

Lennon, A.G. Andy 1986 *R/C Model Airplane Design* Littlehampton: Chart Hobby Distributors Ltd.

Peacock, Ian 1988 *Introduction to Electric Flight* Hemel Hempstead: Nexus Special Interests

Selig, Michael, Donovan & Frazer 1989 *Aerofoils at Low Speeds* Virginia Beach Va USA: Soartech

Simons, Martin 1996 *Model Aircraft Aerodynamics* Hemel Hempstead: Nexus Special Interests

Simons, Martin 1988 *Model Flight* Hemel Hempstead: Nexus Special Interests

Sutherland, Alasdair 1995 *Aeronautics for Modellers* Upton-upon-Severn: Traplet Publications Ltd.

Technical Services Dept. 1988 *Strand Guide to Glassfibre* Wellingborough: Scott Bader Co. Ltd.

Thomas, David 1989 *Radio Control Foam Modelling* Hemel Hempstead: Nexus Special Interests

Walsh, Douglas E 1990 *Do It Yourself Vacuum Forming for the Hobbyist* Lake Orion, Ml. USA: Vacuum Form

Warring, Ron H. 1989 *Glass Fibre Handbook* Hemel Hempstead: Nexus Special Interests

# Index

## A

ABS, 103, 132
adhesive, 101, 103, 108, 109, 149-151
adverse yaw, 28, 88, 138
aerobatic, 2, 13, 14, 22, 31, 43, 48, 52, 55-58, 67, 73-86, 129
aerodynamic mean chord, 29-32
aerofoil, 14, 46-66, 70-78, 84, 85, 115-128, 155, 156, 163
aileron, 3, 9, 28, 56, 64, 88-90, 94-96, 131, 137-143, 158, 161
    drag, 88
    reversal, 89
air speed, 16, 46, 47, 55, 73, 81
airbrake, 87, 91, 140
airflow, 18, 45-53, 61, 79, 80-84, 115
airframe, xi, 23, 34-37, 41, 45, 74, 94, 103, 111, 126, 130, 145
all moving tail, 26, 93, 97, 146, 161
aluminium, 2, 38, 106, 107, 114, 125, 128, 129, 132
angle of
    attack, 18, 51-64, 71, 77-84, 88, 163
    incidence, 15, 51, 54, 68, 84, 95, 119, 121, 125, 128, 134
aspect ratio, 13-15, 24, 26, 47, 48, 61-66, 80, 89, 94-97, 102, 107, 117-119

## B

balancing, 37, 78, 92, 94, 95, 97
ballast, 25, 29, 99, 142, 160
balsa, 17, 43, 99-103, 108-128, 132-137, 140-148
battery, 25, 35, 41, 42, 43, 68, 74, 75, 130, 142
beech, 37, 38
bell crank, 88, 137, 138, 144
biplane, 3, 8, 9, 14, 16, 24, 31, 32, 67, 124, 126, 137

boundary layer, 45, 46, 65
brass, 39, 108, 129, 140
butterfly tail, 3, 27, 28, 87, 91, 128, 137

## C

CAD, 2, 122, 154
camber, 51-57, 69, 70, 74, 77, 80
cambered section, 56, 77
canard, 6, 15, 32, 73, 82
carbon fibre, 99, 106, 114, 129
cardboard, 102, 103, 123, 129
centre of
    gravity, 14-19, 23-38, 43, 53, 73-86, 92-99, 107, 126, 134, 136, 142, 159-164
    pressure, 52, 53, 58, 64, 65, 77-81, 93, 94
Clark Y, 55-58, 84, 118
clevis, 126
closed loop, 131, 144, 145
cockpit, 7, 8, 103, 147
control surface, 16, 22, 73, 83, 87-97, 126, 127, 137, 142-146, 161
coverings, 103, 149
crutch, 113

## D

delta, xiv, 3, 6, 11, 15, 24, 31, 37, 47, 55, 61-66, 73, 82, 91, 124
diesel, 3, 35, 36, 40, 105
differential, 28, 88, 138, 139, 144, 146
dihedral, 9, 66, 68, 73, 79-88, 102, 124, 128, 165
directional stability, 75, 79-82, 89
divergence, 76
down
    thrust, 37, 38, 83, 86, 164
    wash, 51, 84
drag, 14, 15, 18, 19, 24-27, 45-64, 69-74, 78, 80, 84-91, 126-134, 139, 141, 147, 163
    aileron, 88

form, 45-47
induced, 24, 45, 47, 61-63
interference, 126
parasite, 45-48, 62
drawing, 1-3, 9, 116, 153-156
duration, 34, 42, 48, 74
Dutch roll, 82, 83
dynamic stability, 76

## E

electric motor, xi, 3, 41, 43, 130
elevator, 2-9, 16-19, 25, 27, 73-78, 83-94,
107, 108, 126, 128, 137, 140-145, 159-164
elevon, 3, 58, 87-91, 137, 139
engine location, 16
mount, 7, 35-38, 41, 107, 110, 114, 132
Eppler, 56, 57
expanded polystyrene, 102-104

## F

fin, 1-9, 13, 15, 17, 24-27, 45, 47, 73, 79-82,
86, 89, 93, 95, 126-128, 140, 160, 165
flap, 69, 70, 141
flaperons, 90, 91
float, 14, 133, 134, 163
flutter, 14, 26, 49, 92-97, 121, 144, 145, 163
flying wing, 6, 14, 15, 24, 31, 52-55, 58, 90,
91, 124
foam, 4, 17, 36, 66, 99, 101-107, 115-123,
128, 130-134
folding propeller, 43
form drag, 45-47
former, 15, 22, 35, 77, 111, 119, 120, 131, 154
four stroke, 3, 33-40, 115
Fowler, 69,70
Frise aileron, 88, 138, 139
fuel, 5, 16, 17, 25, 31-41, 48, 49, 73-78, 107,
108, 111, 114, 148-151
consumption, 34, 35
proofer, 149, 150
tank, 16, 25, 34-38, 75, 108, 111, 148, 151
fuselage, xi, 4-31, 36, 37, 45-51, 61, 67, 74-
86, 93, 99-105, 111-118, 124-148, 155, 160

## G

glass reinforced plastic, 99
Göttingen, 58
gravity, centre of 14-19, 23-38, 43, 53, 73-86,

92-99, 107, 126, 134, 136, 142, 159-164
GRP, 38, 99, 104-106, 114, 123-132, 144,
149, 156

## H

hatch, 23, 103, 148
hinge, 70, 88, 91-97, 138-142, 145
horn, 88, 92-94, 138, 140, 145, 146

## I

incidence, 15, 51, 54, 58, 68, 84, 95, 111, 119,
121, 125, 128, 134, 160
induced drag, 24, 45, 47, 61, 62, 63
interference, 14, 27, 45, 126
drag, 126
internal combustion engine, xi, 5, 16, 33, 38-
41, 111, 112, 151
inverted flight, 39, 56, 61

## K

keel surface, 79, 80
Kevlar, 106, 107

## L

landing, 10, 16-19, 26, 41, 69-74, 110, 120,
126-134, 162,163
lateral
axis, 75
stability, 9, 68, 75, 79-82, 133, 165
leading edge, 10, 31, 51-53, 60, 64, 65, 71,
89, 92, 101, 117-128, 137, 142
lift, 14-18, 45-85, 89, 91, 95, 96, 118-120,
134, 140, 159, 163
lift/drag ratio, 54, 57, 62, 63, 70, 163
liteply, 101, 111, 112
longitudinal
axis, 75
dihedral, 85
stability, 67, 75-78, 163

## M

mainspar, 121-124, 155
mainwheel, 19, 131
manoeuvre, 15, 64, 65, 73, 74, 79, 81, 87
mass balance, 92, 93
materials, 1, 6, 32, 40, 99, 100, 104-114, 144,
149, 150, 155
monocoque, 113, 114, 123

monoplane, 3, 13-16, 22, 24, 31, 67, 117, 124
multi engine, 117

**N**

NACA, 55-58, 84
nicad, 41, 42
noseleg, 10, 18, 38, 131, 132
nosewheel, 10, 18, 19, 74, 131
nylon, 36, 126, 149

**O**

obechi, 103, 123
offbeat aircraft, 3
oscillatory instability, 82, 83

**P**

paint, 1, 34, 149, 150
parasite, 45-48, 62
paxolin, 38
payload, 3, 73, 74, 75
pendulum stability, 67
piano wire, 107, 108, 114, 125-134, 140
pilot, 19, 32, 55, 73, 74, 82, 83, 87, 93, 133, 147, 163
plastic, 11, 38, 99, 103, 104, 142, 145-148
ply, 38, 43, 101-103, 111-117, 125-128, 132-135, 140-144
polycarbonate, 104
polyester, 104
polystyrene, 102-104
pressure, centre of, 52, 53, 58, 64, 65, 77-81, 93, 94
profile, 45, 111, 135
propeller, xii, 9, 10, 16, 22, 34-49, 74, 86, 113, 143, 161, 162
publication, xi, 40, 157
push rod, 34, 88, 137, 138, 144
pusher, 10, 15, 16, 37, 40, 81, 143
PVC, 104
pylon, 2, 15-18, 37, 74, 86

**R**

radio, xi-xiii, 1, 3, 6, 14, 16, 23, 25, 35, 43, 67, 75, 83, 105, 111, 113, 139, 142, 148
rate switch, 161
retract, xi, 129, 130
reversal, 89
Reynolds' number, xii

rib, 115-118, 122-127, 155
rigging, 84, 86, 125, 126, 160
rotation, 9, 10, 22, 26, 61, 86
rudder, 2-9, 16, 17, 27, 28, 68, 82-95, 126, 131-145, 161-165
ruddevator, 87, 91, 137

**S**

scale, xi, 1-4, 7-11, 17, 18, 28, 31, 33, 48, 55, 68-70, 83, 118, 129, 148, 151, 154, 161
seaplane, 133-135
semi-symmetrical, 54-57, 118
side
    slip, 79, 80, 89
    thrust, 38, 86, 160, 164, 165
silencer, 10, 34-38, 49, 114, 115
ski, 45-48, 108, 111, 123, 135, 150
slat, 71
slot, 37, 71, 111, 132
    propeller, 37
snake, 131, 143, 144
spar, 120-122, 126
spat, 132
speed, xii, 13-15, 18, 32, 40-55, 60-74, 78, 81-99, 117-121, 137, 151, 154, 161-163
    range, 14, 15, 48, 49
spin, 56, 74, 78, 81, 82, 163
spiral instability, 82
spruce, 99, 112, 128, 137
stabiliser, 78, 83, 84
stability, 9, 11, 25, 26, 66-68, 73-83, 89, 105, 133, 134, 163, 165
    directional, 75, 79-82, 89
    dynamic, 76
    lateral, 9, 68, 75, 79-82, 133, 165
    longitudinal, 67, 75-78, 163
    pendulum, 67
    static, 75
stall, 26, 53-66, 67, 71, 73, 78, 89, 163
stalling
    angle, 15, 53, 60, 63, 69, 71
    speed, 48, 49, 55, 68, 70-74, 163
static stability, 75
steel, 100, 106, 107, 126, 140
stores, 126
streamlining, 46, 128
subsidence, 76
symmetrical, 53, 56-58, 118

semi, 54-57, 118

## T

tail dragger, 7-10, 18, 19, 74, 131, 162
tailless, 14, 48, 57, 58, 64, 90, 91
tailplane, 4-13, 23-31, 45, 47, 64, 67, 73, 77, 78, 81-95, 103, 111, 126-128, 137, 160
tailwheel, 7, 8, 18, 19, 131
take-off, 9, 10, 15-22, 37, 48, 68-74, 110, 128-134, 159-164
taper, 66, 89, 113, 115, 119, 120
taxying, 131, 162
thickness, 45-60, 102-107, 113, 118, 123, 127
throttle, 2, 3, 9, 18, 35, 55, 78, 83, 86, 131, 143, 163, 164
thrust,
    down, 38, 86, 164
    side, 38, 86, 160, 164, 165
    up, 37, 86
tip float, 134, 135
tissue, 108, 149
tractor, 15, 16, 37, 86, 112
trailing edge, 24, 31, 52, 65, 66, 69, 70, 88, 89, 101, 102, 116-126, 137, 138, 155
tricycle undercarriage, 7-9, 18
trim, 16, 54, 78, 86-91, 140, 144, 161, 163
turbulent boundary layer, 46
turtle deck, 103, 113
two stroke, 22, 28, 33-40, 115

## U

undercarriage, xi, 3, 7-10, 15-19, 26, 27, 37, 40, 64, 71, 102-114, 123, 128-136, 162
up thrust, 37, 86

## V

V tail, 27, 48
vertical axis, 55
video, 162
vortices, 46, 61, 62, 65

## W

washout, 64, 66, 115, 116, 119, 123
waterproof, 133, 134
weight, 6, 11-16, 22-28, 34-49, 63, 68, 73-81, 86, 92, 99-113, 121-137, 142-151, 157-161
wheel, 19, 74, 104, 105, 130, 131
    well, 130
wing, xi, xii, 3-18, 22-32, 36-41, 45-143, 148, 150, 154, 155, 160, 163
    loading, 6, 13, 22, 32, 40, 41, 55, 68-77, 82, 160
    planform, 26, 47, 49, 60, 64, 66, 115, 120, 122, 163
    position, 8, 67
    span, 6, 14, 21-24, 47, 61, 88, 99, 133

## Z

zero lift, 58, 61